Justine Ford is ... ...nd journalist. Her first ... ... on the
top-rating *Austr...* ... ed the
Melbourne gangl... ...omicides
and missing perso... ...ue Justine has won the
trust of many fam... who are victims of crime, and developed deep access to police all over Australia, enabling her to
bring crucial, never-before-published case information to her
reporting. Justine has written three books, *Missing You, One
Piece of the Puzzle* and *Unsolved Australia* (Pan Macmillan,
July 2015). www.justineford.net

Also by Justine Ford

Missing You
One Piece of the Puzzle
Unsolved Australia

The Good Cop

JUSTINE FORD

The true story of Ron Iddles,
Australia's greatest detective

PAN
Pan Macmillan Australia

First published 2016 in Macmillan by Pan Macmillan Australia Pty Ltd
This Pan edition published 2018 by Pan Macmillan Australia Pty Ltd
1 Market Street, Sydney, New South Wales, Australia, 2000

Cataloguing-in-Publication entry is available
from the National Library of Australia
http://catalogue.nla.gov.au

Typeset in 12.5/17 pt Fairfield LH Light by Post Pre-press Group, Brisbane
Printed by McPherson's Printing Group

CONTENTS

RON'S POLICE FORCE TIMELINE

1973	Joined the Victoria Police
1980	Started at the Homicide Squad
1983	Completed Sergeants' Course
1985	Seconded to the National Crime Authority (NCA)
1986	Awarded Chief Commissioner's Certificate for Bravery and Courage on Arrest on 29 May 1984
1987–88	Seconded to the Drug Squad
1989	Returned to the Homicide Squad
1989	Resigned from Victoria Police
1994	Rejoined Victoria Police and returned to the Homicide Squad
1999	Awarded the Blue Ribbon Foundation Angela Taylor Scholarship to study Criminal Profiling and Serial Killers at the FBI Academy, USA
2001	Awarded the Australian Police Medal (APM)
2007	Awarded Certificate of Recognition by Victoria Police for Subject Matter Expertise in Suspicious Death Investigations

2008	Awarded the Chief Commissioner's Ethical Leadership Certificate
2010	Awarded Commendation for Investigation into the Murder of Erwin Kastenberger on 8 March 2005
2012	Awarded Policeman of the Year by the Blue Ribbon Foundation
2012	Awarded the Mick Miller Detective of the Year
2014	Finished at the Homicide Squad
2014	Appointed Secretary of the Police Association Victoria
2015	Awarded Order of Australia Medal (OAM)

FOREWORD

It wasn't a great beginning for the new homicide detective who would go on to become a legendary murder investigator.

It was June 1980 when Ron Iddles stepped into a Thornbury bookshop where owner Maria James had been stabbed sixty-eight times in a frenzied attack that remains unsolved to this day.

It was to be one of the few cases that Ron Iddles would leave as an open file in 2014 when he finally stepped aside from the Homicide Squad to become Secretary of the Victoria Police Association.

When he walked away a veteran senior sergeant he had investigated over 300 murders and checked hundreds more suspicious deaths. He left with a Bradman-like success rate of around 99 per cent.

In a business where detectives can easily become hardened to human tragedy Ron Iddles remained passionate, emotional and committed. Physically brave and mentally tough, he is brought to tears recalling some of the tragedies he has encountered.

While Ron had the brains, the dedication and the energy

to become a first-class investigator, he also had the essential emotion needed to be a murder cop – empathy. The ability to relate to the victim he would know only after death, the family devastated by their unspeakable loss, and importantly, the ability to understand why the offender chose to kill.

By building a relationship with murderers, Ron was able to take them on a journey that began with trust and ended with a confession.

'Most are not bad people, they have just made bad choices,' he says.

His refusal to condemn killers has fostered unique relationships with some suspects. When one was released after nearly twenty years, his first call was to Iddles – to thank him. 'He said he was spiralling out of control and was never going to stop committing crime until he was caught. He says he is determined to take his second chance now.'

Ron's methodical style meant that, when he laid charges, they tended to stick. He lost only three Supreme Court cases and each time went to the dock to shake hands with the man he believed had got away with murder. Each time he gave the same piece of advice: 'You have just copped the biggest break you will ever get, so take advantage of it.'

It was a long way from the lounge room of the family dairy farm near Echuca where as a schoolboy he would sit and watch episodes of the TV drama *Homicide*.

In drama, the police managed to solve a murder in sixty minutes. In the reality it could take decades.

A few years ago Ron asked me to join him for a charity fundraiser in Echuca – for years he has quietly raised a small fortune for good causes around the state.

On the way he said we would be meeting Tammy Mills, a *Shepparton News* reporter who had persuaded him to open a local cold case homicide investigation.

It was the murder of Michelle Buckingham, sixteen, who disappeared in October 1983. She was last seen walking towards the Strayleaves Caravan Park on 21 October. Like Maria James, she had been stabbed repeatedly without obvious motive.

Mills' idea was to bombard Shepparton with the story in the hope that someone with inside knowledge would finally come forward.

It was a million-to-one chance but sometimes long-shots actually win.

'I kept telling her we didn't have the staff or resources to work on it but she kept calling me and kept asking questions. Eventually I agreed to reopen the case, and that if she wrote about it, any leads would be followed up,' he says.

And she did, writing a comprehensive series for the *Shepparton News* in August 2012 that covered the murder, the initial investigation and the aftermath.

Police received thirty tips, but only one intrigued Ron. It was from a man who agreed to meet the veteran detective at the Shepparton East Football Club ground. His name was Norman Gribble and he would tell Ron the secret he had kept for decades.

Someone he knew had confessed to the murder and that someone was his brother-in-law, Stephen Bradley.

In May 2014, Bradley was charged, extradited from Brisbane and eventually committed for trial.

In 2015, no longer a homicide squad detective, Ron gave evidence in a Supreme Court murder trial for the last time.

Bradley was convicted and more than thirty-two years after Michelle was stabbed to death he was sentenced to twenty-seven years with a minimum of twenty-one.

While Ron's first case remains unsolved, he had the satisfaction of closing his last.

The true crime bookshelves are filled with stories about the worst people in our society. And so Justine Ford's profile on one of the best is a welcome and refreshing addition.

John Silvester
Senior Crime Reporter
The Age

PROLOGUE

In a career at the Homicide Squad spanning twenty-five years, Ron Iddles has investigated about 320 murders, with a 99 per cent clear-up rate.

Tonight he is talking to a packed auditorium in Essendon about the 1983 stabbing murder of Shepparton teenager Michelle Buckingham, a case that has taken the Homicide Squad until 2015 to finally solve. He explains that while some murderers are locked up within hours, other cases can take years to crack. Ron has been doing these talks since his early days in the force, discussing crime and its effects to members of the public. Any entry fees are donated to charity. He has never accepted a cent.

Ron always plays to full houses; some in the audience tonight haven't missed one of his talks in a decade. Tonight, he walks on stage to thunderous applause. Then silence. No one wants to miss a word.

The audience hears the fine details of how the celebrated detective closed in on a man he'd accused of the sixteen-year-old's murder. Ron's PowerPoint presentation shows photos of police in the scrub at the crime scene, and a video of Ron interviewing a suspect. It is edge-of-the-seat stuff, a gripping way to spend forty minutes. Will the suspect confess?

Ron sees these engagements as an opportunity to educate the public about important issues such as violence against women, family violence, and the overwhelming need in today's society to keep each other safe. His charity work – for which he has raised $1.5 million – would see him recognised with one of the nation's highest awards, an Order of Australia Medal in 2015.

It was also one of these talks that would see him out the door of his beloved Homicide Squad.

*

It all began in 1980. One of the parents on his daughter Joanne's school council asked Ron if he would talk to the school about drugs. Who better to talk about drugs than an officer who had worked the junk-riddled streets of St Kilda? Convinced that his talk might educate others, Ron decided to give it a go.

While he was used to giving evidence in court, addressing a group of mums, dads and grandparents was a new experience. 'I was probably fairly nervous and I had a lot of notes,' he says. 'I got asked a lot of questions and noticed that people have a fascination for police work.'

A few months later, another Neighbourhood Watch group asked him to talk about his role as a homicide investigator, having heard about his noteworthy speech at the school.

For that talk, he presented an in-depth case study during which he discussed clues found at the crime scene, the investigation and the judicial process. Ron also took along a booklet of crime-scene photos but warned the audience about its graphic content.

'I said, "You don't have to look at the pictures of the person who's been shot",' he recalls, but everyone wanted a gander. 'People were intrigued to see the photos but I didn't go so far as to show them the post-mortem pictures. Even though it was what I dealt with every day at Homicide and was part of my life, I probably didn't appreciate that many people haven't seen a dead body.'

After that, word kept spreading. Probus groups began asking Ron to speak to their members. Word of mouth travelled a long way and he was soon a regular on the state's speaking circuit.

'In the end I saw it as a good community thing, and it gave people a good sense of what you did as a homicide investigator,' he says.

At the end of each presentation, Ron always gave the audience something to ponder. 'I have given you the facts of the case,' he would say. 'You're the jury. It's up to you to determine what happened. Ladies and gentlemen of the jury, now you are to go and consider your verdict.'

Generally, they did it over tea and light refreshments.

Until he first left the police force in 1989, Ron found himself addressing around ten groups a year. The number of engagements doubled after his return to the job in 1994, when he was asked to speak to at least twenty groups a year, including Rotary and Lions clubs. By this time his presentations were even more dynamic.

'Technology had changed by then, so we had audiovisual recordings of interviews with suspects,' he says. 'People wanted to be immersed in the investigation process from start to finish and they were fascinated to hear a suspect saying, "This was what I did".'

Ron also showed clips from the television news, photos of exhibits and, sometimes, footage of the offender being arrested. 'There were numerous TV shows about homicide and police investigations but this was taking people into the real world of a homicide investigator,' he says. Ron was a one-man show connecting police with the public, which explains why a growing number of senior police endorsed his presentations. Arguably more interesting than a night at the flicks, the requests for Ron Iddles the public speaker kept pouring in.

As time went by, he became known as a man with a message.

'We are caught up in the fastest-paced world we have ever seen,' he'd say. 'We are going like a missile out of control, but sadly it is a world you and I helped create. Maybe it's time to put the handbrake on. Maybe it's time to start a conversation. Maybe it's time to engage. I'm not asking you to go home on a Sunday night and sing "Kumbaya" and hold hands. But, I am saying, *look after each other.*'

In a homicide context, Ron explained that the combination of lust, greed and revenge produced a fertile environment for murder. He had seen it so many times – people resorting to violence when they could have resolved their problems with words.

Ron had created such a buzz on the public-speaking circuit that the Blue Ribbon Foundation established 'Insight' nights, at which detectives demystified their work to members of the general public. Eighty-five people came to the inaugural

Insight night. They told their friends, and the next year 180 people came, followed by 250 the year after. Any money raised went to a local hospital to purchase equipment and, according to Ron, 'The events were also in memory of police officers who had died, so it was a good cause all round.'

Ron was so popular he could have charged thousands of dollars for his services but, for him, it was all about educating people about his job and serving the community. Everyone who came to these nights knew they were getting stories about real-life murders and their solution and the events were clearly billed as such. In thirty years he'd never had one complaint. But times were changing.

*

As one of the highest profile cops in Victoria, Ron could easily have worked his way to the top of the organisation, but he wanted to solve murders, and he couldn't do that from behind a desk. It troubled him that all his fellow senior sergeants had left the Homicide Squad due to a controversial rotation policy. 'In late 2009, after what was known as the "Boston" review of the Crime Department, Charlie Bezzina and Lucio Rovis were moved. In the end they both took sick leave due to stress and never returned,' Ron says. In 2010, Rowland Legg was rotated and he too ultimately resigned. 'Then in 2011 Jeff Maher decided to leave rather than be pushed out the door. He went to the Arson Squad and retired in 2016.' With decades of specialist experience gone, they were grim days for what was once considered Victoria's most elite squad.

'The whole library was going. The last encyclopaedia was Ron,' says former Homicide detective Allan Birch, who hoped Ron would be spared after winning the 2012 Mick Miller Detective of the Year award. 'We couldn't lose him. That would be devastating.'

But you can't fight City Hall – or police policy gone mad. Ron Iddles was the last man standing. How long could he avoid the dreaded rotation? And if he did leave Homicide, where would he go? When the secretary of the Police Association of Victoria, Greg Davies, announced his resignation in September 2013, several officers suggested Ron apply for the role.

'I thought about it as the possible next chapter of my life, and the final one of my full-time working life,' Ron says. 'I asked myself if I could make a difference, and the answer was yes.'

So he applied for the job. It wasn't a lay-down misère that he would get it, and it was possible he might be permitted to stay at Homicide for another couple of years.

He was, after all, their top cop and prior to being honoured as Detective of the Year had been awarded the Australian Police Medal and Policeman of the Year. Victoria Police had recognised him for his expertise in suspicious death investigations and he had received a Chief Commissioner's commendation for ethical leadership. The longest-serving detective at the squad, he was at the height of his investigative powers and had no real desire to leave. He just hoped he would have the choice.

*

On Friday, 15 November 2013, Ron and his wife Colleen drove to Bendigo for the Biggest Blokes Lunch – an event to raise money for prostate cancer – at which Ron was keynote speaker.

'Ron started his talk and at the very beginning he made the point that some people might be offended or upset by the graphic nature of some of the pictures, so they could either look away or come and discuss their concerns with him after his presentation,' says organiser and MC Keith Sutherland.

'You may see some photos,' Ron clearly warned. 'I'm not asking anyone to look at them.'

As usual, no one budged. Ron also asked any members of the media present that evening to identify themselves so he could make sure they understood the context of the presentation, that it was insight into a homicide investigator's work, the same kind of lecture he had been giving for years.

'The audience knew he wasn't there to bake cupcakes!' Ron's wife Colleen says.

For more than an hour Ron gave a speech themed around the need to look after each other. 'I spoke about a whole range of social issues that impact on us in society, and how some of those issues – depression, alcohol and drugs – often cause homicides,' he says.

'Ron's very clear message was to "look after your mates", and if anyone missed that point they clearly did not understand what the presentation was about,' Keith says. 'It was not about dead bodies or graphic photos.'

Rather, it was about how there can be tragic consequences if people don't take care of each other. Keith adds, 'Ron went on to highlight some cases where people were looking for help and their friends missed some of the triggers.'

Ron's short case study was the high-profile murder of Irish woman Jill Meagher. On 22 September 2012, serial sex offender Adrian Bayley abducted the 29-year-old ABC employee from the inner Melbourne suburb of Brunswick, before raping and strangling her to death. It was a crime that outraged the nation, including Ron, whose speeches invariably turned to society's need to better protect women. On this occasion his message was particularly apt as it was White Ribbon Day, a day to raise awareness about preventing violence against women.

Ron acknowledged the only person responsible for the crime was Bayley, but again urged the audience to take care of each other, especially when they go out for a few drinks. 'Jill had a very high blood alcohol reading, something like 0.230,' he told the audience. 'If young people are going to go out and drink, you've got to look after each other.'

During the case study, Ron showed a photo of Jill Meagher's obscured, partially clad body in a shallow grave. It was on screen for less than two seconds. Blink and you'd miss it.

'His message was: if you go out drinking with your friends, make sure you get each other home, and do not go alone as there are predators out there waiting to take advantage of your vulnerability,' Keith says.

It was a powerful speech, and one Ron hoped would inspire those who had heard it.

'That was fantastic,' Keith said to Ron when he walked offstage. 'You could have heard a pin drop.'

Ron then took his seat next to a local councillor, who said to him, '"That is the best presentation I've ever seen".' Ron felt satisfied his important safety message was well received by yet another respected community member.

*

About the same time as the Jill Meagher talk, Ron was scrutinising evidence in the unsolved case of Michelle Buckingham, alerted to the unsolved murder by reporter Tammy Mills from the *Shepparton News*. After Tammy wrote a story about the case, a man came forward with crucial information, enabling Ron to identify a suspect named Stephen James Bradley. He took Bradley in for questioning in Brisbane on Tuesday, 27 November 2013.

As he was taking Bradley to the Queensland Police Homicide Squad office, his mobile phone rang. It was a staff member from the Victoria Police Media Unit asking if Ron had shown a photo of Jill Meagher at a fundraiser. The staffer told him someone had tipped off the *Herald Sun*.

'He said they're going to run a story about it on the front page, saying how insensitive it was,' Ron recalls.

Ron was mystified because no one had complained about the photo to him. *What am I going to do?* he wondered. *I've done nothing wrong.*

'I'm pretty sure I said, "I don't think you get it",' Ron recalls, adding that he was outraged and speaking in a raised voice while Bradley sat next to him in the police car. 'I said, "I've given my time as a public speaker for more than twenty years and have raised one and a half million dollars for charities, and I can tell you, I ain't done anything wrong!"'

Aware that he was uncharacteristically flustered in front of a suspect, he turned to Bradley and said, "'It's all right, Steve. I'm a bit pissed off and a bit upset but I'm not going to treat you that way".'

Ron knew he had to stay focused on the interview with Bradley. He did, but it wasn't easy. Afterwards, he called the media officer, who told Ron he didn't think they could stop the story running. Ron says, 'But no one from the *Herald Sun* had the decency to ring me! It was a disgrace. I then told my inspector he could go to my desk, find my PowerPoint presentation and make an assessment himself.'

It was unknown who had complained; no one had had a bad word to say on the night.

Later, in his hotel room, Ron phoned Colleen to tell her the bad news, warning her that the story about his talk would be plastered all over the front page of the paper tomorrow. 'Batten down the hatches,' he told her.

Colleen was mortified, but what made matters worse was that Ron was still interstate and she couldn't comfort him in person. 'I just felt sad for him,' she says. 'It was going to detract from all the good he'd done for other people. I felt this was the thing people would remember him for.'

Ron said a superior at Victoria Police told him that showing the photo probably hadn't been appropriate. Certain he had not acted improperly, Ron rang the assistant commissioner to reiterate he'd done nothing wrong.

'Are you going to throw me under the bus?' he asked.

'He said, "No, we'll say you are a great detective and have done a lot of good work, but this was an error of judgement and we need to publicly apologise".'

Next, Ron rang George and Edith McKeon, Jill Meagher's

parents. Members of his crew had investigated Meagher's death and Ron had met her family in court. The McKeons had stayed in contact with Ron after the murder trial and knew he was a public speaker and fundraiser. The first they'd heard of the incident was when a media officer from Victoria Police phoned them to say one of their members had done something dreadful, without explaining who was responsible or the context. All they said was a policeman had shown a naked photo of their daughter in a talk.

Ron told the McKeons the whole story.

'George said, "If I'd been told it was you, I'd have said there was not a problem",' Ron recalls. 'I said, "Can you tell [Jill's widower] Tom?" And I got a message back to say he supported me.'

George also offered to call the newspaper, hoping he could stop the press.

Ron didn't sleep at all that night.

At 5.45 am, he couldn't help checking his mobile phone, and there it was, the front page of the newspaper screaming at him: *Top Cop's Jill Insult.*

Ron was gutted – and angry. 'For the journalists not to call me was nothing short of disgraceful,' he says. 'I was aware the story would cause huge television and radio coverage and this would impact on my family.'

Every major television station in the country ran the story, and in Melbourne, the Jill Meagher photo was the only subject being discussed on talkback radio.

'Neil Mitchell [from 3AW] said I'd done it in poor taste; that he didn't know what I was thinking and that I was a disgrace,' Ron says. But Mitchell's listeners were taking Ron's side.

'They said things like, "I heard Ron Iddles speak at a fundraiser. I've seen the photos. There's nothing offensive about what he does. He's giving a community message".'

Colleen noticed that no one was complaining about the photos of *other* victims Ron had used before, even though, in the context of the other images, Jill's photo wasn't nearly as graphic. 'She was seven-eighths buried under dirt. You couldn't see anything really,' Colleen says. But Jill Meagher was big news. Her opportunistic abduction and murder had so shocked the community that it prompted ten thousand people to march down Sydney Road in Brunswick demanding an end to violence against women. The case continued to fascinate, and every newspaper knew it.

At 10 am Ron learnt that Victoria Police was going to hold a media conference without him. 'My argument was, "Don't I get a right of reply?"'

As news spread, Ron was inundated with calls, especially after the premier, Denis Napthine, was doorstopped and described Ron's use of the photo as 'sickening'. But the premier was not expressing the views of his colleagues. 'My phone went berserk,' Ron says, 'I had senior members of the Liberal Party ring and say, "I don't know why he said that".'

All the *Herald Sun* crime reporters called Ron too. 'They said they were not part of the story. They had tried to stop it and didn't want to be a part of it,' he says.

The crime writers had told their superiors that Ron was a good contact who always made himself available to them. Their pleas not to burn him fell on deaf ears.

At around 10.15 am, Victoria Police called Ron again. They had decided he could speak to the media. 'But they put me in an awkward position because they were apologising. I said, "You don't need to apologise because I've got the support of Jill's family".'

Colleen, who knew Ron was exhausted, was firmly against her husband appearing on television. 'I just had a bad feeling about it,' she says.

Ron's media conference was scheduled for 11.30 am at Brisbane's Police Headquarters.

'I hadn't slept in thirty hours. I looked like shit,' he says.

The only consolation was that two of his faithful crew members, Detective Sergeant Allan Birch and Detective Senior Constable Paul Bubb, were sitting in the back of the room to support him.

As the cameras rolled and snapped, Ron looked drained. 'I said in no way did I want to demean her,' he recalls. 'I said that the people who are making the judgements weren't there. I said I was trying to make good out of bad.'

Colleen remembers the broadcast well. 'Ron wanted to show people he didn't need to make an apology because he had the approval of Jill Meagher's family,' she says. 'He believed he was a tall poppy and people were out to get him.'

Later that day, Ron flew back to Melbourne.

'I was really sad that night because it affected the whole family,' Colleen says. 'I couldn't go into work for about two days because I was traumatised by what my husband had been subjected to. I felt so sorry for him. He didn't deserve it. I knew how hard he had worked for the victims' families.'

Ron's adult children, Jo, Matt and Shae were also bombarded by people asking about their dad.

By the next morning, as Ron drove to work, Neil Mitchell had had a change of heart and said he had got it wrong, telling his audience that he had received about 320 emails overnight, all supporting Ron. Newspaper reporters who knew Ron also showed their support for him in print.

But the fallout wasn't over. Victoria Police announced that all police public-speaking engagements were suspended until they could put an appropriate policy in place.

Veteran fundraiser Keith Sutherland stood by Ron on television, in the newspaper and on radio, reiterating that Ron had been trying to deliver a message about looking after your mates, but the media weren't interested in that.

Fortunately, Ron's support from the community never waned, and Keith invited him back to address another fundraiser the following year. When Ron took to the stage, four hundred men gave him a standing ovation.

THE BOY FROM THE BUSH

*'Growing up in the country gave me values,
shaped my character and gave me a work ethic.
And watching the TV show,* Homicide, *made me
think,* I want to be a policeman.'
– Ron Iddles

The fifties in Australia were a time of great opportunity and prosperity. After the hard years of the Depression and two world wars, there was optimism in the air and stability in the leadership of Prime Minister Robert Menzies. New businesses were set up and many flourished, not just in the city but in country towns like Rochester, near Echuca in northern Victoria.

Many returned soldiers from World War Two settled in the area on 100-acre farms known as 'soldier settlement blocks', financed by government loans. Often they became dairy farmers, who drove into Rochester's town centre once a week for supplies.

There were five pubs in town, three butchers, two bakeries, a fruit shop, a newsagent, two stock and station agents, and three supermarkets, one which sold groceries on one side, and clothing and drapery on the other.

Pride of place in the main street was Iddles Brothers Shoe Store, a few minutes' walk from Woodlands' Garage, one of several petrol stations in the thriving little town.

With a population of just over two thousand people, Rochester was the kind of place where most of the locals knew each other, so it was no surprise when the Iddles family met the Woodlands.

*

Good with numbers, Phyllis Woodland worked as one of the first female tellers at the Union Bank after she finished school. Phyllis had lived in Rochester all her life and her brothers owned Woodlands' Garage. Airman Bill Iddles had ridden his bike past Woodlands' countless times, but didn't meet the mechanics' sister until he was introduced to her at a Christian youth group.

Phyllis had three other admirers at the time – a pilot, a banker, and a farmer – but Bill's sense of humour won her over. 'He used to throw pebbles at the window of the Union Bank to get her attention,' says Ron's sister, Nancye Lees. 'He would play jokes and she was always happy, laughing.'

In May 1950, after a three-year year courtship, twenty-three-year-old Bill Iddles, and twenty-six-year-old Phyllis Woodland tied the knot. They honeymooned at a guesthouse in rural Ferntree Gully, which is now one of Melbourne's outer suburbs. 'After they got married, she left the bank and Dad started driving a bus from Rochester to Melbourne,'

Ron says. 'It was a passenger service that would leave at seven in the morning, get to Melbourne at eleven, then return home at night.'

After a while, Bill quit driving buses and took a job as a mechanic at Woodlands' Garage. He was a man from the land however, and left a short time later to work as a share farmer on a nearby sheep and wheat property. The Iddles family – along with Bill's widowed dad, Bill Iddles Senior (better known as Pop) – lived in a weatherboard house with an enormous back-yard in Rochester.

Two years after getting married, their first child, Nancye, was born in 1952, followed by non-identical twins Ronald and Barry Iddles (both eight pounds four ounces) at Rochester War Memorial Hospital on 10 March 1955.

Shortly after the twins were born, the nurses asked Phyllis what she wanted to call them.

'Mum said, "Iddles is a terrible name to put anything with",' says Nancye. '"My initial is P. for Phyllis, and my husband's is W. for William, which makes us sound like Piddles and Widdles."' Amused, the hospital staff decided to call the babies Piddles and Widdles while they waited for their real names. When Ron was named, his first initial and surname spelled out, appropriately, Riddles – of which he would solve many.

Although Phyllis used to dress them in identical clothes, Ron and Barry had very different characters from an early age, as their sister Nancye confirms.

'Ron was always outgoing and interested in anything that was going on. He was the stronger of the twins because Barry had a health condition, so Ron was more active.'

A cyst on Barry's throat was diagnosed when he was eighteen months old, and he had his first operation a year later. After that, his mum took him to a Chinese herbalist who treated him with a foul-smelling black poultice, then he referred Barry to a plastic surgeon who removed his hyoid bone when he was nine. For two weeks after the surgery, Phyllis stayed with the younger twin in hospital. It was a worrying time for the whole family, especially for Ron and Nancye, who wrote him a 'get-well' letter on a brown paper bag.

When he was discharged, Barry was not allowed to play sport or take part in any activities that might aggravate his condition, so he spent time baking with their mum, while Ron helped their dad outside.

By the time they were ten, Barry was fully recuperated. Nonetheless, 'We were different,' Ron says of his twin. 'Because he was sick, he didn't do things that were rough and tumble. Back then, he'd be happy doing something with Mum and was more into cooking, whereas if Dad was going out, I'd go and potter outside or get on the tractor.' The more rugged activities suited Ron, who was content so long as he was active. 'I had mates I could play with, but often they were doing the same as I was, which was helping around the farm.'

The Iddles kids had plenty of fun times together, though, and the boys played with each other or with their big sister.

'Monday night was special because we'd put a rug on the dining-room table and play a game called "Bobs",' Ron remembers. The younger members of the family would use a homemade cue to shoot a ball with a numeric value across to the other side of the table, while Pop would watch and clean his pipe. 'The winner was whoever got to fifty first,' Ron says.

One of the greatest joys in the Iddles household – particularly at Christmas time – was Phyllis's lavish country cooking. Her powder puffs, jelly cakes and golden syrup dumplings were the envy of the district. 'Sunday, we always had a cream sponge – ginger fluff – with four layers of cream,' Ron recalls.

The Iddles family lived amid premium dairy country and had a cow in the backyard, which meant an ample supply of milk, cream and butter. 'My dad would milk the cow by hand and it was my job to make the butter,' Ron says. Ron enjoyed farm life and it instilled in him a work ethic he carries on to this day. 'Some jobs on the farm were chores but others I did because I enjoyed them, like driving the tractors and ploughing. I was able to see the end result of my work: for example, when I cut the grass, I'd rake it and then make hay bales. It taught me that work gave you a sense of self-worth, and to get anywhere in life you have to put in an effort.'

Christmas was always a big family affair, shared with grandparents, great aunts and uncles, neighbours and anyone they knew who had nowhere else to go. It was a traditional, country Christian family in which Bill was the breadwinner and Phyllis stayed home to care for the children.

'We used to collect beer bottles from the side of the road,' Nancye says, recalling how the Iddles kids realised from an early age that teamwork pays off. The money from the bottles helped save towards a caravan that would be a family holiday fixture for the next ten years. 'Dad would sell them for a halfpenny each and the money we made contributed to the caravan. We sold *a lot* of bottles!'

Come January, Bill would hitch the family's yellow fibreglass caravan to his pink-and-grey DeSoto, and the whole family – including Pop Iddles and Phyllis's mum, Nanna Woodland – would set off at six in the evening on their annual family holiday to Barwon Heads on Victoria's Bellarine Peninsula.

'We left at that time because the car would overheat,' Ron says. 'Then, after about an hour and a half we'd hop out, and while the adults had a cuppa, Dad would open the bonnet to cool the engine off, then off we'd go again.'

Bill and Phyllis would sleep at one end of the caravan while Nancye shared a double bed with Nanna Woodland, and Ron, Barry and Pop occupied the annex.

'There was a lot of love and family life,' Nancye says. 'And that's been Ron's foundation. That's what's made him who he is.'

When the boys were eight and Nancye was ten, the family moved to Bamawm, twenty minutes' drive away, where Bill worked for a dairy farmer. Bamawm was where the Iddles kids first learnt to drive. Bill bought a 1938 Ford Pilot V8 from a solicitor as a paddock basher and, in no time, the boys were doing wheelies around the haystack.

'It was polished black with big round silver headlights and leather seats,' Ron says before wincing, 'Dad took an axe to it and pulled the seats out so that it could carry hay.'

The Iddles also owned a Plymouth, which, according to Ron, was 'built like a tank'. Around that time, Bill also taught Ron how to remove a bung motor from a car and fix it. 'He was always very mechanically minded,' Bill observes.

Ron drove the Plymouth until it blew up and later his dad purchased a mint condition Standard Eight for $24. 'We had a long gravel driveway with a right-hand bend,' Ron recalls.

'We'd go as fast as we could up the driveway and then as fast as we could around the corner!'

The kids rarely acted up at home; hardworking Bill wouldn't have tolerated it.

'He was pretty strict,' Ron says. 'There was a fair amount of discipline in the home. You didn't backchat or play up or you got the strap. Looking back, I wouldn't say I was overly close to my dad but I don't feel badly about that. He had to work hard to provide for his family. But would he kick a footy with me? Yes. He also made me a fishing rod out of the branch of a tree and was always happy to teach me mechanics. I don't think it was tough love, but fair love. In those days it was just the way we were brought up. We were expected to obey our parents and do chores. We came to understand you had to work if you wanted to get ahead.'

For Bill, it was all about instilling strong values in his children.

'It was about knowing right from wrong and being respectful,' Ron explains. 'We were never allowed to call an adult by their first name, for example; it was always Mr and Mrs, or Aunty and Uncle.'

Devout Presbyterians, Bill and Phyllis took their children to church every Sunday, where Phyllis sang in the choir. 'While my parents were very religious, I think church in the country was where people got to stop for a little bit,' Ron says. 'It was a social thing. It was, for the families, a day of rest.'

According to Nancye, church also provided a formal framework for the morals the children were being taught at home: the importance of caring about others, and sharing with those in need.

'Our family always tried to help local families who struggled,' Nancye says. 'We would take a trailer of wood to them, or food. Mum and Dad would kill a sheep or pluck a chook or duck, and we would take our hand-me-downs. We've all inherited our parents' caring, generous nature.'

From third grade, Ron attended Lockington Consolidated School. Lockington had one primary teacher and two secondary teachers – one who taught English, history and geography, and another, Ted Coleman, who taught agricultural science, science and maths.

'About ninety per cent of the kids at that school were off farms,' Ted recalls. 'Farmers have a pretty dry sense of humour; they're pretty honest, pretty direct, and their livelihood depends on accuracy. Everything's a challenge in a rural community, and the kids reflected that.'

Ted loved his students, of whom, at the start, there were only sixteen. 'There was mutual respect for one another and Ron was looked on by the others as a bit of a leader,' he says. 'He spoke his mind.'

Ted first started teaching Ron in Year Nine (known then as Third Form) in 1969. 'Ron I admired as a student because he was trustworthy, he was honest,' Ted says. 'He had that rural integrity. But he had the capacity to challenge you in the way a farmer would; for example, he might ask, "Would you have that many sheep in a paddock, or that many cows per acre?"'

Ron's intelligence, Ted says, was unique to those who lived on farms and he could apply it in practical ways. 'To city people it's not easily understood,' Ted says. 'It's a kind of intelligence that allows you to seek answers.'

Lindsay McMinn (who Ron nicknamed 'Fungi' because of his mushroom-coloured hair) was one of his best mates, and has kept in contact ever since. 'Ron was a keen footballer and he also played cricket,' Lindsay says. 'We all wanted to be on his team because he was so big and strong. He was bigger than everyone in the school!'

What really stood out to Lindsay about Ron was his humility. 'He didn't think he was any better than anyone else,' Lindsay says. 'He was very kind to everyone and he was a very generous bloke too. He'd give you anything. He was the same to me now as he was then – a bloody good bloke and a mate, always.'

Ron never got into any trouble at school. Lindsay says, 'I used to get the lash but he never did. I don't think he ever got the cuts at school – he was too nice a person. And he was always in the top-notches in the class all the time.'

When Ron was twelve, his dad bought a farm of his own at Lockington. The children were allowed countless pets – dogs, cats, ducks, turkeys, 'special' cows and even a featherless, sulphur-crested cockatoo that they raised on porridge. 'We were also each given a calf, and when they grew up, we sold them,' Nancye says.

As is the bush way, Bill enlisted his children's help to run the farm. 'I used to get up at half-past four,' he remembers. 'The three of them were on a roster system, so they'd be in the dairy at five, have a shower, then ride to the school bus.'

They were long days. 'Before I went to high school I'd milk 120 cows,' Ron says. 'I didn't get home until nearly five. Then on weekends I'd be cutting hay, carting hay and slashing paddocks with a tractor.'

Once the cows had calved, it was the siblings' job to teach them to drink from a bucket, but rather than feed them one at a time, Barry invented a 'Calfeteria' made from a forty-four-gallon drum, cut in half, with rubber teats and hoses that could hold forty litres of powdered milk. It enabled Barry, Nancye and Ron to feed twenty cows at once.

Barry says that Ron has only acted dishonestly once, and even then, it was more of an omission than a lie. Concerned that a crow in a gum tree had been menacing a lamb, Ron decided to blast the blood-hungry bird with a twelve-gauge shotgun. Unexpectedly, the gun went off and hit the front passenger door of Nanna Woodland's car.

Rather than tell her he'd blown a two-inch hole in her car, twelve-year-old Ron figured that, with a little ingenuity, he might just get away with it. 'He panel-beat it with a hammer,' Barry says, recalling how their grandmother's car was green, as was their house, so Ron fetched a tin of house-paint and began applying it to the car. It was a dubious colour match, however, and for the rest of the week, their grandmother tried to wash the strange green mark from her 1964 Zephyr sedan. 'He admitted it once he was sprung,' Barry laughs, 'but he'd tried to cover it up!'

Nancye remembers her brothers were always respectful but occasionally teased her. 'We used to swim in the irrigation channel on the farm,' she says. 'If it wasn't fresh flowing, you'd get leeches on you. Ron and Barry would chase me with the leeches!'

Throughout his teenage years, Ron's love of football continued to blossom, and he played for the Bamawm Under Sixteens, then for Echuca, first as a ruckman (which didn't surprise anyone, as he was fast lurching towards 194 centimetres), then in the forward pocket. He played in the firsts, but would back up for the seconds when they didn't have enough players. 'Quite often I played two games on a Saturday,' he says.

'I was talking to his football coach recently and he said it was a shame Ron went to Melbourne because he would have been a good footballer,' Bill says.

Things might have been very different had Bill Iddles not purchased a television set. 'I was one of the last to come to television because I could see it was going to be a hindrance to work,' he says. 'But we got a black-and-white set when Leonard Teale was in *Homicide*, and you could be sure on the nights it was on, they'd finish up early and watch that.'

Ron mostly kept his ambition of joining the police to himself, but one day in class, when Ted asked his students what they wanted to do after school, Ron casually mentioned it.

'I thought, *Where would that have come from?*' Ted wishes he had pressed Ron to find out why he wanted to investigate murders, but admits that, in those days, teachers rarely discussed students' future plans in much depth.

Ted found the teenage Ron to be kind and community-minded, someone who put others before himself. 'He's not a vain person. He never was at school, either,' Ted says. 'He was not, "Look at me, look at me". There's a consistency about the boy that is in the man, and that consistency reflects those underlying principles as a result of his family experience and genetic make-up.'

By the time Ron was fifteen, he wanted to quit school. There were only four secondary students left at Lockington Consolidated, which only went up to Year Ten. He'd had enough and leaving school would not prevent him from one day joining the police. 'Mum and Dad said, "No, that's not happening, you're getting a certificate," so they enrolled us in Echuca Technical School, which went up to Year Twelve,' he says. Nancye had already completed her studies and was helping out on the farm, but that wasn't what Bill and Phyllis had in mind for the boys.

On their first day, Phyllis – who made sure the twins were neatly decked out in their new school uniforms – drove them to the bus stop at Lockington, from where it would take them an hour to get to their new school. 'We were wearing new short-sleeved shirts, shorts that went nearly to the knee, white socks and black shoes,' Ron says. 'But when we got on the bus, everyone was wearing long pants.' Unfortunately, the childishly dressed teenagers would have to endure the walk of shame onto the bus for at least another week. 'I remember getting home and saying, "Mum! You've got to get me some long pants!"'

Ron was surprised to find there were teachers for every subject. 'There were probably six hundred students and at least four Year Eleven classes, so I felt that the pressure was on,' he admits.

When they returned to school, Ron continued to feel weight on his shoulders. 'You had to perform, so I worked hard,' he says. It paid off when he became dux of Year Eleven.

Ron toyed briefly with the idea of becoming a railway station assistant. 'But I realised I'd be putting sand in ashtrays and blowing a whistle when a train came in.' And that just didn't excite him, not in the way that Leonard Teale and John Fegan's fictitious adventures did.

2

THE BIG SMOKE

*'I hadn't been in the police cadets for very long
when I met Colleen. She was a diamond in the
rough who would turn out to be my rock.'*
– Ron Iddles

In Ron's day, there were two ways to get into Victoria Police.

If you were eighteen-and-a-half, you could join directly and go into training as a recruit. The other option was to complete Year Eleven and start as a cadet. Unable to wait, Ron applied to join the cadets while he was in Year Eleven, and travelled to Melbourne for a fitness test and interview.

'I was very excited when I received the letter to say I'd been accepted,' he says. 'Mum and Dad saw it as a very good profession and I remember other relatives being at the house that day and congratulating me.'

And so it was that Ron Iddles, just shy of seventeen, left Lockington in February 1972 to live in Melbourne, two hundred kilometres and a world away. 'Mum and Dad brought me down in their 1966 HR Holden station wagon and Mum was in tears,' Ron recalls.

Ron moved into a boarding house in Hawthorn, six kilo-metres from Melbourne's CBD. The boarding house was run by a small-framed woman called Ada who worked tire-lessly upstairs while her husband ran a real-estate agency downstairs. 'I paid fourteen dollars a week and that included breakfast and dinner at night,' Ron recalls. 'And for an extra dollar I got my washing and ironing done, although being young, sometimes I held onto the extra dollar and did it myself.'

The routine at the old boarding house was the same every night. 'At six o'clock, Ada would ring the bell, and for half an hour we sat and yakked,' Ron says. Ada always ate with her four lodgers, while her husband, perhaps tired after talking to clients all day, dined alone. 'Normally we had meat and three veg, but occasionally Ada served ox tongue with white sauce,' Ron says with a shudder. 'I couldn't handle that.'

Ron's twin, Barry, who still lived on the farm, recalls going to see his brother at the boarding house. 'I was very excited to go and visit him in Melbourne,' he says. But Barry's excitement turned to disappointment when he compared Ada's lacklustre cooking to their mum's. 'The cakes would be dry and the bread stale, so Ada would plunge them in water and stick them in the oven to freshen them up,' he says. Barry didn't care for his brother's new digs at all. 'The boarding house was long, narrow, dark and cold, like a city miner's cottage. It cost two cents an hour for a heater. It didn't feel homely.'

City life was vastly different from life on the farm, where Ron woke to the sound of cows mooing, dogs barking and tractors ploughing the soil in a distant paddock. 'Our neigh-bour would start to round up his cows for milking at 5.30 am and they would walk along the road outside our house,' Ron recalls. It had been the most bucolic of lifestyles.

Now, Ron was waking up to cars, trucks making pre-dawn deliveries and the sound of early-morning trams rattling by. Welcome to the big smoke.

And then there was cadet school. 'We had the shortest of hair-cuts and the drill instructors would yell at us, telling us we were out of step,' Ron says. 'Our shoes had to be spit-polished so every day I'd catch the tram back to my boarding room and spend at least forty-five minutes polishing them with Kiwi Parade Nugget and an old stocking. It was the first thing we all did when we got home. Everyone had their own technique, but if you couldn't see your face in the toecap, you weren't up to standard. Most of us thought, *What have we gotten ourselves into?'*

Part of a cadet's training was to carry out mundane jobs at police stations. Ron's first placement was at Kew, where he worked for three months. 'I was sent to supervise school crossings in the morning, and in the afternoon, I did the filing,' he says.

His next placement was at the Dawson Street Transport Branch, where, again, he filed documents. 'I'd come in in the morning and they'd give me a pile of cards – hundreds of them – to put in big steel filing cabinets,' he says. 'And that's what I'd do all day.'

Frustrated by cadets, Ron quit in February 1973. He had given it a year, but promised himself he'd be back when he was old enough to return as a direct entrant.

But by now there was another reason Ron was desperate to climb the ladder.

Her name was Colleen.

*

On 24 October 1972, one of Ron's fellow boarders asked if Ron wanted to accompany him to a church service in Malvern. Eager to get out of the boarding house, Ron said yes.

The church was so packed when they arrived that there was little room to move. There was only one seat left, next to a striking girl with honey-coloured hair. She didn't even look at Ron, but from that day on, Ron started attending church regularly.

'On the third or fourth night, we ended up sitting together,' Colleen says. 'He was so different. He was so straight and well dressed with polished shoes and a straight back and sides, while I was wearing torn jeans which had been texta-ed all over, a kaftan top and leather sandals.'

But Ron didn't care that sixteen-year-old Colleen Drought was a city girl or a self-confessed hippy – he wanted to see her again. Colleen told him that her mum wouldn't let her go out until she had finished Year Eleven, so Ron rang her on the last day of school, three months later.

'She said, "Who are you?"' Ron recalls, cringing. 'Clearly I'd made a big impression on her.'

Ron and Colleen went on their first date in late 1972. 'We went into the city and saw a movie with Goldie Hawn in it, called *Butterflies Are Free*,' Colleen recalls. 'He was respectful.' She pauses, grinning like a teenager. 'I also liked his gorgeous blue eyes and winning smile! From then on, I thought, *That's it, I'm done, he's mine!*'

Colleen recalls meeting Ron's parents for the first time about six months later. Even though she had met Ron in a church environment – much like the way Bill had met Phyllis – she suspected they didn't entirely approve. 'I was wearing a pair of flared purple cord jeans and a tight black blouse, and I had long hair at that stage,' she says. 'I was probably not the kind of girl they were expecting Ron to marry. I think they always had visions of the boys marrying country girls.'

Ron found it even more nerve-racking when he met Colleen's mum, Jean Bannister, and her stepfather, James Bannister, at their home in Caulfield in Melbourne's south-east. After he rang the large metal bell outside, Jean and James ushered Ron into a plush sitting room.

'They had white shag pile carpet and special armchairs,' Ron says, recalling how fancy it seemed compared to his family's utilitarian farmhouse. 'Her mum put out Barbecue Shapes, and at three o'clock they had sherries. I couldn't believe I was allowed in there! I was a bit out of my comfort zone.'

Jean and James took to Ron instantly. 'They really liked him because they knew he was going to be a police officer,' Colleen says.

A few months later, *she* proposed. 'It would have been sometime in 1974,' Ron says. 'She asked me to marry her because I was too slow! She told her mum and her stepdad and they nearly choked. I was nineteen and she was eighteen. But then we had a sherry to celebrate.'

*

A few months earlier, in October 1973, Ron, having come of age, had returned to police training. It was timely because recently a brand new Police Academy had opened in Glen Waverley, supplanting the old training facilities on St Kilda Road in the city. The new academy was housed in a draughty former Catholic monastery, where all the recruits were expected to live from Monday to Friday. For Ron, that meant giving up his room in the boarding house, so on weekends, he'd return to the farm in Lockington, or sometimes sleep on a mattress at the nurses' quarters at Kew Cottages where Colleen, who'd become a student nurse, was now living.

'None of the girls knew he was there,' Colleen says. 'He came in late at night and he snuck out in the morning.'

The Police Academy was no less rigorous and just as militaristic as the cadets, but Ron kept reminding himself that soon he would be a policeman. 'At 6 am we'd get up and do fatigues for an hour,' he remembers. 'We all wore the same thing – grey pants and a jacket that had to be starched, even though we'd be weeding the garden, hosing concrete, digging the garden bed, and a whole range of jobs that were manual labour. After that, we'd shower and have breakfast in the mess hall.'

The similarities to the military didn't end there. The recruits had to keep the floors polished and dinner was served promptly at five. 'Not only that, but you had to have your socks and underpants all lined up,' Ron says. 'Every now and then they'd spring a room inspection on us, wiping their finger on the surfaces looking for dust. They'd yell, "This is a disgrace!" if it was dusty, or if your books weren't lined up, or if you hadn't made your bed properly. Everyone looked forward to Friday because you were allowed to go home.'

Only under very special circumstances were recruits allowed to leave the campus during the week, and classes ran all day. 'You had to do law, which was a big component, and there were two to three periods of that every day,' Ron explains. 'You had to learn what your power of arrest was, what theft was, the nature of summary offences – things you'd encounter as a constable on the street.

'We learned English and wrote essays,' he continues. 'We were taught to touch-type, and back then, we used type-writers with carbon paper. There was also physical exercise, drill training, firearm training and defensive tactics. Back then police had a handgun and a baton, whereas now they have capsicum spray as well.'

Ron was a member of Recruit Squad Seventeen, an all-male outfit of twenty-four, which included recruits who went on to esteemed careers, a couple who ended up in jail, and one cop, Denis Tanner, who was twice investigated for murder, although no charges were ever laid against him.

At eighteen-and-a-half, Ron was one of the youngest non-cadet entrants at the academy, where the average age was twenty-one (these days, it is almost thirty).

'What I remember about Ron was his maturity,' says Paul Evans, a former recruit squad member who would later become an assistant commissioner. 'The rest of us were silly eighteen-and nineteen-year-olds, but Ron was one out of the bag. I heard him speak and thought, *God, he's mature for his age.*'

According to Evans, Ron had a flair for his studies, and was a natural born cop. 'He was good, honest, and straight down the line,' he says. 'He could talk to people and he had a passion. You just knew he was made for the job.'

The other thing that stood out about Ron was that he knew where he wanted his policing career to take him. 'He wanted to be a detective,' Evans remembers. The rest of us didn't know what we wanted to do. He was just the complete package.'

What Ron didn't tell his fellow recruits, however, was that it was the television show *Homicide* that had inspired him. Had he said so, he would have found himself in good company. 'I think a lot of us were influenced by the TV shows in those days – *Homicide, Division Four* and *Matlock Police*,' says Evans. 'I was influenced by *Matlock Police* and *Homicide*. When you're sixteen, seventeen, eighteen, nineteen, you do get influenced by all these wonderful things.'

Yet even though Ron knew what he wanted to do, he maintained his humility. 'Ron was never full of himself,' Evans says, acknowledging that a few of their peers were 'loudmouths'. 'He was down-to-earth and very level-headed. And he was so good to the rest of us. He was interested in everybody and always had a smile on his face. He was one of those fellows you couldn't help but like.'

John Moloney, from the country town of Donald in northern Victoria, was Ron's closest friend at the academy and agrees their squad was made up of some 'bonzer fellows and some that weren't so good in life'. Moloney's father had died when he was young, so he returned home as often as he could to help his mum look after his seven siblings. It couldn't have been easy, but Moloney could count on Ron's support. 'Ron was one of the reasons I passed at the academy,' Moloney says. 'I've modelled myself on him, I can tell you that. His values were great, he had that natural ability and his mind would be ticking away all the time. He had an older head on his shoulders.'

The two boys from the bush formed a bond that year that would last a lifetime. 'We became such good friends at the academy, and I became a friend of the family,' Moloney says. 'I'm very blessed to call him my friend. The greatest decision I ever made was to join the police force, because I met him.'

In February 1974, his training complete, Ron graduated from the Police Academy, earning seventh place in his squad, and topping the class in law.

'Graduation day was exciting because you invited all your family,' says Ron. 'We'd march on the parade ground and then get called up to be given our certificates. Then we'd march off, and it was a tradition that everyone would throw their white hats in the air.'

Colleen delighted in the pageantry of the ceremony, to which she wore a new outfit she'd bought especially from Sussan. She did feel a pang of sadness, however. 'Because I was engaged at the time and not yet married, I wasn't allowed in the family photo. That's how things were in those days.'

After the ceremony, dinner and drinks were held at a function centre. Ron invited a friend from school, his brother and sister, and Colleen, who turned heads in a black-and-silver floor-length lurex gown with a halter neck.

There was another tradition that also told the world Ron Iddles was now an officer of the law. 'After the celebration it was pretty normal to hang your jacket in the window of the car to let everyone know you were a policeman, that you were the real deal,' he chuckles. 'So of course I hung my jacket in the window of the car!'

With training at the academy now over, Ron now had nowhere to live. He crept into the nurses' quarters at Kew Cottages to sleep on Colleen's floor many more times, but it was far from ideal. The logical solution was for the couple to live together, so they found a furnished one-bedroom flat in Thornbury and set up house.

Ron and Colleen feared their devout parents would disapprove, but the backlash was even more intense than expected.

'The parents didn't take it well,' Colleen remembers. 'Ron's dad and mum came down with the Bible and read a passage to us about fornication. We didn't even know what it was – we had to look it up in the dictionary!'

Regardless, the young couple continued living together while Ron took up his first posting as a member of Victoria Police. But it was no dream job.

*

After graduation, the new members' names were pulled out of a hat to determine who would be stationed where. Most were sent to Russell Street headquarters to perform active duties while living in the barracks. Fewer than a handful of others were sent to Government House and Parliament House. Ron drew the short straw, and was sent to work as a security guard at Government House. 'All I'd ever wanted to do was be a policeman, and after five months' training, I ended up at Government House. It was disappointing, to say the least,' he says.

Ron was willing to do the hard yards, but not this. 'When I got there I was basically read the riot act,' he remembers. 'It was my job to patrol the grounds, and there were morning, afternoon and night shifts.'

On morning shift, Ron's first job was to climb the tower and raise the flag to full mast (assuming all the state's dignitaries had made it through the night). Between nine and one, he was positioned at the back gate in a guardhouse not much bigger than an outside toilet.

'Around eleven o'clock the only vehicle for the day would arrive – the Baker Boy bread van,' Ron says, citing it as the highlight of the shift. 'I'd take a sheet of paper with me to the guardhouse and write on it what time I thought the Baker Boy would come. That was about the extent of the excitement.'

Ron wasn't allowed out of the guardhouse except for a toilet break, and only when the sergeant sporadically dropped by to see if he needed one. After lunch, he would work until three, and was sometimes stationed out the front of the building to take down details of any cars that might arrive.

Ron's yearning to do actual police work only grew stronger, and after a week, he got his chance. 'One day I was there when a guy came in who was drunk, and being drunk in a public place was an offence,' Ron explains. But rather than chide the man and tell him to go home, Ron did as he'd been taught. 'I arrested him. I called South Melbourne Divisional to come down,' he says. 'My boss was furious because it meant I'd have to go to court. But I thought that's what police work was about.'

As punishment, perhaps, Ron was then rostered onto night shift, which meant a whole new level of boredom. 'You had to walk around the grounds of Government House on the hour, and you had to be at the back gate on the half-hour,' he says. 'Sometimes the inspector – who would visit once a night – would be there waiting for me on the half-hour.'

By now an expert at making surfaces sparkle, Ron had to mop the brown cork floor before buffing it to a high shine.

He had no intention of slacking off, but had he been so inclined, he would have been caught. 'Sometimes the inspector would park a hundred metres away then sneak up to make sure I wasn't asleep,' Ron says, rolling his eyes. 'So after a week, I'd had enough.'

He knew there was a way out. 'Every Friday a government gazette came out, and in it were vacancies at police stations,' Ron says. 'So I applied for Collingwood and Fitzroy.'

And after just a month at Government House, he was offered a job at Collingwood.

*

Three months before he turned twenty, and three months before her nineteenth birthday, Ron Iddles and Colleen Drought got married. The reception, at the Monash Hotel Motel at Clayton, was a great success, which was just as well given it cost a hefty $5.50 a head, the same price as a Gary Glitter ticket at Festival Hall.

Colleen's uncle, Church of England minister Reverend Thomas Drought, performed the ceremony with another relative, Canon Alfred Miller. It was all very formal. 'Even though I'd been living with my husband, I still wanted to wear a white dress,' Colleen says. 'In those days you weren't supposed to wear a white dress unless you were a virgin.'

So, on Saturday, 21 December 1974, in an ivory gown inspired by Princess Anne, Colleen walked down the aisle towards the man with whom she'd spend the rest of her life. 'I looked terrible,' Ron remembers. 'I was wearing blue flared trousers and a matching jacket with velvet trim.'

Colleen wore a pale blue silk pantsuit as her going-away outfit, and couldn't wait to find out where Ron was taking them on the first night of their honeymoon. Around nine o'clock, the pair set off in their car, which the wedding guests had covered in graffiti, tin cans, toilet paper and confetti, as was the custom. Ron insisted they drive a hundred miles before stopping, as his father had always done on family road trips. At the end of the journey, the young Mr and Mrs Iddles made it to Euroa, where Ron booked into what Colleen describes as 'one of those really horrible old motels'.

'She sat on the edge of the bed and cried her eyes out,' Ron remembers.

'He had no idea,' Colleen says. 'He was very young though, and we didn't know we could go anywhere posh. And his dad had always said, "You've got to get the one hundred miles!"'

Even though the newlyweds would go on to enjoy the rest of their honeymoon in Canberra and Sydney, the morning after the wedding was a let-down too. 'Ron got up really early in the morning to clean the car,' Colleen says, still astounded. 'I was lying there thinking, *Where's my husband?* The magic moment just went!'

Shame it was too early for a sherry.

3

THE THIEF CATCHER

*'I was very excited and apprehensive because
Collingwood was busy and, at times, violent. There
were police members who'd been there for eight or
nine years who were reasonably experienced. As the
new boy on the block, how was I going to fit in?
What was the culture? But at the same time
I thought, I finally made it. I'm finally here.'*
– Ron Iddles

In 1974, inner-city Collingwood was tough. Hardworking and hard drinking, it was the kind of place where if you said the wrong thing in the wrong pub, your beer would be served with a knuckle sandwich. Collingwood's rough-house reputation was nothing new, and over the years, all sorts of colourful characters had called it home, including the flamboyant 1920s gangster Squizzy Taylor, who'd once lived in Johnston Street.

Ron's new boss, Senior Sergeant Ivan Smith, was tall like Ron, wiry, and super-fit from playing VFL in the country, and later, a season for Fitzroy. Smith was in charge of fifty-five officers who worked across three shifts. He was a fair, methodical and neat leader who insisted that his staff wear their hair as short as his. Ron laughs, 'He had a crew cut like Gomer Pyle.'

Within days of starting at Collingwood, Smith's paternal nature made Ron feel at home. 'Ivan treated everyone like they mattered,' Ron remembers. 'He didn't have children of his own but he used to say, "The members are my children". It was great to have such an understanding boss who cared about his officers. Collingwood was a difficult area to police, but Ivan provided the support and guidance a young police officer required.'

Part of Smith's job was to identify areas in which his charges could improve. He even remembers asking Ron how to spell words from time to time, to make sure the young constable's spelling was up to scratch. Typically, Ron was prepared. 'He'd say, "I'll get my ready-speller",' Smith recalls. 'He used to carry a ready-speller in his pocket!'

Not that Ron needed his ready-speller on Collingwood's mean streets. Riding around in Divvy Van Five, he quickly discovered there was always something going on. 'There were seventy-six hotels operating in the area at the time, high-rise commission flats and many family violence issues. It was also a Painters and Dockers area.' The Painters and Dockers were a (now defunct) trade union that represented shipbuilding labourers, and were alleged to have criminal ties.

Sometimes even the cops were crims, and Ron remembers his first encounter with one like it was yesterday. As Collingwood's newest officer, it was Ron's job to drive one of the sergeants out on patrol. 'We went to the Retreat Hotel in Abbotsford, which was known as a Painters and Dockers pub,' he says. It was ten minutes before closing time. 'The sergeant said to me, "We're going there to show the flag", which was a police term that meant we were going to walk through in our uniforms to show a police presence.'

The sergeant told Ron to make sure everyone left the hotel on time, and that the doors were closed behind them. *Mission accomplished,* thought Ron, as the patrons filed out quietly. Afterwards the sergeant turned to him and said, 'What do you want to drink?' Ron was startled – they were both in uniform – and said he didn't drink. 'You sure you don't want a beer?' the sergeant pressed. 'I'm going to have one.'

Ron relented and allowed himself a pony (a five-ounce glass), but it didn't sit well with him. 'He was the sergeant, so you did what you were told,' Ron says. 'I didn't agree with it but it just seemed to be accepted. Looking back now, I wouldn't have done it. We all have a set of values and I think it would have been easy to become involved in situations that went against your beliefs.'

Encouraging the newcomer to drink a beer on duty wasn't the worst of the sergeant's crimes. Near the police station was a sandwich shop, owned by a justice of the peace. One day, when Ron went to the shop to buy his lunch, the JP said, 'There's something in the sandwich for you.'

Ron realised what he meant when he went to bite into his ham-and-salad sandwich and found a wad of cash. He went straight back to the shop to confront the owner. 'There's $150 in my sandwich,' Ron announced. 'What's that for?'

'I've been told by the sergeant you can fix something for me,' the JP replied.

'I don't fix anything up,' Ron said, handing back the money, along with the sandwich.

Sometime later, Ron wasn't surprised to hear the dodgy sergeant was caught out, and ended up spending time in the Big House for drug trafficking.

*

With so many pubs in Collingwood, there were also a lot of drunks.

In the early to mid-1970s, cases of public inebriation were heard during a session at Collingwood Magistrate's Court known as 'Drunks' Court'. It was well known among uniformed police that the magistrates there frowned on officers who referred to their notes while giving evidence. 'So you had to be able to say, for example, that on whatever date, you saw the defendant swaying down Smith Street, Collingwood; that you approached them and asked them for their name; that they gave their name; that you noticed a strong smell of alcohol; and that they'd urinated in their pants,' Ron recalls. 'You'd then say you conveyed that person to Collingwood Police Station, where they were lodged in the cells for four hours. You had to know it verbatim.'

Collingwood Police Station had its regulars, most of whom Ron came to know. 'There were two or three we locked up all the time for drinking methylated spirits, or "White Lady", as it was known back then,' Ron recalls. Without fail, when it came time to release the metho drinkers from the lockup, they'd all ask the same question, 'You haven't got a nip there, have you?'

'The metho drinkers also loved Royal Reserve Port, which was really cheap and had a high alcohol content, and

McWilliam's sherry,' Ron remembers. 'So if we had a bottle there, we'd give them a nip and off they'd go. But they'd be back two or three days later.'

Sometimes, Ron would lock up metho drinkers for sleeping in a doorway, not to give them a hard time, but out of compassion. 'Just to give them a bed,' he admits.

There was also the problem of drink-driving, which, back then, society tended to tolerate, even though it was dangerous and against the law. To charge a motorist with driving under the influence, police would first call in the Breathalyser Unit to perform a breath test, but the early technology was inconclusive. 'So we'd also test the person by getting them to touch their nose, walk heel to toe, do a sum or draw three circles on a twenty-cent piece,' Ron says. 'We'd present that to court in addition to the breath analysis to show they were impaired.'

Ron believes the process failed those with disabilities. 'What if that person had a condition that meant they couldn't write properly, or if they had had a cognitive impairment which meant they couldn't walk heel to toe? But that's how it was done.'

One of the worst things about working in an area where there was so much grog was the amount of violence that accompanied it. 'Thursday night was a big night because it was pay day, and it was back when people used to get paid in brown envelopes,' Ron remembers. 'Some men would go to a hotel, stagger home at ten o'clock, behave aggressively or sometimes violently, and then the police would be called.'

Ron suddenly found himself lecturing men twice his age. 'Here I was, a skinny country kid of nineteen, telling guys who'd been married twenty-five years what they should be doing and how they should be treating their wives. They'd yell, "Who do you think you are? You think you can say that just because you've got a uniform!" It was a little confronting.' But Ron had a knack of defusing potentially explosive situations. 'I learnt early on in my career the greatest weapon I had was the ability to talk to people. I'd say something like, "Mate, I understand that shit goes on, the best thing you can do is move out for four or five hours, have a sleep and then come back".'

But there was still the danger that a violent husband could turn on police. 'There were some occasions when I was frightened,' Ron admits. 'But the more incidents you went to, the more you learnt communication skills. You weren't taught it, but you'd learn to separate the parties, and talk to them.'

Unfortunately, Ron says, there was no focus on family violence in 1974, so police powers were limited. 'The best we could do was arrest the bloke for being drunk in a public place and lock him up for a few hours,' he says. 'We'd advise the women to take civil action and see the Clerk of the Courts, who could issue their partners with a summons for assault, but the women never did it. It wasn't a police matter then unless it involved a physical assault, in which case you could charge the male, but it relied on the victim coming to court and making a statement. And because family violence wasn't spoken about in the public arena, the women wouldn't do that.

'The only thing that worried me was where a woman may have had a serious injury, but we still couldn't do anything and we'd have to leave her there for it to happen all over again,' Ron continues. 'It was disturbing that men would treat women the way they did. I'd never been exposed to it. I always thought it showed that some men had a weak character; they would never attack a male, but were happy to have total control over a female.'

*

As time went by, Ron got to know the streets, the dodgy haunts and the colourful Collingwood characters. More than anything, he loved the night shift, when he saw them all. 'Night shift was exciting because the only people who were out between one and four were crooks and coppers,' he says. 'You always caught a crook. You always caught a drunk driver. It was fun.'

Two nights out of seven, Ron would man the station, cleaning the firearms and catching up on the clerks' unfinished typing, but it was out on patrol where he did his best work. Back then, there was very little traffic after dark, so the sight of just one vehicle on the road was enough to raise suspicions. 'It was pretty quiet by one in the morning, so any cars I saw moving round, I'd pull over and check,' Ron says.

Unfamiliar vehicles also attracted his attention. 'After several shifts I soon became aware of where vehicles were parked in particular streets,' Ron says. 'While I didn't know every car, if I saw one I hadn't seen before it often stuck out, and if it was still there two or three days later, it would warrant checking out.'

Back at the station, when Ron looked at the police reports, he often discovered the unfamiliar cars were not where they should have been. 'They'd usually been reported stolen,' he explains. 'We found many stolen cars just by knowing our area.'

Ron quickly realised that working in the one place for a length of time was giving him an advantage. 'If you were stationed there for a while, you got to know the people of Collingwood, the crims and the behaviour,' he says.

Ron worked out that the best way to catch a crook was to patrol the streets at a snail's pace, keeping a sharp blue eye on his rear-vision mirror. He knew that he might not notice suspicious behaviour at speed, and sometimes he'd simply park in a shadowy alcove, wait, and watch.

There were signs that told Ron when folks were up to no good. 'If we were driving along a street and a car turned off in the opposite direction, chances were there was a reason why they didn't want to go past a police car,' he explains. So whenever a car tried to avoid him, Ron tailed it, and more often than not, he'd discover the driver had been involved in a burglary or the vehicle had been stolen.

Ron was also wary of men carrying sports bags in the middle of the night; he knew they weren't going to jazzercise. 'I'd check them and find pliers and jemmy bars in their bags,' he says. Invariably, he'd find out the men toting tools had just broken into a nearby house or factory. 'I don't think there were many night shifts where I didn't catch a thief.'

'He was the best thief catcher I've seen in my whole life. He was fearless. Tireless,' says Ivan Smith. 'It's unbelievable to think someone could be that good. We were very glad he walked through the door.'

No one was happier that he'd walked through the door than Ron, but he admits there were times he was apprehensive. 'You'd feel that way sometimes when you were going into the unknown,' he says. 'You might get a call for an "Offender's On", which meant someone was breaking into a house or a factory, so you'd drive there like crazy and hope to catch them in the act. It was an adrenaline rush as it meant you drove fast without any siren as you didn't want to alert potential suspects.'

But an 'Offender's On' could also be downright creepy because police never knew who they were going to find when they got there, or what kind of mood they'd be in. 'On arrival you'd always find the premises had been broken into, so you were on edge,' Ron says. 'We always expected the worst – in other words, some kind of confrontation with the offenders. But if you entered a building with that in mind, at least you were cautious.'

Often, by the time police arrived, the criminals had fled, but other times, Ron – who'd usually called for backup so that the front and rear of the premises were covered – caught them red-handed. And what he came to learn was curious: 'They were often more frightened than we were,' he says.

*

After a couple of years, it was Ron's job to take a new recruit on patrol. 'Ron, can you help me catch a car thief?' the rookie, who'd heard about Ron's growing reputation as a thief catcher, had asked.

'So we backed into an alcove and I told him what to look for,' Ron remembers. 'I said if a car goes by and it looks like the quarter-panel window at the front is open, more than likely it's been smashed. If there were three people in the front of a car sharing a bench seat, that was also a clue the car had been stolen.' Ron didn't know why thieves huddled together like that; they just did. 'Within an hour we'd caught one, just by looking out for those clues.' It was a buzz for the rookie but just as exciting for Ron, who felt like he'd won Tattslotto every time he nabbed a crook.

Ron received four commendations for thief-catching during his time at Collingwood, and frequently passed on vital information about illegal activities to the Collingwood CIB. His impressive record attracted the attention of the other officers at the station. 'After a short space of time when he was showing his thief-catching ability, people wanted to work with him,' his former boss Ivan Smith says. 'They learnt from him.'

Ron's instincts for the job could have come from all those episodes of *Homicide* he'd watched growing up. Smith offers an interesting perspective: 'He must have so much suspicion. I come from the country myself and I think we have a bit of an advantage. It's a combination of country knowledge and city cunning.'

It wasn't just on the night shift that Ron shone. 'He brought thieves with him to work that he'd caught along the way. There was crime all around. All you had to do was look for it, and that was what Ron did. He had an unerring instinct for it. It's a natural instinct, I suppose,' says Smith.

Colleen was proud to see her husband thriving. 'While he was at Collingwood he became admired for being a good cop,' she says. 'A fair cop.'

'The thing with Ron, everyone said he was a lucky crook catcher, but I don't think he was,' says Leigh Gassner, a fellow constable at Collingwood who became a friend. 'He didn't let up for eight hours. He was always out there, constantly pulling over cars. It was his instinct combined with his commitment, which is why he quickly got a name for himself for catching crooks and finding stolen cars.'

The other thing that stood out to Gassner about Ron was his integrity. 'Very quickly with Ron, you pick up on his values and authenticity,' he says. 'He would never dip into any behaviour that could be called into question. And you never got the impression he was driven by ego.'

The Collingwood days were a time Ron will never forget. 'I was having fun but I was also seeing another element of life,' he reflects. 'I was seeing violence, death, suicides and major car accidents where people were maimed or harmed, and I saw the pain. As a police officer, you see things that no one else sees in their lifetime. In my time at Collingwood I certainly saw more about human behaviour than when I was growing up.'

*

While Ron was at Collingwood, Colleen was working as a nurse's aide at Willsmere, a mental health hospital in Kew, a job she held until she was pregnant.

The first house they lived in after they got married in 1975 was in Abbotsford. 'The managing director of Phoenix Biscuits went to Ivan Smith and asked if a policeman could live at the back of his house in Abbotsford, like an unofficial security guard,' Ron says. 'So we went to live there for $15 a week rent.'

During that time, Ron took in a boarder so that he and Colleen could save for a home of their own. 'I didn't like the idea, but Ron talked me into it,' Colleen says. 'Ron charged him $15 a week in rent, even though that's what we were paying!'

Soon, however, the boarder set Colleen on edge. 'I just sensed there was something about him that wasn't right. He was weird,' she says. 'He stayed in his room all the time and he didn't change his sheets. I didn't like him.'

He didn't seem to have a job either. 'He'd initially told me he was a company director,' Ron recalls. 'Back then I thought it was a big deal, but I later learned you can be a director of your own tin pot company.'

'He was the entrepreneur of nothing,' Colleen adds.

Despite the boarder's unwelcome presence, Colleen fell pregnant in August 1975. 'I wanted a baby quickly,' she reveals. 'I think we got rid of the boarder about halfway through my pregnancy. It got to the stage where I finally kicked him out.'

Colleen went into labour ten days after the baby was due, but didn't realise it at first. 'That day, Ron took me to Dimmeys in Richmond to go shopping,' she says. 'By the evening, I thought something was definitely happening.'

Ron drove his twenty-year-old wife to Cabrini Hospital in Malvern, where the labour lasted twenty-six hours. During that time Colleen's mum, Jean, insisted Ron join her for breakfast, but Ron made sure he was back when his baby girl came into the world.

'He was really moved and he cried,' Colleen remembers, though he'd found the trauma of watching her through labour very intense.

The couple named their daughter Joanne Elizabeth, and even though Ron wanted to spend as much time as he could at the hospital with his wife and daughter, back then, hospital protocol restricted new dads' visits to 'father's time', a measly half-hour every night. He wasn't even allowed to hold the baby; he had to look at her through a glass window.

Colleen didn't get to see much more of their daughter during her seven-day stay in hospital, either. 'I didn't even know for sure that Joanne *was* a girl!' Colleen says. 'I wasn't allowed to change her nappy or dress her; the nurses just brought her to me to breastfeed – ten minutes on one side and ten minutes on the other. They were quite ruthless in those days.'

The night after Colleen gave birth, Ron asked if the boarder could come back to stay for one night. 'For some reason he came back because he had nowhere to stay,' Ron recalls. 'It was a bad decision on my part because it caused stress for Colleen. And I worked out that he was strange, too. Women have a better antenna.'

After a short stay, Colleen again ejected him, but while Ron was at work he'd sometimes turn up unannounced. 'He used to come and bang on the door,' Colleen says. 'It got to the point where I had to have the house in darkness at six o'clock so he'd think I wasn't home. It was scary, and I don't think Ron realised that until later.'

Eventually, the boarder tired of his unfulfilling visits, but Colleen always remembered what it was like to feel frightened in her own home.

*

When Joanne was seven months old, Ron and Colleen fulfilled their dream of home ownership, and on Boxing Day 1976 moved into a three-bedroom brick house at Launching Place, a picturesque rural township an hour's drive from

Collingwood. Other young families had started to move there but infrastructure was poor, public transport almost non-existent, and the closest major shopping centre was twenty kilometres away. Being so far from the action did, however, make Launching Place affordable. 'Interest rates on home loans had risen to eighteen per cent, so this was where we could afford to buy a new home without overcommitting,' Ron says. 'The house-and-land package cost $21,000.'

To make ends meet, Ron worked a second job, five days a week. 'After a night shift, I'd leave Collingwood at seven, arrive home at eight, then work as a bricklayer's labourer until 1 pm,' he remembers.

Ron also did all the gardening, built a shed, concreted the driveways and paths, and took another job driving tractors and slashing grass on the roadside and on vacant blocks. 'We used to have a great time,' says Harry Derix, who rode a tractor alongside Ron, and lived two doors down. 'And Ron always used to make sure the equipment was in tip-top shape.'

When he wasn't working, Ron, Harry and Harry's brother, Matthew, who owned the tractors, would catch up over a barbecue, and soon became firm friends. A while later, they even played together on an indoor cricket side they called 'The Yobbos'.

'At six foot four, Ron's such an imposing figure,' Harry says. 'But we used to joke that, even though he looked like Tarzan, he bowled like Jane!'

Ron's bowling skills were the only thing Harry could fault in his friend. 'He was a fabulous fella,' he says. 'He was so dedicated to his job and a nice fella to get on with. You knew he'd get all the way to the top.'

Even though Colleen was excited to move into their own home, she felt isolated initially. As she says, 'There were no shops! And the roads were unmade – they were dirt.'

The young family didn't have a telephone either, which meant they had to go to a public phone booth to make calls. 'I had no contact with Ron at work so I didn't know when he was coming home,' she says. 'Not only that, but we didn't have a TV for at least six months, just a radio. In those days you couldn't go out for a coffee because coffee shops didn't exist, and there were no mothers' groups.'

They were tough circumstances for any young mum, let alone one used to the hubbub of the city. Colleen missed nursing and wanted to return to study, and was desperately lonely. 'Visits from our families were rare, unless it was a special occasion,' she says. 'And the only friends that visited were the ones I made at Launching Place.' Adding to her loneliness was the fact that her husband was always at work.

'Sometimes he would work for fifty or sixty hours at a time,' she remembers. And while she accepted he had an important job, Colleen felt alone even when her husband was at home, because he seemed distracted. 'It's such a strain on the relationship, the police force. And in those days there were no support groups. I'm not surprised there are so many divorces and separations.'

Colleen became so upset one day that she briefly left Ron. She bundled Joanne into the backseat of her car and headed to her mum's in Caulfield. 'I only walked out once, but it was really hard,' she says, adding that she returned home that evening. 'I just wanted to shake him up, because he was working all the time.'

Ron remembers the day: 'I remember Colleen pulling me up, and basically giving me an ultimatum, which was that I had a family and needed to engage and be part of it. Being a police officer puts you in a hyper-vigilant state every day. You experience massive dumps of adrenaline, and then when you get home you're the opposite – tired, quiet and detached. This is something you don't have control over, and your body undergoes a biological change. You accept it as part of the job, but it does have an impact on your personal life.'

Ron knew something had to give. 'Police work had become all-consuming,' he admits. 'Slowly I changed, Colleen went back to study, and I supported her by working around her nursing shifts.'

Colleen was much happier, but quietly acknowledged Ron was always going to work harder than most. Still, she says, she would never have left him. 'I felt that Ron would always be my protector,' she says. 'I always felt he would never desert me. I always felt he would never have an affair. I always felt he was genuine with me.

'He's safe,' she says. 'Very safe.'

*

In those five years at Collingwood, Ron saw everything, including his first dead bodies when he was nineteen. He suspects the very first was someone who had died from a drug overdose or natural causes. Having seen so many bodies over the years, he cannot be sure. 'If it was an overdose or natural causes, they generally looked peaceful and just like someone sleeping,' he says.

But there were other scenes the young policeman was called to that were more confronting. 'I remember being called to three or four suicides where people had jumped off the high-rise buildings at 229 and 253 Hoddle Street. At 241 Wellington Street in Collingwood too,' he adds. All were public-housing units.

'I remember one call in which a male had jumped from the eighteenth floor,' he says. 'By the time we arrived someone had put a blanket over him, but you could see a lot of blood and skull parts. Was I horrified? At times those things can affect you, but back then it didn't really worry me. It was part of the job.'

There were also the times when Ron and his fellow officers were called out to conduct welfare checks on people no one had seen for two or three weeks and had passed away, decomposing in their own house. 'The smell was horrible,' he says.

Ron was stationed at Collingwood when the notorious Easey Street murders were committed. Twenty-seven-year-old Susan Bartlett and twenty-eight-year-old Suzanne Armstrong, who had also been raped, were ferociously stabbed to death at their Easey Street home on Monday, 10 January 1977. Two days later, their bodies were discovered in the house, along with Armstrong's sixteen-month-old son, who had not been harmed, but was in a cot not far from his mother's body. News of the horrific crime spread across Australia.

As a uniformed officer, Ron didn't work on the case, but his suspicious nature led him to make a significant discovery. He was out on patrol, so it was his job to search cars for drugs and other prohibited items. 'I stopped someone one night who was known to me and the local police and I found a bloodied knife in the boot of his car,' Ron says. 'The guy claimed he'd found it at Victoria Park railway station, which was a short distance from Easey Street.'

The Crime Department at Russell Street arranged for the knife to be tested and found the blood matched one of the slain women. It didn't look good for the driver Ron had pulled over, but he was telling the truth: he'd merely found the knife, but had not murdered the women.

*

You couldn't be a cop in Collingwood in the 1970s without encountering the Painters and Dockers, members of the Federated Ship Painters and Dockers Union. In the 1960s and 1970s especially, the waterfront was a hotbed of industrial unrest and, at times, blatant thuggery. There were rumours that bodies of murder victims had been buried at the docks beneath tonnes of concrete. The union's activities eventually led to a royal commission in 1980, before its deregistration in 1993.

The Painters and Dockers members frequented four or five hotels around working-class Collingwood. There was the Ivanhoe Hotel, the Royal Hotel and the nineteenth-century Grace Darling Hotel, named after a lighthouse keeper's daughter who saved a group of sailors from drowning after they were shipwrecked off the Scottish coast.

Most popular amongst the Painters and Dockers, however, was the Retreat Hotel in Abbotsford, where Crawford's wartime TV show, *The Sullivans*, was filmed. It is a charming, cosy, wood-panelled pub with a colourful past. 'Back in those days, the carpet in the main bar was dirty and the rubber flooring around the bar was sticky where beer had been spilt,' Ron says. 'Smoking was permitted in bars in the 1970s, so it was a smoky environment. And there were no women allowed in the public area.' Times have certainly changed.

Ron regularly charged the Painters and Dockers with driving offences. 'Often they drove without a licence and under the influence of alcohol,' he says. But it was Ron's way of killing two birds with one stone because, once he'd pulled them over, he often discovered they had been handling stolen property too. 'It was an effective way in which you could charge a well-known criminal and obtain a prison sentence without much effort.'

Ron was just playing by the rules and the Painters and Dockers respected him and the police in general. 'If you caught them, they'd never admit anything, but they'd accept it if it was proven and they'd do the time,' he says. 'I also caught them for house break-ins.'

They were tough people but there existed a mutual respect between the unionists and the police. 'If there was an issue in a hotel where a police officer was getting attacked, I reckon the Painters and Dockers would have stood up for you,' Ron continues. 'They weren't affected by drugs and they weren't irrational, whereas now, people are affected by a whole range of substances and don't have the same respect for police.'

*

Even though he was a Geelong supporter, one of Ron's favourite jobs as a uniformed officer was attending Collingwood games at Victoria Park. Collingwood played at the ground between

1892 and 1999, and it remained their home until 2005. In the 1970s, when Ron was stationed at Collingwood, eighteen police from Collingwood, Richmond and Fitzroy stations were on duty during the games.

'Our job was to patrol the grounds,' Ron says. 'I often ended up at the eastern end where there were no seats, lots of mud and, back then, the fans could drink whatever they wanted. If it rained it was like a pig-pen.' The eastern end was inhabited by a small group of away fans hemmed in by a teeming mass of black and white. 'It often ended up like a bloodbath,' Ron says. 'By half-time there was always a blue at the back of the goals. On average, we'd lock up fifteen to twenty people for brawling.'

Even though there wasn't a Collingwood fan among them, the games were a highlight for the whole Iddles family. 'We'd watch them on telly,' Nancye says. 'We liked seeing our brother, or in Dad's case, his son, between the flagpoles with his police hat on!'

But no one got as much of a thrill as Ron himself. 'On the days the football was on, we'd use the special brawler van which would fit six policemen and up to fifteen people we'd arrested in a pod at the back,' he says. 'We'd also walk through the hotels and if we found anyone drunk we arrested them and put them in the brawler. We had a sense of power because there were six of us together. And we were usually big blokes of six foot and over, so when we all walked into a pub, it was a good signal that we meant business.'

There were one or two hotels in the area known for serving drunks, and they were especially busy when the local team had lucked out. 'If Collingwood won, it was like a full moon.

The hotels went off!' Ron remembers. 'But if they lost, you could shoot a gun through the street, because they all went home to sulk!'

*

Knowing who was who around town meant that anyone Ron hadn't seen before stood out like a sore thumb.

Ron recalls turning up late one night in 1976 or 1977 at a Turkish coffee club in Victoria Street in Abbotsford. There were two or three of these sparsely furnished clubs in the area, and they were open all hours of day and night. Inside, middle-aged men sat around laminex tables playing a game called Red Aces. 'They would have a piece of paper as a score sheet, but it was actually a betting sheet,' Ron says.

'I went away and found out it was an offence to gamble in a public house or shop,' he continues. 'So if it was really quiet we'd back up the van to the front door, swoop in and arrest everyone in the building. 'I'd often go there, charge the owner with suffer gaming – allowing illegal gambling to take place – and everyone in there with being found in a common gaming house. The maximum I arrested was twelve at a time. It was a good experience, as not many police got to arrest people for illegal gaming.'

Ron started dropping into the Turkish clubs so frequently he got to know the patrons by name. It was like the future American sitcom *Cheers*, except they served thick, strong coffee instead of beer. Then, in the late 1970s, Ron noticed an Australian-born man in their midst. It signalled to him that something was changing, but what?

'Through my observation and information I received from men who attended the clubs, I found out they were dealing large amounts of heroin,' Ron says. 'This was when heroin was beginning to be a problem. It was coming in through our ports. In the Collingwood area, for some reason, a group of Turkish men became more involved than anyone else. The guys I dealt with did not deal with the day-to-day user. They sold heroin to mid-level dealers from St Kilda, who distributed it in the streets.' Ron was aware of the occasional overdose in Collingwood but points out that, 'Most of what was purchased was going back to St Kilda.'

What Ron was seeing marked the start of powder drugs in the 1970s – and a whole host of new policing challenges. Police saw a rapid rise in house burglaries and street prostitution – crimes which helped pay for heroin users' habits.

Suspecting the Australian man was behind the drug dealing at the club, Ron and a sergeant staked it out, waiting for him to leave. When he did, 'We pulled his car over and what do you know, there was half an ounce of heroin inside,' Ron says.

Ron and his sergeant passed on the information to Detective Senior Sergeant Bob Falconer at the Drug Squad, who was always grateful for a tip-off. 'Any detective worth their salt will tell you that when you're a detective, the uniformed police are your best source of information,' Falconer says.

'The Drug Squad then arranged large-scale raids,' Ron says. One morning, a group of three, including Ron, raided two or three of the clubs, but didn't find the stash of drugs they were expecting. 'We believe they knew in advance we were coming,' Ron says. 'When we got there, they were all playing cards.'

Worse, it looked like whoever had made the call had paid with his life: that night a Turkish man was murdered outside the Builders Arms Hotel in Fitzroy. The police suspect it was payback for talking to them.

*

After five years at Collingwood, Ron had spent the requisite time in uniform to become a detective. It was the only way to edge closer towards his dream of becoming a Homicide investigator. 'So I applied for a detective's spot and got a post at Russell Street,' he says.

'I was ready.'

4

THE NEW DETECTIVE

*'Learning how to be an investigator was another
step towards my dream of going to Homicide. I soon
learnt that books could only teach you so much; it
was often about understanding human behaviour.'*
– Ron Iddles

The moment Ron arrived at Russell Street Police
Headquarters in 1979, he was herded into the 'Bull Ring',
a large office on the third floor for new detectives. 'It was like a
resource pool,' he says. 'There were about twenty who worked
there in the morning and twenty in the afternoon, and as
vacancies arose, they left. For example, if Carlton CIB wanted
a couple of detectives, they would take them from there.'

Ron was moved into 'Special Duties', which was considered
a detective's job even though its officers were still waiting their
turn to attend Detective Training School. 'The work generally
involved investigation of a particular target followed by surveillance on them to build up a profile,' Ron explains. 'Often the
work was around drug trafficking, and once Special Duties
officers established their targets were dealing they'd conduct

a raid, and hopefully arrest the offenders and seize drugs and money.'

Aware that Special Duties was a plainclothes job, Ron wasn't surprised that his new boss looked nothing like the clean-cut Ivan Smith from Collingwood. His name made him sound more like an embattled comic-book character than a police officer: 'My new boss was Sergeant Charlie Brown, and he had long black hair and a beard, and wore black horn-rimmed glasses,' Ron says, recalling how, instead of wearing crisply starched uniforms, he and his colleagues worked in jeans and t-shirts.

'We drove unmarked cars and our role was to work on low-level drug dealers, look for stolen property and get information on people who'd committed burglaries,' Ron explains. 'We were proactive, not reactive. In other words, we'd act on information that we'd received or obtained ourselves from criminals.'

From the back of a parked panel van, Ron and his team of three spent up to eight hours a day conducting 'static' surveillance, which involved photographing suspected drug dealers through a gap in the van's heavy black curtains. In the days before all cars came off the production line with air conditioning, the van could become stifling hot or freezing cold, depending on the weather. The Special Duties officers stepped outside only for quick toilet breaks, and made sure they brought a cut lunch and a thermos to get them through the day. Once they'd collected enough evidence, they moved in – and out of the cramped panel van.

Ron recalls that the crooks used all sorts of underhanded tricks, and would even involve their own children in criminal activity. 'I remember once, we sat off a house in Heidelberg then followed as a drug dealer drove to a car yard with his two kids,' Ron says. 'The kids were running around the car yard while he was breaking into the office. They were his cover.'

After four months tailing low-level crims, Ron moved another step closer towards proactive detective work when he was transferred to Fitzroy CIB. 'It was across the road from Collingwood,' he points out. 'That was an advantage for me, because I knew Fitzroy and I knew Collingwood.'

As Ron continued to wait for a place at Detective Training School, he was moved into 'Crime Duties' at Fitzroy CIB, where he helped investigate offences committed overnight. The first officers at the scene – uniforms – were hardworking and diligent, but some of the detectives at the CIB were less committed. 'It was the norm for detectives to work and drink,' Ron says, explaining how the detectives often met their informers at the pub, or got on the tiles together during work hours.

'Quite often, at twelve o'clock, the sergeants would write in the duty book that they were going out to conduct inquiries, and wouldn't come back until five o'clock,' Ron says. 'Some of the hardworking detectives were on to them, and they'd write "Gone to Lunch" in the duty book next to the sergeants' names.'

Ron never went out for a long lunch, 'But it didn't take long to work out who was keen and dedicated, and who wasn't. Coming from a structured, disciplinary environment, it was important to align yourself with the hard workers because some didn't work as hard as they should have. And it caused a bit of friction.'

After two months, Ron was accepted into Detective Training School where, for the next three months, he didn't have time to think about his tanked-up superiors; he was too busy studying towards his ultimate dream.

*

An ounce of information is worth a ton of investigation.

A written note will outlive a mental note.

Failure to search is failure to find.

The whiteboard at Detective Training School was crammed with punchy sayings, designed to give the student investigators an advantage in the field. Ron was quick to learn the mantras by heart, and years later came up with many of his own.

There were thirty-four officers in Ron's class at Detective Training School, otherwise known as 'Bonehead College'. Established in 1938, it was Australia's first investigators' training course, located at the Police Depot on St Kilda Road in the city. The men were broken up into syndicates of about six members. Ron remembers, 'Detective Sergeant John Hill was my syndicate leader, so he was my "go-to" instructor.'

Ron quickly came to regard Hill, a former Homicide detective, as his mentor. 'I remember him speaking about how to interview suspects, and I later adopted some of his techniques,' Ron says. 'Nothing was ever a problem. He was always prepared to listen, and he understood where you were coming from. He'd stay back after class to assist you if required. He was known as a very thorough investigator, and I wanted to model myself on him.'

One of the students in Ron's class was his former workmate from Collingwood, Leigh Gassner. Gassner, who sat next to Ron in class, was not surprised that Ron was drawn to Hill. 'He was very much like Ron,' Gassner says. 'He was a quiet, methodical detective who attracted people. They were probably of similar character and I imagine Ron was attracted to him because he could relate to him. He was a very good investigator.'

Every now and again, Gassner would drive Ron to class, as they both lived north-east of Melbourne. 'I had a Honda Scamp,' Gassner says, a tiny, second-hand car that couldn't have been comfortable for a man of Ron's stature.

The course was broken up into a few key units: law, investigative techniques and practical exercises. Ron says, 'Once a week we'd do an exercise where there'd be a dummy in a room that was set up as a crime scene. The practical exercises always involved homicides and forensics, and it was our job to conduct a seven-point crime-scene examination.'

The first step in the seven-point crime scene examination was to visually examine the scene. 'We were taught to look, but not touch,' Ron explains. Then trainee detectives had to photograph the crime scene and closely examine it, looking for any physical evidence. 'Once you'd located any evidence, you had to photograph it in situ. You then had to label and collect your exhibits.' The trainees also had to explain what they were doing and what their next step would be after leaving the scene. 'You might say you were suspicious of the person next door, so you might then be asked how you were going to interview him,' Ron adds.

The instructors drilled other important procedures into the group too. 'You had to know how to conduct an identity parade, you had to be able to tape confessional evidence, and you also had to be able to do a tape recording of a read-back interview,' Ron says. 'In those days, if police had a suspect, they would type up their record of interview with them. We were meant to type as quickly as the person spoke. Then you'd get the suspect to read it over, and tape-record him reading it back. He'd say it was true and correct, and then he'd sign it. That was a read-back interview.'

Every Monday – even on their very first day – the would-be-detectives sat an exam made up of fifty multiple-choice questions. 'If you hadn't studied, you wouldn't pass,' Ron says. 'And we had to learn a lot of definitions verbatim. For example, if you were asked to define assault, and there were three or four words missing from your answer, you didn't get a mark.

'On the second week you were allowed to fail the weekly test, but at four weeks you had to pass. At eight weeks you had to pass, and at twelve weeks you had to pass,' he continues. 'If you didn't get over sixty-five per cent in your exams, you failed. And back then, you didn't get a second go. It was an enormous amount of pressure.'

'It was really full on,' Gassner concurs. 'It was none of the adult learning techniques of today. It was a really hard slog. But Ron was always really conscientious.'

Every Friday afternoon, classes wound up at four, which wasn't a moment too soon. 'It was tradition that everyone went to Friday-night drinks,' Ron recalls. Most trainees went to the nearby City Court Hotel, but there was a group of five, including Ron and Gassner who, because they lived so far away, drove halfway home before stopping in at the Frognell Airforce Base in Camberwell. 'We'd have a game of billiards, those who drank would have three or four beers, and then we'd go home,' Ron says.

Friday night was the only night Ron allowed himself to take it easy. The rest of the time, he and his friends hit the books hard, determined to pass. 'I'd study till ten, eleven, twelve at night,' he says. 'And in the morning, I'd read over my notes. I wrote *lots* of notes. I also had definitions on hand-cards so that I could get them word perfect, and a book of notes that précised every subject. Everyone had a different method, but we all put in massive hours.'

The overall feeling among the trainees was that they were in it together. 'It wasn't everyone for themselves,' Ron explains. 'It was twelve weeks you'd never get back. So if you could help someone, you would.' Ron tutored a student he'd known since the Police Academy: Denis Tanner.

'It's ironic that a guy who struggled there who I helped out was Denis Tanner,' Ron says of a classmate who was later to come under internal scrutiny. 'But he was a guy from the country. He was a nice enough bloke. He struggled a little with the concepts at Detective Training School, but he'd acknowledge that.'

During week twelve, the last week of the course, the student detectives sweated it out in their final exam. Everything rode on it. 'You had to be good to get through,' Gassner says, 'and if you didn't get through, you got chucked out of the CI [Criminal Investigation Branch]. It was cut-throat.'

On the final day, a panel of three instructors called the students in, asking them one by one to identify a fingerprint pattern through a magnifying glass. The instructors wanted to know if it was a delta, composite, whirl or loop pattern.

'You had five minutes to identify the fingerprint,' Ron says. 'If you got it wrong, it didn't go so well for you.'

Ron got it right, but wanted to find out how he and his classmates had fared overall in the course. He knew he'd done reasonably well, but with everything coming down to the final exam, it brought out the trainees' competitive spirit. 'We ran a book!' Ron says. 'We each put one or two dollars in and the winner took all.'

There was a funny saying at Detective Training School about those who didn't come first, second or third. 'They'd say you came equal fourth,' Ron says.

But Ron Iddles – even though he wasn't the favourite – didn't come equal fourth. He came first – and won a few bucks off his mates in the bargain. 'I took the lot in the end,' he laughs. Once again he was the dux.

*

The following Monday, exhausted and with 'total brain drain' from the gruelling detectives' course, Ron returned to Fitzroy CIB as a Detective Senior Constable. *I now have these wonderful skills,* he thought quietly to himself, bursting to use them.

The new detective immediately learnt, however, that books can only teach a detective so much. 'Straightaway, I was sent along to a factory burglary in Wellington Street, Collingwood,' he recalls. 'An air-conditioner, worth about $15,000, had been stolen.'

As soon as he got there, Ron carried out the seven-point crime scene examination he'd had drilled into him over the past three months. 'I knew that, first of all, I had to look at the scene and get someone in to photograph it, so I called in Forensic Services,' he says.

When the team arrived, the crime scene examiner, who seemed surprised to be there, asked Ron what he wanted him to do. 'I asked him to take an overall photograph of the factory, and to photograph the burglars' point-of-entry, the damage caused on entry and where the industrial air-conditioner was taken from,' Ron remembers.

More experienced detectives would have considered it overkill to call in Forensic Services, but Ron was only two days out of the investigators' course and already his natural thoroughness was cutting through. 'Having just completed Detective Training School, I thought I had to do those things every time,' he explains.

With his usual hawk-eye, Ron noticed tyre marks from a small truck in the factory's laneway. He knew it was suspicious because a truck would have been needed to take away the sizeable air-conditioner. 'So I asked them to make a cast of the tyre tread,' Ron says.

Upon his return to the station, Ron made sure the exhibits – including the impressive metre-long plaster cast of the tyre pattern – were promptly listed in the property book and locked in store. 'When the boss saw them, he said, "Who put this shit here?"' Ron recalls with a chuckle. He then explained it was evidence from the crime scene he'd just attended. 'What did they teach you at Detective Training School?' the boss demanded. 'If you bring this much stuff back, I'll have a property office full of crap!'

'Eventually I started to learn what you should do and what you shouldn't do,' Ron says. 'I learnt that the plaster cast would only have been useful if the vehicle was found, or if someone rang in with information. That plaster cast would never have been enough to solve the job; it could only have been corroborative evidence. And while my boss was a bit hard on me, it was about putting theory into practice. I eventually worked it out, and it became second nature.'

As soon as Ron adapted to his new role, he solved crime after crime, and his colleagues couldn't help but be impressed. Fellow detective Ken O'Connor says that not only had Ron's reputation as a thief catcher followed him from Collingwood, but he continuously built on that reputation. 'Ron was the best policeman I've seen in my whole time. The best,' Ken says. 'And he was exceptionally popular. Anyone who's ever worked with him will say that's a common theme.'

O'Connor recalls attending a violent demonstration with Ron at the Marjorie Noonan Nursing Home in North Fitzroy in 1981. The then prime minister, Malcolm Fraser, not the flavour of the month, had arrived to officially open the facility, at which time protesters began hurling fruit at him. 'I remember the first guy we arrested,' says O'Connor. 'He was wearing orange overalls and he was throwing tomatoes at the prime minister from a little haversack. We thought, *We'll have him.*'

According to O'Connor, the man in the overalls provided 'the spark that ignited the rest of them'. Suddenly, harder fruit like apples and oranges were being hurled at the PM. 'So we arrested a few of them,' O'Connor says. Among those pinched was a man who turned the protest on the fuzz. They arrested him for assaulting police and other street offences.

The protesters pleaded not guilty, and one even tried to discredit O'Connor in court. O'Connor had told the court that during the affray he was holding one of the protesters by the right arm, and gave evidence to that effect. He was surprised when the protester suggested he was lying and produced a photo that told a different story to his own. 'It had me holding his left arm,' O'Connor remembers.

'When police are asked questions in court, the accused are entitled to attack our credibility,' Ron explains. 'In other words, they can challenge an account which we have sworn on oath is the truth. And in this case, from memory, I think the man who attacked our credibility was acquitted.'

The photo niggled at the detectives because they knew they had told the truth. When they looked at the image more closely, their doubts about the protester were justified. 'They'd developed the photo in reverse!' O'Connor says. 'In the background, you could see the word "Milkbar" in reverse!'

There was no way now that Ron was going to let the dishonest protester off the hook. 'I took out a warrant, proved he'd turned the negative around to make the photo look different, and charged him with perjury,' Ron says. 'Then he was convicted.'

The moral of the story: don't try to outsmart the sharpest senior conny in town.

*

After three or four months back at Fitzroy, Ron's mate Leigh Gassner gave him a call. 'He said, "Do you want to come here? It's a fantastic place to work".'

Gassner doesn't remember trying to persuade Ron at all. 'I don't know why I convinced him,' he says. 'It was a pretty silly thing to do, actually!'

'He talked me into it,' Ron says, recalling how Camberwell was closer to home, and that another mate was stationed there too. But after working in one of the city's busiest crime hubs, how would leafy, middle-class Camberwell measure up? 'After the first week, I thought I'd done the wrong thing,' Ron admits. 'It was like a rest home.'

For the locals, the tranquillity of the suburb was probably its attraction, but for an energetic thief catcher like Ron, it was dead boring. 'It was a dry area,' he says, explaining how there were no hotels in Camberwell. 'So it didn't have brawls and there were minimal assaults,' he adds. Not that Ron *wanted* people to assault each other; he just wanted to be there to catch them when they did.

What Camberwell *did* have, however, was a tonne of house burglaries. 'That was because it was affluent,' Ron explains. 'It was a totally different area to Fitzroy and Collingwood where there were lower socioeconomic groups. There, you'd come down to people's level, but in Camberwell, where there were doctors and lawyers, you'd have to come up to their level.'

It didn't improve Ron's sense of dissatisfaction that many of the home owners treated the police like second-class citizens. Often, when they turned up to investigate a report of a break-in or stolen jewellery, they weren't even allowed through the front door. 'Complainants would ring up and say, "Can you use the tradesmen's entrance?"' Ron remembers. 'It didn't always happen, but when it did, it was offensive because we were there to help them.'

Frustrated by the lack of action, Ron took it upon himself to go find some. *There's got to be some shitheads around here,* he thought. So when he discovered there were boarding houses in the area, he started dropping in. He learnt that some of the residents were unemployed, while others were straight out of jail. 'I started to work out who was living there, and when I'd knock on the door of their bedsits, I'd casually look around from the doorway to see if anything was out of place.'

Sometimes Ron would find a resident on a warrant, which at least gave him the satisfaction of an arrest. Other times he charged boarders with possession of drugs or theft. 'I'd often find stolen milk crates in their rooms,' he says. 'Some people had up to a dozen because they used to put their belongings in them.'

While charging down-and-outers with stealing milk crates may have seemed over the top, Ron maintains that, 'It was stolen property and costing the milk company money. But I probably just needed to be back on the mean streets!'

The most unruly the neighbourhood seemed to get was when parents went away and left their teenagers home alone. 'Every now and then we'd get called out to a noisy party and find a house full of sixteen- and seventeen-year-olds,' Ron says. '"Where's Mum and Dad?" we'd ask. And they'd say, "They've gone skiing for the weekend".' Ron felt like he was on another planet: he'd never met anyone in Collingwood or Fitzroy whose parents could afford to go skiing for the weekend – or ever.

While at Camberwell, Ron and Gassner investigated a troubling report from a teenage girl from a well-off local family. 'A young girl came forward with her mum and said she'd been raped,' Ron remembers. She told the detectives that nine boys had been responsible for the brutal attack. 'She said they had carved initials into her leg.'

Ron and Gassner immediately arranged for the Police Medical Officer, Dr Peter Bush, to examine her. They took her statement and started looking for her attackers.

After a couple of weeks and with no sign of the rapists, the girl started calling the detectives with new information every second day. On one occasion, she told them her assailants were still stalking her, which Ron and Gassner knew they had to act on quick-smart. 'She told us that a green panel van was often parked outside Camberwell Girls High, where she went to school,' Ron says. 'So we went and spoke to her school friends who said that, yes, she'd talked about it, but that they'd never seen the van.'

It wasn't until the detectives next saw Dr Bush that they realised they might not actually have a crime on their hands. The doctor confirmed that letters had indeed been carved on the girl's body, but something about her story did not stack up. 'He said that all the initials were straight and that they had all been carved at the same depth,' Ron remembers. 'Dr Bush said that if the letters had been carved while she was being held down, they would have been cut at different depths. "Sadly," the doctor said, "I think she's done it herself".'

It came as quite a shock to the men, but it didn't mean the investigation was over. 'I remember saying to her mum we don't believe it, and having her ask the girl if she'd made it up.'

Soon after, however, they received a report that the girl had once more been attacked. Again, Ron and Gassner rushed to her aid. 'But when we told her about the evidence we had, she admitted she'd made it all up.'

Even though Ron and Gassner effectively closed the case, it saddened them, and they never forgot the privileged but lonely girl. 'I'd seen things at Collingwood, but this was something new,' Ron says. 'She had just wanted some attention and her story had developed as we'd taken an interest in her, had gotten stronger. Initially we believed her, and it wasn't until the medical evidence showed otherwise that we doubted her story. It just taught me that every day, we're still learning.'

Ron and Gassner made sure the girl received counselling, and even though Ron was glad to have helped, he believed his skills could better be used elsewhere. 'I said to the guys, Camberwell's not for me. I'm going back to the rough and tumble,' he recalls.

'So I went back to Fitzroy, where I stayed until I went to Homicide.'

5

WELCOME TO THE BROTHERHOOD

'My first case at Homicide as the primary
investigator was important to me. It was very
complex because it involved the underworld,
it involved armed robbery, and it involved
criminals giving evidence against other criminals.
It was also about a young woman's innocence.'
– Ron Iddles

Ron had been back at Fitzroy CIB for just four months when the trusty *Police Gazette* listed two vacancies at the Homicide Squad. As soon as he read the advertisement, Ron pounced. 'You had to write a two-page document setting down your skills and then you had to wait until you got an interview,' he says. Not that everyone was granted an interview. 'Realistically, you had to know somebody,' he acknowledges. 'It was a bit of a brotherhood.'

On paper, no one could doubt Ron's credentials: renowned thief catcher, dux of Detective Training School, and while at Fitzroy, he'd even spent a couple of nights helping out on the 1979 murder of heroin dealer Victor Allard, who was gunned down in St Kilda. But senior investigators, especially those given the responsibility of hiring, usually require verbal references too.

They must have liked what they heard, because the head of the Homicide Squad, Detective Chief Inspector Paul Delianis, invited Ron to attend an interview before a selection panel including himself and two crew leaders, Detective Senior Sergeant Brian McCarthy and Detective Senior Sergeant Jimmy Fry. 'Ron was very impressive and he spoke confidently and well,' Delianis remembers. 'He was self-assured and had a lot of experience for a young detective.'

But to secure one of the jobs, the candidates had to do more than present well. They had to know the legal definition of homicide and manslaughter, and explain how they would react on the job under various circumstances. Ron recalls one of the senior sergeants showing him a series of photos of a dead man covered in blood. 'Jimmy Fry said, "What can you tell me about these photos?"' The most obvious response would have been that there was a lot of blood, but the photo told Ron something more. 'I said there was a possibility it was a suicide.'

He was right, and it was just the answer the older detective, who'd been at the Homicide Squad for nine years, was looking for. Fry had investigated the case himself, and the 'victim' had indeed taken his own life. 'They wanted to find out whether you'd just assume every case was a murder,' Ron explains.

Next, the panel asked Ron how he would respond if he was the most senior officer at a murder. He told them he would take charge of the scene and consider who to call in, such as

Snowy-haired: Ron as a baby with his 'pop' Victor William Iddles, circa 1955.

Early gun play: Bill Iddles taught Ron (right) to shoot tin cans with an air rifle when he was ten. After that Ron shot sparrows for his cat's dinner.

Smiling for the camera: (left to right) Barry, Nancye and Ron.

School days: Barry and Ron at Lockington Consolidated. His teacher recalls: 'Ron was a leader . . . he spoke his mind'.

The apples of her eye: Phyllis Iddles with her twin boys, Ron and Barry, and daughter Nancye.

Sunday best: (left to right) Ron, Phyllis, Nancye, Bill and Barry before church. Ron had the mole on his left cheek removed before he turned ten.

Summer holidays: For a decade of summers, the Iddles family took their yellow fibreglass caravan to the Mornington Peninsula. Front row: Barry, Nancye, Ron, Nanna Woodland, Phyllis. Back row: Bill, Pop.

Time out: The Iddles kids taking a break from their chores on the farm.

The Iddles twins with Barry's dog, Spot. The boys had another dog named Lassie after the collie in the TV series. A year or two later Ron stopped watching *Lassie* and tuned in to *Homicide*. It made him want to investigate murders.

Big fish: Ron has caught them all his life. He still owns the fishing rod pictured.

Two men and a truck: Ron atop hay bales, with his Uncle Herb below. This 1950s Ford V8 with a five-speed crash gearbox was the first heavy vehicle Ron learnt to drive. He still dreams about it.

All dressed up: Ron first wore this pinstripe suit when he joined the Police Cadets in 1972. He thinks it is 'the kind of suit an old man would wear'.

Ron's graduation from the Police Academy in February 1974. (Left to right) Nanna Woodland, Bill, Ron, Phyllis, Barry, Nancye.

Engaged: Ron and Colleen in 1974.

Awarded: Ron with Colleen and Joanne after he received the Chief Commissioner's Certificate for Courage following a violent run-in with a prison escapee in St Kilda in 1984.

Proud dad: Ron and daughter Joanne on her wedding day. It was a rainy day but the sun came out in time for this photo.

Like father, like son: Ron with newborn Matthew in 1988. Gifted at school, Matt grew up to become a pilot but also considered becoming a detective.

Run-ins with Uncle Chop Chop: Ron and his family often used to run into Mark 'Chopper' Read at the pub. (Left to right) Shae, Chopper, Ron. Chopper credited Ron with helping him turn his back on crime.

Family first: When Ron left Homicide, Colleen insisted he spend more time with his children and grandchildren. Now, family holidays like this one keep everyone close. Back row: Matt's girlfriend Paige, Matt, Shae, Keenan, Jo, Ron. Front row: Ella, Darcy, Marcus, Colleen.

Men from the land: Bill Iddles and Ron in Rochester, 2010.

photographers, videographers and ballistics experts, 'although,' he says, 'not much blood spatter analysis was done in those days.'

The interviewers asked Ron what he would do if he found out the suspect had fled the scene and turned up at a nearby railway station. He said that would be a secondary crime scene, and aside from the usual crime scene analysis he would search the suspect and separate him from others, 'to avoid him concocting a story'.

'You really have to use your brain in the Homicide Squad and you have to nut out the cases and the people involved in them,' says Paul Delianis, who'd taken over as head of the Homicide Squad in 1978.

'You'd also have to take your arrest sheet, which showed what arrests you'd made and what for, and what court experience you'd had, for example, if you'd appeared in the County Court or the Supreme Court,' Ron says. 'They'd also ask you about post-mortems and whether or not you'd been involved in an inquest.'

'It was important as far as the selection process was concerned that these people knew how to give evidence in the superior courts,' Delianis explains. 'And Ron had given evidence in the Supreme Court *and* the County Court.'

'They also asked whether you could work any hours, whether you could work at short notice, whether you were prepared to do country travel and sometimes be away for two or three days at a time, and they asked you how you and your wife would cope,' Ron adds. 'The point of it was to see how you'd fit in and if the chemistry was right, because you'd be working in a team environment.'

Not surprisingly, Ron ticked all the boxes – and more. There was just one thing that bugged Brian McCarthy and Jimmy Fry: the fact that Ron lived at Launching Place. 'It was some fifty-five kilometres from Russell Street and, as a Homicide investigator, you get called out a lot,' Delianis says. 'Getting into the city in some haste is a bit of an issue, but we decided he was good enough to overlook that.'

And so it was that Delianis – in a decision that would influence police history – phoned Ron and said the words he'd longed to hear: 'You've got the job.'

Curiously – given how long Ron had yearned to go to Homicide, and that he has an almost photographic memory – he can't remember exactly how he felt when he received the news. 'I would have been excited,' he says.

One thing's for sure: Leonard Teale and John Fegan would have been proud.

*

In 1977, Detective Senior Sergeant Brian McCarthy was working as a general operational detective at Russell Street Police Headquarters when he was transferred to the Homicide Squad. 'They sent me up to the Homicide Squad because no other bugger wanted to go there!' he says. 'There was a bit of a bad mark on the Homicide Squad because of the Abortion Inquiry.' Seven years earlier, the Abortion Inquiry, headed by William Kaye, QC, had investigated an abortion protection racket involving three high-ranking Victoria Police officers, including Inspector Jack Ford, once the head of the Homicide Squad. It was found that doctors had been bribing the officers in order to carry out illegal abortions. As a result, and for perverting the course of justice, the officers were shipped off to Pentridge. Others were investigated but not charged and, for a while, it left the Homicide Squad looking shady.

It was fortunate that no one else had wanted the top job, because it suited McCarthy perfectly. He was a dedicated, methodical and sympathetic investigator, whose very nature proved an inspiration for Ron. 'I called him Father McCarthy,' Ron says. 'In one way he was priest-like because he was caring and sharing.'

A particularly notable McCarthy characteristic ended up inspiring the screenwriters of the first *Underbelly* television series. 'He always had a tin of biscuits that his wife Betty had made. They were chocolate chip or shortbread,' Ron says. Charmingly, Frankie J. Holden's fictitious Homicide Squad boss, Garry Butterworth, used to offer his younger charges his wife's homemade shortbread.

Conveniently, all of McCarthy's crew, including Ron, Jack Jacobs and Rowland Legg, lived fairly close to one another, so Ron used to pick them all up on the way to work, starting at the boss's place. 'I'd leave Launching Place at five-thirty in the morning and get to Brian McCarthy's around six,' Ron remembers. But McCarthy was rarely ready on time, which explained his nickname, Scratcher. 'His wife Betty would be up when I got there and she'd often say, "He's just scratching around",' Ron remembers fondly.

Ron also recalls how every now and again, McCarthy – an avid rock collector – would ask him to stop the car. 'If he saw a rock on the side of the road that was an unusual shape or colour, we'd go and pick it up for him,' he says. It was a regular occurrence and often involved heavy lifting. 'Some were like boulders!' Ron adds.

It was important for the crew to have moments of levity because day in, day out, they investigated the most violent of murders, and an effective crew's strength came not just from their investigative skills, but from their unity.

Ron's bloody entrée to the Homicide Squad, when he first worked under McCarthy's supervision, was the Maria James murder in June 1980. By that time, the squad had recovered from the Abortion Inquiry.

'Right from the start Ron was a good operator, very conscientious and meticulous,' McCarthy says. 'He was just a very good crew member. He's probably the best operator I've ever struck, and I was in the police force for thirty years.'

McCarthy knew from the start that he had Ron's respect, and the feeling was mutual. 'Any ideas he'd suggest were useful,' Brian says. 'He always told you what he thought. He didn't pull any punches. He was so efficient and he wasn't over-proud about it. He was just matter of fact and liked to get the job done properly. He was a great bloke to work with.'

Ron also impressed the big boss, Paul Delianis, who tried to spend as much time as he could at the Thornbury bookshop where the mother-of-two had been murdered. 'Ron was energetic, enthusiastic, professional and had a great desire to succeed,' Paul says of Ron's investigative skills. 'He worked well in a team and his demeanour of strength and determination was well known, while he recognised he was the new kid on the block.'

Towards the end of 1980, Delianis was promoted to Detective Superintendent and soon after became the

Assistant Commissioner of the Crime Department (he ultimately became the Deputy Commissioner). Even though he was no longer involved in the minutiae of every case, he remained in charge of the detectives at Homicide. And as the murders continued to stack up, everything Delianis heard about Ron told him he'd made one of the best decisions of his professional life.

*

At the start of the 1980s, there were five crews of four at the Homicide Squad. It was their job to investigate an alarming number of murders, many of them the result of violent domestic arguments. 'Back in 1980, we were averaging eighty to ninety murders a year and about seventy per cent of them were domestic related,' Ron says, reinforcing the view that domestic violence was prevalent because the governments of the day did not take it seriously. 'Now we average about fifty-five murders a year in Victoria,' Ron says. 'And I would say that fifty per cent of those would be domestic related.'

After the Maria James murder – about which, more later – Ron investigated numerous domestic murders where, often, the murderer – a husband or boyfriend – was still present at the scene. 'As a homicide investigator, you cut your teeth on domestic murders and then move into other kinds of murders, which took a lot of effort and investigation,' he says.

There were police from other squads who didn't take the Homicide Squad seriously, suggesting that investigating murders was not very challenging. 'The Armed Robbery Squad gave us the nickname, "The Heavy Domestic Squad",'

Ron recalls. 'We were perceived by them as not being very tough because they thought we only did household murders.'

But the Homicide Squad – in those days, without computers or DNA technology to help them solve cases – also worked on complex, protracted investigations, including murders related to criminal activity, some of which involved drugs or armed robbery.

Ron will never forget his first major investigation into the murder of an armed robber. 'At four-thirty one Sunday after-noon a guy walking along Britannia Creek at Yarra Junction smelled an awful smell,' Ron begins. 'He went down to the creek and found a body that was pretty badly decomposed. I was the first at the scene because it was only ten minutes from my house.'

The only evidence left at the crime scene were a few twelve-gauge shotgun cartridge cases, but without a wallet or a driver's licence, the victim's identity was anyone's guess. 'So we arranged for the body to go back to the Coroner's Court in Flinders Street,' Ron says. As far as mortuaries went, the one at Flinders Street was less than impressive. 'Even then, it was antiquated. It was just a small room with three or four steel tables and an overhead light. They didn't even have the facilities to do X-rays,' Ron remembers.

The police weren't impressed by the forensic pathologist who worked there either. 'He'd been a medical officer in the air force or the army and now he called himself a pathologist,' Ron says. 'But most of us had some doubts about that.'

Once the so-called pathologist had conducted a prelimi-nary examination, the man's body was taken to Prince Henry's Hospital on St Kilda Road for X-rays. It was protocol that the body be transported under police escort. It was an awful job, no matter how strong an officer's stomach. 'The body was badly decomposed and the stench was unbelievable,' Ron recalls.

After the X-rays were taken, the man's body was returned to the Coroner's Court so the pathologist could determine the cause of death. It was no wonder the detectives had their doubts about him: even the way he read X-rays did not instil confidence. 'Brian McCarthy had to say to him, "You've got them upside-down",' Ron remembers.

Nonetheless, the pathologist was convinced he knew how the victim had met his untimely end. 'He said, "I reckon he's been hit on the back of the head with a lump of wood",' Ron says. It was a surprise to Ron and his fellow crew members, given the presence of the shell casings near the dead man's body.

Fortunately, the detectives were able to find out the victim's name. 'We got him identified from one or two fingerprints,' Ron says. 'His name was Sidney Graham, and he came from Sydney and had been living in a boarding house in Hawthorn, where he'd been a storeman at an electrical wholesaler's. We found out that two weeks before he disappeared, there had been a burglary at the wholesaler's, and that he had some priors for armed robbery.'

With a fellow crew member on leave, Ron's colleague from Fitzroy, Ken O'Connor, was seconded to Homicide to work on the case with him. Soon, they received some most unusual information. 'A Justice of the Peace who lived in Fitzroy came forward with a tape recording,' Ron recalls. 'He said that at night, his phone sometimes tingled. He'd picked up that he'd been hearing a person talking about criminal activity on the other end and so decided to record it.'

What the caller had said during the taped phone call shed light on Graham's murder. 'He said something like, "The cops say we hit him on the back of the 3KZ [rhyming slang for head]. But they've got it wrong because the ARs [the Armed Robbery Squad] took a bag off me with the gun in it a week ago",' Ron says. 'So we went to the Armed Robbery Squad and said, "Did you take a bag off anyone with anything in it?" They said, "Yes. We took it off a Lee Patrick Torney".'

The Homicide Squad investigators were miffed that someone within the police force had leaked a victim's apparent cause of death, but that wasn't their foremost concern; their priority was to find Graham's killer. They took a close look at Torney, and discovered he'd been living in the same block of flats in Fitzroy as the JP. With the likelihood the JP had recorded the known armed robber on the phone, Torney was starting to look very suspicious indeed.

*

From the outset, Brian McCarthy was not convinced that Graham had been bashed to death, as the pathologist kept insisting. Now, with the possibility that Torney's gun had been used in Graham's murder, McCarthy insisted he piece the dead man's fractured skull back together.

Once again, the 'pathologist's' methods were questionable. 'When we got there, he was using Superglue to put the skull back together,' Ron says, marvelling at how the pathologist hadn't realised he could permanently glue fragments in the wrong place. 'So Brian got some plasticine and put on some gloves and put the skull back together himself.'

What the crew leader found justified the grisly procedure. 'He found a large round hole and buckshot,' Ron says. 'Brian could tell from the pellets these were SG [Sellier & Bellot brand], and they were matched to the cartridge case found at the scene.'

The next step was to go to the Armed Robbery Squad and examine the sawn-off shotgun they'd found in Torney's bag. Bingo: it matched the cartridge case and the pellets. 'We knew we were on the right track,' Ron says. There was only one problem he could foresee. 'Lee Torney was a career criminal, part of the underworld, someone to be feared. And we knew he would never tell us anything.'

But if they dug deeper, someone else might.

*

The detectives soon discovered Torney had been regularly visiting a scrap-metal dealer named Albert – or Alby – Renwood, in inner-city Richmond, so they asked Renwood to the police station to find out how much he knew about Torney's affairs. 'He was extremely nervous,' Ron remembers. Even so, he revealed that Torney, along with two other men – Grant Curran and victim Sid Graham – had recently held up the State Bank in Hawthorn. It confirmed to Ron that Torney and Graham knew each other.

'Alby allowed them to come back to his house and whack up [divide] the money afterwards, and get changed out of their balaclavas,' Ron says. But, as Ron well knew, there is rarely honour among thieves. 'The week after the armed robbery, Torney became worried that Graham was going to dob them in, as there had been a dispute over the money.'

And that's when malice turned to murder.

'Alby said a plan was hatched to collect Sid Graham from his boarding house and take him for a drive in the country on the pretext they were going to cut a safe at a bank,' Ron says. The starting point for the 'drive in the country' was a property near Britannia Creek where Curran had once stayed, and where a man known as Beatle Bailey was living at the time.

Bailey, an unemployed man with no criminal aspirations, had no idea what Torney was planning to do after he left his house with Curran and Graham. Torney had told Graham, however, that he wanted him to collect some oxy gear from the banks of Britannia Creek, three minutes' drive away. It was the gear they needed, he said, to cut the safe. When they arrived, Torney maintained the bogus story – if only for a moment.

'They told Sid Graham to get out of the car, go to the creek and get the oxy gear from the creek,' Ron says. 'The others were about ten feet behind, and when Graham got to the creek, Torney shot him. Torney and Curran went back to the house and told Bailey they'd put him off [killed him],' Ron continues. It came as a shock to Bailey, who'd had no idea Torney had been planning a murder. 'Bailey didn't want to know about it and didn't come back to the house again.'

'He knew they'd come looking for him and would have realised they shouldn't have told him,' Ken O'Connor adds.

Ron and Brian McCarthy caught up with Bailey near Morwell, and from the moment he sat inside the police car, he was willing to help and tell the police what had happened.

Rather than wait until they got to the police station, McCarthy, who didn't want his witness to change his mind about assisting police, took Bailey's statement then and there, on the bonnet of the car. 'Brian taught me something that would later serve me well,' Ron says. 'Commit them to a story or commit them to a statement, then and there. Never come back at a later time for a statement, as they may have changed their mind.'

The pieces of the puzzle were falling into place. 'We had the information from the JP, we had Alby's statement, and now we had Beatle Bailey's statement,' Ron says.

*

In his late twenties, Torney had a girlfriend, a cleanskin named Amanda Sinclair.* The twenty-one-year-old customer service officer recalls introducing her boyfriend to her parents. 'They could tell what he was like,' Sinclair says. 'My father was a very good judge of character.'

Yet to Sinclair, Torney had his appeal. 'Because I was very young and naive I thought he was a bit of a charmer, and he was good-looking and paid attention to me.' And even though he was never violent towards her, Sinclair caught a glimpse of his dark side. 'He used to tell me if I ever did the wrong thing, he would find me. I used to be scared of that.'

Torney never told Sinclair what had happened to Sid Graham – she figured it out for herself after hearing strange snippets of his conversations with Curran, who she considered to be 'a normal, everyday guy'. Then Graham's floor rug turned up at her house, along with a few other belongings. But it was when she saw a story on the news about Graham's

*Name changed

93

disappearance that she knew her boyfriend of less than six months had something to do with it. 'I don't know how I knew,' Sinclair says, 'but I did.' She decided not to raise the subject.

'I met Sid a couple of times,' Sinclair continues. 'I'd been to his home in Hawthorn. He was a gentle man – just like Curran. Like a person who was looking for a friend.'

*

As the investigation continued, the detectives discovered that after Graham's murder, Torney and Curran had visited his boarding house. Torney had kept a couple of items, including the rug, but otherwise they'd tried to destroy evidence that might link them to the dead man. 'They cleaned out his flat and chucked his possessions in the Yarra,' O'Connor reveals. 'But the whole flat was dusted for prints and inside one of the dressers was a full handprint of Curran's.'

'All the evidence we were able to collect turned out to be through Ron's brilliance,' O'Connor continues. 'Each night we'd be getting home and we'd know we were getting a bit closer, a bit closer. Then it got to the stage where they could be arrested.'

The police were looking for Amanda Sinclair too, whom they suspected of being an accessory to murder, but she had fled to Brisbane so Torney could not find her. A friend took her in and she unexpectedly fell pregnant. Ron being Ron, it didn't take him long to find her, so he hotfooted it up north, arrested her and took her back on the plane. She was surprised the tall, sharp-eyed detective was so considerate. 'He took off the handcuffs so I wasn't embarrassed,' she says.

'I brought her back to Melbourne and she was terrified,' Ron remembers. When she made a detailed statement, however, the police realised the polite, softly-spoken woman had done nothing wrong. 'She said if Torney found out she'd made a statement, he'd kill her,' Ron says. He felt sorry for the innocent witness, whose only misstep had been to form a relationship with the wrong man. 'What a tangled web we weave,' he muses.

In those days, there was no such thing as witness protection, but the Homicide Squad crew arranged a change of name for Sinclair and public housing, determined to protect her from Torney. 'After we got her from Queensland she was destitute and desperate,' Ron remembers.

Around that time, the Armed Robbery Squad – the first to investigate Torney – arrested him, while the Homicide Squad brought in Curran. 'Curran made a full confession and took us back to Britannia Creek,' Ron says. On the way there, he pointed out places where he, Torney and Graham had stopped along the way. 'So we'd stop the car, get him to point to the scene and take photographs for evidence,' Ron says.

Torney refused to confess. But McCarthy knew there were more ways to kill a cat than by choking it with cream.

While Torney and Curran were locked up in the city watch-house, Brian came up with a plan that was years ahead of its time – to use a listening device. McCarthy decided to keep Torney locked in his cell but allowed Curran to wander along the long bluestone walkway between the cells, in the hope he would find Torney and start talking to him. As the police had a warrant for the listening device, whatever Torney and Curran said would be admissible in court.

'Brian got the listening device put in the food hatch leading to Torney's cell,' Ron says.

The idea was a success. 'One of the first things Lee Torney said was words to the effect of, "I know how I'm gonna beat this. I'll do the same to Amanda Sinclair as was done to Debbie Boundy",' Ron says.

Debbie Boundy, as the detectives were aware, had been poised to give evidence against alleged hitman, Christopher Dale Flannery, when she disappeared on Christmas Day, 1981, believed murdered. Flannery and two other men had been accused of murdering a barrister named Roger Wilson, who disappeared from East Gippsland in 1980. Nineteen-year-old Boundy was in a relationship with one of Flannery's co-accused.

As a result of Boundy's disappearance, the case against Flannery, otherwise known as Mr Rent-a-Kill, was weakened. He and the two co-accused were found not guilty. Ron's fear now was that Torney would try to find a way to permanently silence Sinclair before she could testify against him. 'Straightaway, that heightened everything,' he says. 'Amanda Sinclair's evidence became crucial and we moved her again for her own safety.' Sinclair says not only did Ron save her life, but his practical help and advice got her back on track.

*

Sinclair wasn't the only thorn in Torney's side. As it turned out, his associates weren't backing him either. 'He thought Alby would stay fat and not be a dog, and he thought Beatle Bailey would do the same,' Ron says. Torney was wrong on both counts. 'And Grant Curran had already admitted it and said, "Torney was with me".'

During the course of the investigation, Ron found other damning evidence too. At Torney's parents' home, he found a hacksaw used to cut down the sawn-off shotgun. O'Connor remembers that 'Ron just went all the way to corroborate all the evidence.'

The trial began in Melbourne's Supreme Court on 1 June 1982. 'I spent the whole winter at court,' Ron remembers. Amanda Sinclair, seven months pregnant, gave evidence about Torney's character and activities for half a day. She wished 'the earth would swallow her up', but knew she was doing the right thing.

'After a trial lasting more than three months, Torney and Curran were convicted of murder,' Ron says. 'They both got life but the law changed and life became twenty-five years, so both of them eventually got out.'

More than thirty years later, Amanda Sinclair was watching the news when she saw Ron, visibly upset that the mother of a murder victim whose case he had been working on had passed away. All the memories of the kindly policeman flooded back and she decided to get in contact. 'I decided to write to him and send a photo of me, my children and my grandchildren,' she says. 'I said, "Thank you. We're all here because of you."'

Lee Torney did not enjoy such a happy ending, however, and ultimately he reaped what he'd sown. 'Years after Sid Graham's murder, Lee Torney was re-arrested over a massive crop of marijuana and stolen property,' Ron says.

'Then in 2005 he was bashed to death with a shovel and dumped in a mineshaft near Maryborough.'

6

OPEN FOR BUSINESS

'Every family of a victim has a right to answers.
It is not about closure but about giving them
answers which might explain why.
This case will never be closed and failure
should never be considered as an option.'
– Ron Iddles

Stepping out of the unmarked police car and into the musty second-hand bookshop, Ron Iddles knew he'd arrived. Since he was a boy he had longed to join Victoria Police's elite Homicide Squad, and here he was, about to investigate his first murder. Once inside, the lanky twenty-five-year-old paused to take in the sights and sounds and smells. The shop in High Street, Thornbury, in Melbourne's north, was crammed with works of the imagination: romance novels, science fiction, literature and even a few *Playboy* magazines, wrapped tightly in plastic and hidden discreetly inside a wooden box. A timber door with a daintily curtained window separated the bookshop from a large, dark but well-appointed apartment in which the bookshop's owner, thirty-eight-year-old

Maria James, had lived with her two sons, Mark, aged thirteen, and Adam, eleven.

The daughter of Italian migrants, James was an attentive mother and accomplished home cook. She had maintained an amicable relationship with her former husband, John James, who had remarried, and sometimes she took the boys on outings with John and his new wife. She was much loved by her extended family and friends, and an active member of the St Mary's Catholic parish at Thornbury, where Mark was an altar boy. Adam had cerebral palsy and a mild form of Tourette syndrome which made it difficult for him to communicate, but whenever he had something to say his mum stopped what she was doing to listen and comfort him.

On the day of her murder, Tuesday, 17 June 1980, James packed her boys off to school as usual, but left the 'closed' sign on the front door as she didn't work on Tuesdays. Sometime during that morning, she opened the door to a killer who stabbed her sixty-eight times, at one point pressing a steel potato masher so hard into her face that its unmistakable diamond pattern was left indented in her skin.

It was a relentless attack. James was neither raped nor robbed, yet whoever wielded the knife wanted to make sure their name would never pass her lips.

James's estranged husband discovered her body. He said she had rung him that morning at Fitzroy Town Hall where he worked, asking him to come over, as she was in a spot of bother. She then asked him to hold the line. While he waited, he heard voices in the background, his ex-wife's startled yelps, then silence.

John James drove to the bookshop as quickly as he could, but couldn't get in because the front door was locked. He went around to the back door but it was locked too. *What was going on?* Growing increasingly worried, he fetched a ladder and climbed in a window.

'He walked up to the bedroom and saw a pool of blood, and then Maria, stabbed,' Ron says. In a panic, James raced out the back of the shop to call the police, but when he returned he discovered that the door leading from the residence to the shop, as well as the bookshop's front door, were now open.

'That only meant one thing,' Ron says. 'That the killer was hiding in the bedroom when John arrived.'

The bedroom's cream-coloured shag pile carpet would have been stylish in its day, but by the time Ron saw it, it was soaked with blood. 'There were no crime-scene cleaners in those days,' Ron recalls. 'And when someone has been dead for a couple of days and their blood has congealed, it is a strange smell. It is the smell of death.'

John James was quickly eliminated as he had been at work when Maria was slain and had no motive for her murder. It was now up to John and his new wife to care for Mark and Adam while the police tried to catch Maria's killer.

Senior Sergeant Brian McCarthy led Homicide Squad Crew Three, which included Detective Sergeant Jack Jacobs, Detective Senior Constable Rowland Legg and newcomer Detective Senior Constable Ron Iddles. It was the start of a highly cohesive working relationship. 'It was about knowing each other's strengths and weaknesses, understanding your role, and knowing you could not achieve a result if you were a lone wolf,' Ron says.

In an irregular move, McCarthy decided to run the investigation from Maria's bookshop where the crew would often work from 7.30 in the morning to eleven at night.

'It was the view of Brian McCarthy that it would save time,' Ron explains. 'So rather than going into the office and then to the crime scene, we were there all day and into the night. It was a good idea because a lot of people from the Thornbury/Preston area would come in with information, and the media would come in to talk to us. I guess you could say we were open for business.'

'We were set up in the living room and the kitchen, boiling Maria's jug for tea and coffee,' Ron remembers. 'And in the late afternoon, the crew would have a barbecue and talk over the information they'd picked up during the day.'

But there was no getting away from what had happened in James's bedroom just a few short steps away. 'The stark reality was that we knew she had been stabbed to death in there. It was voyeuristic but we had to go through her personal things and look at the bedroom and think about how she'd lived. I would stand at the bedroom door, replaying over in my head what I thought had happened,' Ron says. 'I'd look at the photos of Maria's body and, in my mind, re-create what had gone on there. From the photo and the blood on the floor, I could see which way she had been lying. What had happened to her was horrific.'

The blood on the bedroom walls told Ron and his colleagues even more about the murder. 'There was directional blood staining which meant the killer plunged the knife in, then each time as he drew it out, blood spatter hit the walls,' he says. 'There was absolutely no doubt that whoever was responsible would have had blood on them.'

It was a high-impact crime scene but Ron was glad to be part of the investigative team. 'Here I was, a fresh arrival, working on the most high-profile case, right in among it. I thought, *I can see what's happened here. I know this is where I need to be.*'

Among the clues that intrigued the detectives were two unfinished cups of tea on Maria's coffee table which suggested she had been entertaining just before she was murdered. 'That told us the killer was someone she knew,' Ron says. 'It was possible,' he adds, 'that her guest had become enraged during their conversation, because she was attacked with a knife from her own kitchen, not a knife the killer had brought himself.' The potato masher was also from Maria's kitchen. 'They were weapons of opportunity which means her murder was not pre-planned.' Ron learnt that the enormous number of stab wounds puncturing Maria's body was significant too. 'The greater the number of stab wounds, the greater the emotional connection,' he says. 'This was a frenzied attack. Most times if you stab someone once or twice, there's not a lot of connection. There was a lot of emotion in this attack.'

Maria James's murder was front-page news, and made the Victorian papers almost every day for weeks, until baby Azaria Chamberlain vanished from Uluru two months later. Every day as the crew entered and left the shop, TV cameras were there to film them. It was a new experience for Ron but he understood the public wanted to know why a loving mum had been murdered with such fury.

The first strong lead came from a Repco employee who'd been at the service station opposite the bookshop on the morning of James's murder. 'At 9.10 that morning he saw a man wearing a pair of fair-coloured slacks and a blue reefer jacket, carrying a small black suitcase, going into the shop,' Ron says. 'He saw this guy knock on the door and go in, which told us that Maria had opened the door and let him in. He was described as being only about five foot seven, with darkish hair which was pulled back.'

Police released the man's description to the media, with immediate results. 'A lot of people rang in and said it sounded like a man called Mario Falcucci, who lived around the corner from Maria's,' Ron says.

Armed with a warrant, Ron and Brian McCarthy turned up at Mario's, a large, one-storey Italianate home. 'When we interviewed him he admitted he had been to the shop and that he was carrying a briefcase,' Ron says.

Inside the briefcase they found a number of American *Parade* magazines. Some of the articles were about sexual killings. 'He'd tried to get Maria to buy his magazines,' Ron says. 'He said that when she wouldn't buy them, they had an argument, then he left.'

But there was something else about Mario Falcucci that piqued the investigators' curiosity. 'Maria's wrists had been tied with hay band, which is used to tie hay bales, and we found out Mario had tomatoes which he'd tied up with hay band,' Ron says.

'We also found out that the day after Maria's murder, he took some clothes – a nice pair of slacks and a reefer jacket – to Fletcher Jones in the city for dry-cleaning,' Ron continues. The investigators discovered that even though Falcucci had once worked at a menswear store in the city, he didn't normally send his dry-cleaning there. 'We went to Fletcher Jones and they made a note that the jacket was stained with what appeared to be blood. From an investigative point of view, it was looking good.'

Even though the neighbour seemed a 'good suspect', Ron was about to learn that, in murder investigations, there is often more than one.

At 12.20 pm on the day of the murder a woman driving south along High Street in Thornbury saw a man run out of Maria's shop, up past where Mario Falcucci lived, to the railway line. 'The guy in the signal box also saw a man running and carrying something, then crossing the railway line,' Ron says. 'He was a man with hairy arms and you couldn't necessarily say that was Mario. And whoever it was ran past Mario's house in nearby Hutton Street. Wouldn't you think if it was Mario, he'd run into his own house?'

The detectives then had to consider whether the killer was a spurned lover. Maria had reportedly requested a prescription for the contraceptive pill and had a small lock on her bedroom door. 'Was that to keep her sons out of her bedroom if she had a male guest? It's a possibility,' Ron says.

'Maria had told some people she was having an affair, and that the guy worked for Telecom,' he continues. 'Two days before she was murdered she received a massive bunch of flowers from a florist in High Street at Northcote but there was no card, so we weren't able to establish who sent them.'

The investigators did, however, track down a man from South Yarra who worked for Telecom and called on her regularly. 'We interviewed him and he admitted he'd frequented the shop and said he knew Maria,' Ron says.

But that lead took them nowhere because a few days after

the interview, the Telecom worker took his own life. On face value, it looked like the act of a guilty man, but the investigators could find no reason why he might have wanted James dead. As far as they could tell, he was just a man who liked to read. But was he? 'In his suicide note, he didn't mention Maria James but he did mention talking to the Homicide Squad,' Ron says. 'What did it mean?'

Ron knew from his days as an inner-city policeman that there's more than one way to gather evidence about a crime. He and his fellow crew members were aware that James was a practising Catholic, and well acquainted with the parish priest, Father Anthony Bongiorno. Had Maria confessed the details of her illicit relationship to Father Bongiorno, who maybe knew her lover's name?

Inside the bookshop, Homicide Squad inspector Brian Ritchie asked the priest about it. Father Bongiorno replied that under church law he could not be forced to say what he had heard in the confessional, and refused to name names. Brian Ritchie must have studied his scriptures because he plucked a Bible from the shelf and opened it to a passage in Psalms. 'He said to Bongiorno, you must obey God's laws as well as the state's laws,' Ron says. 'There was a massive argument.'

Soon after, the crew *did* find the name of a man James had been in a relationship with – a real estate agent. 'Initially he was reluctant to say that he was the person having a relationship with her; he was married and he was concerned about what his wife may say,' Ron says. But the realtor ultimately admitted to the affair and was eliminated after his alibi checked out. 'He was showing someone through a house,' Ron says. 'So we were able to eliminate him without ever having to go and speak to his wife.'

The crew kept digging but after two months at the shop they still had no evidence on which to charge anyone over Maria's murder. They headed back to the office where newer cases demanded their attention.

Time began to pass – years in fact – but Ron never gave up on his first case.

During a quarter of a century at Homicide and with a clearance rate of 99 per cent, it is perhaps more than a little ironic that one of Ron's few outstanding investigations remains his first ever case as a Homicide Squad detective – Maria James's murder, back in 1980.

But by the start of the millennium, Ron was overseeing a Homicide cold case unit and had started to chip away again at the Maria James murder in between hot jobs. With significant advances in technology since her murder, Ron knew that DNA would give him a better chance of cracking the case than before because, he was told, the killer had behind left a vital clue on a pillowslip in Maria's bedroom: his own blood. It indicated the knife had slipped and he had cut himself in the frenzied attack. 'Also,' Ron says, 'bits of information had been coming in, so I decided to take another look at it.'

One piece of information came from former footballer and politician, Phil Cleary, whose sister Vicki Cleary was stabbed to death by her ex-boyfriend Peter Keogh in 1987.

Cleary contended that Keogh – who lived not far from Maria's bookshop – should be investigated over her murder because Keogh's former parole officer had come forward claiming he was the most likely culprit. The modus operandi in the deaths of both Maria James and Vicki Cleary was certainly the same – they were both attacked multiple times with a knife. But Cleary also discovered – after his sister's death – that whenever a woman wanted to end a relationship with Keogh, he turned violent. The question was, had Maria had a relationship with Keogh? It seemed possible, given he was reportedly overheard talking about her and saying, 'I'll kill the bitch.'

Ron found himself investigating a brand new suspect and turned to science for answers.

In 1980, scientists could only determine blood types, but DNA now gave them the ability to identify someone through their blood, hair, skin tissue, bone or saliva.

So in 2001, Ron assembled all the old exhibits and looked at the names of all the suspects who had come to police attention over the years. There were ten in total including Peter Keogh, although police had not been able to find any link between him and Maria James. 'We had no evidence whatsoever that Peter Keogh even knew Maria James,' Ron says. 'We found no evidence that they ever met.'

Regardless, Ron began the methodical process of checking all the suspects' DNA – including Peter Keogh's – against the unidentified blood mingled in with Maria's at the crime scene. Around that time, Keogh committed suicide not far from her bookshop, and Ron gained permission to collect his DNA. 'It didn't match,' Ron reveals. 'So Keogh was eliminated.'

Ron found his original suspect, Mario Falcucci, living in a nursing home, where he took a buccal swab from his mouth. His DNA was not a match either. Falcucci was eliminated and the suspicious circumstances surrounding him were put down to coincidence. 'The hay band we found in Mario's backyard which was similar to that which Maria's wrists were tied up with, was very common at the time,' Ron says. 'Every second house in Thornbury was owned by a new Australian and they used hay band to tie up their tomatoes.'

'As for the blood on his jacket – we had it tested and didn't find any trace of blood. It could just have been dirt.'

The Telecom worker was unable to be eliminated because he had been cremated, but as Ron and his team ploughed through the remaining suspects in between fresh murder investigations, DNA ruled out every one.

So if the blood on the pillow didn't belong to the investigators' best suspects, who did it belong to?

*

Mark James never forgot the day he found out about his mother's murder. He'd been on a school excursion, after which he expected the school bus to drop him off at the bookshop. But the bus drove on and took him back to school at Marist Brothers College in Preston. 'When I got out of the bus, I knew something was wrong,' Mark says. The parish priest, Father Bongiorno, was there to break the news, yet he offered no solace. 'With the benefit of hindsight, there was something wrong with his approach,' Mark says. 'He was cold. There was no warmth, compassion or empathy.'

The news of his mother's violent death rocked the schoolboy to the core. 'I collapsed a bit and couldn't really walk,' Mark continues. 'But I didn't find him much help at all.'

When Mark thinks back, he realises it wasn't the first time the priest had behaved in an un-Christian manner. 'There'd been a scandal a few months before Mum was murdered, about three, six, or maybe nine months before,' he recalls. 'A lot of bookshops had started to sell *Playboy* and Mum had a box of them hidden away, but they were wrapped in plastic so you couldn't open them.'

Father Bongiorno had got wind of the racy magazines and took it upon himself to publicly shame Maria James. 'Mum was sitting there in church and he said something like, "Maria James has those dirty porno books in her shop!" She was hurt by that. It was spiteful, it upset her.'

What made the priest's remarks really sting was that she had been raised to respect men of the cloth. 'Back then, things were a bit different,' Mark says. 'These guys were demi-gods.'

In 2007, the respected crime journalist Keith Moor wrote an article about the not-so-saintly priest and his link to Maria James in the *Herald Sun*. The story exposed Father Bongiorno as a paedophile.

Several years later – in 2013 – a family friend asked Mark if he had ever been touched by Bongiorno. 'I said, "No, I had sat on his lap and maybe he was thinking dirty thoughts, but nothing happened".'

The family friend persevered and asked about Mark's brother. The question took him by surprise because he'd never suspected his brother had been abused. But then again, he'd never asked.

'I knew how to relax him and soothe him, and get him to talk,' Mark says of his intellectually impaired younger brother, Adam. 'So I asked him.'

What Adam told his big brother left him aghast. 'He told me Father Bongiorno had been touching him down there and it was just before Mum was murdered.'

But there was more.

'Mum had sensed something was wrong with him,' Mark says. 'She asked him and he told her. Mum said to him shortly afterwards, "Adam, I'm going to do something about this".'

Mark discussed the shocking news with Ron who took a statement from Adam – the first ever. 'Adam said his mum went over to the church and challenged Father Bongiorno about the fact he'd sexually assaulted him,' Ron says. 'So if Maria was going to expose him he had a motive to silence her.' Ron also had to admit – Father Bongiorno looked an awful lot like the police sketch of the hairy-armed man seen running from Maria's shop.

Ron knew there was only one way to inculpate or exculpate the paedophile priest: DNA. But Father Bongiorno died in 2002, aged sixty-seven. Ron's best bet was to collect DNA from his sister, but she refused.

The only other alternative was to exhume the priest's body, but to get permission from the Coroner's Court, the police needed a stronger case. 'Ron had a novel way of going about it,' Mark remembers. 'He said, "It's not an exhumation, it's a search warrant!"'

Unfortunately, Ron's request to dig up the priest's bones was rejected and, in 2015 – after he left Victoria Police – a new team of cold case investigators used confidential DNA techniques to eliminate Bongiorno. Still, it was not a closed case and Ron's involvement was not over.

In 2016, an ABC journalist, Rachael Brown, approached Ron and asked him to take part in a podcast about Maria's murder. Ron agreed, knowing, after twenty-five years at homicide, that the media is a helpful investigative tool.

During her investigation Brown spoke to hundreds of people and unearthed other victims of Father Bongiorno. Her podcast also revealed that Adam James had been sexually abused by a second priest, Father Thomas O'Keeffe. She discovered O'Keeffe had an interest in knives, raising the question – was *he* involved in Maria's murder?

But Father Bongiorno was thrust back in the picture when detectives, going back over the crime scene photos from 1980, made a shocking discovery: the pillowcase which the investigators were led to believe had the killer's blood on it came from another crime scene altogether. Ron says it is possible that when police moved out of Russell Street Police Headquarters in 1994, someone accidentally put a blood-stained pillow from another crime in the same bag as the pillows from Maria's bedroom. 'It turns out that the DNA of the person we believed was responsible has nothing to do with Maria James' death whatsoever,' he says. 'And that means only one thing: that everybody who was eliminated is now back in the frame.'

That includes Father Bongiorno, who, as Brown's investigation spectacularly revealed, was seen with blood on his hands and face on the day of Maria's murder. An electrician working at the presbytery only put two and two together after seeing a newspaper article about the murder in 2013. 'He said he saw Father Bongiorno covered in blood and asked him what happened,' Ron says. 'Father Bongiorno said, "I fell in the rose bushes."' The electrician offered to wipe off the blood off the priest in his van but no sooner had he turned his back than the priest had disappeared.

Ron says a detective took a statement from the electrician but did not believe he was credible. Ron wishes he had spoken to the electrician himself because he disagrees. 'Considering this in light of Father Bongiorno's motive for murder,' he says, 'it's nearly the smoking gun.'

Tuesday, 17 June 1980 is a date Ron will never forget. Visiting Maria James' grave with her elder son Mark almost forty years later, his eyes mist with tears as he assures Mark the answer is out there somewhere and to never give up hope.

'I think all homicide investigators have this view that failure's not an option,' Ron says. 'If I was to re-investigate this case I'd want to re-examine all the exhibits. I'd want to know if there was any DNA there that was foreign to the scene. I would then want the inquest re-opened and I'd want to produce the evidence of Adam and the electrician. On the balance of probabilities I'd want to ask the coroner, could you say that Father Bongiorno was responsible? That's where I think this should go.'

Even though the case remains unsolved, Mark James says it would never have progressed as far as it did had it not been for Ron. 'He's still giving me hope,' Mark says. 'It's amazing how he won't give up and that's given me the confidence that one day this will be solved.'

7

'TIS THE SEASON

'I have a lot of memories growing up of listening to him on the phone in the middle of the night. He wasn't around a lot – not because he didn't want to be there but he just worked and worked and worked.'
– Joanne Iddles

Joanne Iddles, snowy-haired like Ron was as a child, was just starting kindergarten when her dad started catching killers. Ron tried to shield his little girl from the horrors of his work so that her early childhood was as it should be – full of fairies and princesses and special occasions spent with her family.

Christmas, for instance, never lost its magic for Ron, even though he was, by now, a non-believer. As a policeman who'd already witnessed countless autopsies, he'd concluded that once a person is dead, they're dead. 'Every year, we'd watch *Carols by Candlelight* on Christmas eve. They'd always sing "Silent Night, Holy Night" and it was like the world had stopped, almost as though a line had been drawn and everything went into a quiet space.

I always hoped the next day would be a time to spend with my family, but it rarely happened. I knew as soon as the phone rang I was going to work.'

Christmas was not always so happy for others, which was why, Ron says, 'On-call homicide investigators are always on edge at Christmas.' During his twenty-five years at Homicide he worked as many as eighteen Christmas Days and often investigated murders in other parts of the state. It was tough because Ron wanted to make Christmas special for his little girl, but other people needed him more. 'It was disappointing if I was called out when Joanne was young as it meant she was left at home with Colleen, which happened during many of her early years. It would have been better if I was home, but it was not the case.'

The call from work usually came during the late afternoon or early evening, after families had had too many egg-nogs and started getting on each other's nerves.

'In the early days we had pagers, and later, telephones, and when I'd receive a call from a particular number, I knew I was going to work. It would be the supervisor from D24 [police communications],' Ron says. 'One of the things about Homicide is that while you can plan for things, you can't plan for anything. Even on Christmas Day you'd always be packing up to go to work.'

Such is the life of a homicide cop – often sacrificing family life to go to the aid of a family who has lost a loved one under the worst of circumstances.

Ron remembers the first time he was called to a murder during the so-called festive season. It was Christmas Eve 1980, and a woman had been stabbed to death at a caravan park in Springvale South, in Melbourne's south-east, because the husband thought the wife had spent too much money on Christmas presents.

'Throughout my journey at Homicide, there was often a murder on Christmas Day, and it normally revolved around families that were somewhat fractured – yet someone had decided they should all get together,' Ron says. 'When they mixed alcohol into the situation, there would be an argument. At one stage there was a murder on Christmas Day for eleven years in a row.'

Not all spouses would find the cop's life easy to accept, but Colleen was different. 'I couldn't have done it without an understanding wife,' Ron says. 'Colleen knew what I did, she accepted it. She totally understood and supported me if I had to go to work. At the time I did appreciate it, but looking back I appreciate it far more now because in my career I've seen relationships break up because a wife or partner hasn't totally understood the nature of being a detective.'

Ron particularly remembers the tragic death of a man at Rye on the Mornington Peninsula one Christmas. 'It involved a fifteen-year-old boy who'd been given a new archery set,' Ron says. 'He had a lot of experience.'

That day, more than thirty of the boy's family and friends were spending Christmas at his house. And, as Ron would discover, this was no feuding family: they all got along well, and were grateful to spend time together and exchange gifts. Then things went terribly wrong.

'The fifteen-year-old boy went outside with some other teenagers,' Ron begins. 'He took his new crossbow and set up some hay bales to fire into them.'

It seemed like a fun thing to do while he waited for his mum to serve a roast lunch, and as an experienced archer who understood that his arrows, once fired, would embed themselves safely in the hay bales, there was no obvious cause for concern. At the same time the boy was setting up the hay bales, his next-door neighbour went out to his backyard to enjoy a can of beer while he waited for his lunch; it was too windy out the front. It was a fatal mistake.

'Just as he sat down in a plastic chair, an arrow came through the fence and went through his back and heart,' Ron says. The teenage boy – despite his experience and ability – had looked through the wrong side of his crossbow, which had sent the arrow flying through the fence instead of the hay bale.

'The boy saw the man on his back and called his dad,' Ron continues. Panicked, the father and son jumped the fence to their neighbour's aid. 'They took out the arrow – which was probably not the best thing to do – and the man died.'

'By the time we got there, at about two or two-thirty in the afternoon, the table was set with all the Christmas trimmings,' Ron remembers. 'We had to say, "Sorry to meet under circumstances like this, but the fifteen-year-old will have to come to Rosebud Police Station with his dad".'

Once the interview was over and Ron was thoroughly satisfied the man's death had not been deliberate, the shaken teenager was allowed to go home at around 10 pm.

'Christmas didn't happen for them,' Ron says. 'I felt bad for everyone, especially the guy who was dead, and his wife.'

'Two seconds either way, the man wouldn't have died and it wouldn't have been a tragic accident,' Ron reflects.

*

The hardest cases to deal with were the ones in which the victims were children.

Ron recalls receiving one call – which, like so many others – came at 2.30 in the morning. D24 was telling him that a woman had killed her three children and husband. That mild September night in 1982, Pina Zikos had slain her husband Nick, their daughters Tracy and Wendy, and their son Mark. The image of their dead bodies has haunted Ron ever since. 'I can still see that bedroom where it happened all these years on – it's a vision that never leaves you,' he says. 'In the bedroom were the three children. There were two single beds in there and one child was dead in each bed. The oldest child, a girl, was lying on the floor.' She was the one closest in age to Joanne.

'When you deal with grief and death all the time, you want to shield those closest to you,' Ron says. 'It can distort your view of the world, so throughout my career I basically put a fence around Colleen and the kids.'

Colleen will never forget the Zikos case either. 'In the old days, homicide cops used to bring home crime-scene photos,' she reveals. 'I could cope with that because I was a nurse and I saw a lot of things. But I can still see the Zikos children lying on their beds . . .'

The children's father had been unable to protect them. 'He was behind the door, slumped in the corner,' Ron recalls. 'They'd all been stabbed twenty-six, twenty-seven times.'

Ron pieced together how it had happened.

The previous night, the family had gone to Cockatoo in the Dandenong Ranges to visit friends, in whom a troubled Pina had confided. 'She had said to them, "I feel like I'm going like my mother" – Pina's mother suffered from paranoid schizo-phrenia – "and I think I need help".'

Pina's friends did all they could. 'They rang Lifeline and Pina spoke to a counsellor, and they made an appointment for her to go and see someone the following morning. I think even though she made the appointment to go to Lifeline, she knew what she was going to do that night,' Ron says, adding that even though the children each had their own bedroom, Pina decided to settle them all in the same room when they returned home. After the children were in bed, she and Nick turned in themselves. 'Then, once the husband had fallen asleep, she got up and got a Staysharp knife.'

'I had to treat the scene as a jigsaw puzzle,' Ron says, to figure out what happened. 'Part of it was clinical, but when you go to reconstruct what happened in the bedroom, then it becomes personal and emotional.

'It was like a bloodbath,' he says. 'It looked like the young boy, who was about four, had been stabbed first whilst in bed, as he hadn't moved. You could tell that the next one killed, who was about six, had woken up because she had defence marks. You could see that she'd put her hands up and been stabbed. The eldest girl, who was about eleven, was on the floor. It looked like she'd woken up after the first child was killed, and that she'd stood up, been stabbed, and fallen on the floor.'

It was a terrible scene, but there was nothing their father Nick Zikos could have done to stop it. 'I knew the husband must have heard the commotion because of the way the bedclothes were thrown back as if he was in a hurry,' Ron says. 'Then he ran down the long hallway and into the bedroom, where she stabbed him about twenty-six times in the heart.'

While at the crime scene, Ron couldn't stop to consider his feelings; he had a job to do. 'We did the normal things – we got the photos, and I think we had video, even though it was pretty basic. To some extent you were process-driven. But on jobs like this you'd sometimes go home and bawl your eyes out.'

'I don't think any police officer likes to deal with children's death,' Colleen says. 'And some of them affected Ron more than others. The Zikos case was really terrible. That one affected him so much. Maybe because the mother was left behind and she was so distraught.'

The murders threw a light on Ron's own family life. 'Seeing the children stabbed to death made me realise how amazing Colleen was with Joanne,' he says. 'I was so lucky to have her.'

When the police told Nick Zikos' brother, George Zikos, what had happened, he was understandably devastated. 'He asked, "Can I go to the house?"' Ron says, recalling how he warned George about the horrendous scene inside. 'I said, "We don't have cleaners".'

But George was politely insistent. 'He said, "It was my brother's blood – I've got to clean it up",' Ron remembers.

So, around eight o'clock that night – after Ron had been working on the case for more than seventeen hours – he went with George to clean the house. 'We lit a fire in the back-yard and carried the mattresses out, then burnt them one by one,' Ron says. 'Then we carried the wooden beds out. We cut the carpet up and burnt everything, and then we cleaned everything up.'

Today, it is unimaginable that a detective and a grief-stricken victim's relative would have to clean up a murder scene themselves. 'How can you let a brother clean up his own brother's and nephew's and nieces' blood?' Ron asks, still incredulous.

To this day, Ron feels deeply sorry for George Zikos and the good friends who had tried to help Pina. 'How can her friends from Cockatoo ever get over it? She left their house at eleven or eleven-thirty, and by two-thirty, the whole family was dead.'

'She pleaded not guilty on the grounds of insanity and was kept [in prison] at the Governor's pleasure,' Ron says. 'To my knowledge, she's served her time.'

8

NO HARD FEELINGS

*'This case fascinated me because when someone
I'd put away got out of prison and back in the real
world, I was the first person he contacted.
Why did he want to have contact?'*
– Ron Iddles

Ringing Ron Iddles was always a safe bet, even if you were a criminal. With a reputation for playing it straight with everyone – from victims' families to crooks – Ron has never promised anything he could not deliver. 'Criminals have always felt comfortable ringing me because they know I'm not going to somersault them. I never lied to them,' Ron says. 'It's a big thing for a criminal to pick up a phone and call Crime Stoppers but it's a bigger thing to call a police officer about something that might implicate them. They might think, *What are the consequences of doing this?'*

Increasingly, criminals were drawn to Ron because they knew he was honest. And it never hurt his investigations. 'I always considered everyone as a source of information regardless of their status in life,' Ron says. 'It was not a matter of cultivating them, but treating them with respect and letting them know I was always available for them.'

It's that quality that may well be the greatest secret to Ron's crime-solving success. Take the following case from 1981.

The East Keilor market gardener's day began much like any other – tilling the soil, planting seeds and harvesting brussels sprouts. The peace was shattered when a young man named Thomas Kyte turned up on his doorstep, begging for help. What made the stranger's presence even more confronting was that he had been shot in the back and the groin and was bleeding profusely. 'So the gardener called the police, the police attended, and Thomas Kyte was taken to hospital,' Ron says.

Kyte survived but he wasn't the only one on the wrong side of a shotgun that day. One of his mates was also gunned down but didn't live to tell the tale. 'The local police found the body of a man named Garry Jennings near the river,' Ron says.

When Ron was called in to investigate Jennings' murder and Kyte's attempted murder, he expected Kyte to tell him who was responsible. It wasn't that simple. 'Initially he didn't want to cooperate at all,' Ron says. 'Even in the early 1980s it was still fairly common that you didn't cooperate with police, especially if you'd been shot, because they'd always think someone would come and even up the score. So the attitude was usually, "Tell the police nothing".'

After a while, Kyte had a change of heart and turned witness. 'Through information he and others gave us, we worked out that three men took Tom Kyte and Garry Jennings from a home in Albion Street, Brunswick, at gunpoint,' Ron says. 'They were taken to the river and made to stand against the river bank and were shot with a shotgun.'

Jennings died straightaway but Kyte hung on. 'He basically played dead until the three men left,' Ron says. 'Then when he thought it was safe he crawled down the road for 1.5 kilometres to the gardener's house and raised the alarm.' It was an incredible effort and Kyte was lucky to survive.

With Kyte's help, Ron identified the three men responsible for the bloody showdown, and Ron learnt they'd kidnapped Jennings and Kyte over a drug debt.

He vividly remembers going with Brian McCarthy to a house in Broadmeadow an alleged where one of the suspects, twenty-seven-year-old Bruce Nicholls, lived with his mum. They hoped to find Nicholls there or at least some clues to his whereabouts. 'We knocked on the door and heard a rustle inside,' Ron says. 'An elderly lady – Bruce's mum – opened the door and invited us in. She said, "Would you like a cup of tea?" Much to Ron's surprise, his boss said yes. 'He would have been happy to sit down and engage in conversation to get some information, but first and foremost, we were there to search the house,' Ron says.

Before Mrs Nicholls could put on the kettle, Ron caught McCarthy's eye and motioned towards the rear of the house to suggest they look back there for the wanted man. 'As it turned out, Bruce was in the wardrobe,' Ron says.

After tracking down all three of the men, the police charged them with murder. 'And after a lengthy trial, the three of them were convicted,' Ron says. 'They were each sentenced to life, but it came down to twenty-five years, from memory.'

*

Bruce Nicholls, like a lot of men jailed for murder, had thought long and hard about the man who'd locked him up.

'I never held it against him,' Bruce says. 'He'd done his job and my aim was to walk out the front gates the same way as I went in – as a free person – and I thought, *I'll ring him when I get out*.'

'Bruce Nicholls rang me within a week of getting out,' Ron remembers. 'I said, "How can I help you?" He said, "I just want to come and meet you".'

Ron knew it was prudent for a homicide investigator to be on his guard when meeting a man he'd put behind bars. 'I thought, *Is he going to be bitter? Is he going to be twisted? Is he vindictive? Is it possible he's setting me up?*' Ron says. 'But I went because I knew that after all those years in prison he'd have a lot of knowledge about a lot of things and might give me information. When you work in Homicide it's good to have a network of people who are hooked into criminal activity.'

It turned out to be a pleasant meeting. 'We went and had a cup of coffee and there was no animosity,' Ron recalls. 'He thanked me for what I'd done for him and said if there was any way he could help out in the future, he would.'

One of the reasons Nicholls regarded Ron so highly was because Ron had spoken plainly and honestly during the 1981 investigation 'as he tried to get behind the truth of it all'. There was no heavy, bad cop act. 'He was just his normal self,' Nicholls says. 'He just asked the questions correctly and as far as I was concerned he did a good job and that's why I respect him. I never felt like any injustice was done.'

Nicholls spent his entire sentence in Pentridge. 'Even when I was in jail I used to follow his story and think, "Keep up the good work",' Nicholls says. 'Every chance I could, I read about him [in the newspaper]. I always paid attention to what cases he'd been covering and I'd think, *They've got the right person.*'

Nicholls also credits Ron with keeping him on the straight and narrow after his release in 1997, aged 41, after having served the minimum eighteen of his twenty-five-year sentence. He says that even though he and Ron are about the same age, he sees Ron as the father figure he never had. 'I always wanted to be like him. I didn't want a criminal record,' Nicholls says. 'You couldn't have a better role model than Ron.' When he was first released, Nicholls, who was on an invalid pension, lived in Shepparton before moving back to Melbourne. He stayed in contact with Ron throughout.

As the years went by, Nicholls phoned Ron whenever he came upon information about a crime, or sometimes just to invite him for coffee. He says when he turned up at Ron's office with a hot tip, Ron always treated him with respect.

'The greatest gift you can give anyone is the ability to listen,' Ron says. 'And you never know what someone might tell you. Information about a crime might come to light or a life might be saved.'

Which was exactly what happened when Nicholls phoned Ron late one night to report that his best mate's de facto had died of a drug overdose and that the dead woman's baby was alone in the house with her body. Nicholls' friend hadn't wanted to call the police himself because there was an inter-vention order preventing him from visiting his partner and he feared he'd be accused of her murder.

Nicholls could simply have reported the matter to the local police, but he knew Ron would handle things properly. 'Bruce

Nicholls said I was an honest policeman and that he trusted me,' Ron says.

So after Nicholls made his late-night call, Ron arranged for Footscray police to go to the woman's house. 'They found her body and they found the baby,' he says. 'And the story checked out: the woman had died of an overdose.' Fortunately, before he left the house, the woman's de facto had fed the baby, who was in good health when the police arrived.

The incident told Ron he'd been right to meet Nicholls for coffee all those years ago, and that he did the right thing by answering the phone that night. 'Sometimes I think, if I didn't answer that phone call, what would have happened?' he wonders.

'As far as Ron goes, you can't go wrong if you tell the truth,' Nicholls concludes. 'That's all there is to that gentleman and that's what's fascinated me over the years.'

Postscript: Bruce Nicholls died of natural causes shortly after this interview.

9

ST KILDA

*'I went to St Kilda because it was time to move
up the ranks, and to do that, I had to leave
Homicide for a while. St Kilda wasn't everyone's cup
of tea, but I've always enjoyed a challenge.'*
– Ron Iddles

In February 1983 Ron Iddles – no longer a detective senior constable but, at nearly twenty-eight, a sergeant – applied for, and was offered, a job in Melbourne's famous red-light district, St Kilda. The post appealed to the renowned crook catcher because 'St Kilda had the reputation of being a very tough, rugged area, but also police had been involved in minor corruption, prostitution and drugs,' he says. 'As it also had a reputation of having a poor police culture, I knew there'd be a lot of challenges there. I knew I'd learn a lot.'

Ron's reputation preceded him. 'He was well known from Collingwood and the Homicide Squad,' says Paul Hatton, then a senior constable at St Kilda Police Station. 'He was coming to St Kilda with this incredible reputation as a crook catcher. Everyone was saying, *Ron Iddles is coming here?!*'

On his first day, Ron was called into Superintendent Jock Caddle's office. Caddle oversaw policing in the city's inner south-east from his office in Prahran, and told Ron he wanted him to set up a new Special Duties unit. The previous unit, which had been disbanded eighteen months earlier, had been tarnished by allegations of corruption. The superintendent knew Ron was one of the force's rising stars, and would remain unbent despite the colourful suburb's many temptations, outside and inside the station.

Ron's task was monumental. His skeleton crew was to clean up crime in St Kilda, Melbourne's version of Kings Cross in Sydney. 'I had two staff members – Senior Constables Paul Hatton and Mark Caulfield – and we were given an open slate. We could work on drugs, street prostitution, stolen property, whatever we wanted.'

Pretty, bayside St Kilda, dotted with quaint Art Deco buildings, towering palms and tempting European cake shops attracted tourists, bohemians, performing artists and trendy urbanites. Yet parts of the suburb were so seedy it was no wonder the place was rife with illegal activity. The hub of all the action was Fitzroy Street, a commercial and residential strip that ran down to Port Phillip Bay. The street was home to fish-and-chip joints, dingy bars and the now infamous Gatwick boarding house, a slowly crumbling 1930s mansion that housed junkies, street walkers, break-and-enter merchants and other flea-bitten drop-outs.

'Fitzroy Street was surrounded by other cheap accommodation too,' Ron says. 'There were boarding houses in Grey Street and Dalgety Street – single rooms that were cheap and attracted numerous drug users and criminals, so it became a bit like a cesspit.'

It was well known around town that if a man was looking for a good time, Grey or Robe Streets were his best bet. Lurking on corners or perched on brick fences in short skirts, the hookers were value for money so long as you didn't mind risking the clap.

'Down on the Esplanade you had Bojangles nightclub, which was renowned for conflict between bouncers and the public,' Ron continues. 'But other parts of St Kilda were very affluent and the people who lived there would probably never have ventured into Fitzroy Street. A lot of people wouldn't go there for fear of being robbed, bashed or solicited by prostitutes. There were dodgy second-hand shops there too. It really was the hub of evil.'

And thriving like blowflies on top of this pile of human waste were corrupt coppers. 'I remember one crook who said to me, "Are you gonna take my money? The guy before you didn't leave me with enough money for a cup of coffee".'

*

Heroin was St Kilda's public enemy number one. 'One of the biggest dealers was a man who owned a café on Fitzroy Street. He was liked by a lot of police, and he provided them with discount hamburgers and cigarettes,' Ron says disapprovingly. 'But we found out from street prostitutes that he was probably dealing more than anyone in St Kilda.'

By the time Ron arrived in St Kilda, times were changing in the police force. 'I can remember going there with my Special

Duties crew,' Ron says. 'We worked in jeans and t-shirts, so we went in and ordered a cappuccino each.'

The café owner guessed Ron and his sidekicks were police, and told them they didn't need to pay for their coffees. In a flash, Ron eyeballed him, hard: 'I leant across the counter and said, "Just remember this: we owe you nothing and we've paid for the coffee".'

Six weeks later, after the cafe owner sold several caps of heroin to an undercover officer, Ron arrested and charged him with trafficking. 'We closed down the shop, then searched high and low but didn't find any more heroin,' he says. 'We even brought in a dog but he couldn't find the stash either.'

What the police *did* find was a wad of marked notes in the café owner's pocket, and a few thousand dollars under the fish-and-chip paper, sitting around in various places. The unusual locations in which they found the cash suggested to the officers it was drug money.

'Then, back at the police station, the café owner tried to offer me a $5000 bribe,' Ron continues. It was another bad move. 'He was convicted and sent to jail for trafficking, and he got a heavy fine for offering the bribe.'

The café owner might have been done for trafficking horse, but he wasn't the only dealer in town. Ron planned to catch every one he could.

Part of the reason most crooks didn't see the Special Duties team coming was because they looked like everyone else in St Kilda, with their collar-length hair and in their faded jeans. 'Even the crooks would say they didn't know we were policemen,' Hatton says. And when Ron and the crew started driving an old Volkswagen from the Ugly Duckling

Caryard instead of their police-issue Holden, they attracted even less attention. 'We'd be parked in the street and they wouldn't know us as coppers,' Hatton says. 'They'd think we were just crooks.'

Ron occasionally used his colleagues to bait the young men lurking in the shadows of Shakespeare Grove, a secluded street behind Luna Park. 'I would leave the crew members on the street just standing there, and wait until they were approached by a young male,' he says. 'Once there was an offer and a request for payment, the young males were arrested for loitering for the purpose of prostitution.'

Sometimes Ron acted as bait. 'It was about trying to clean the street up, but at times trying to help those who were affected by drugs,' he says. 'On one occasion I arrested the son of a prominent judge, who was charged and convicted. I am sure he never worked the street again because I spoke to his father, who offered great support for his son.' It was a quiet victory Ron never forgot.

The Special Duties crew couldn't help but feel sorry for the street workers they picked up. 'We felt like it was a victimless crime,' Hatton says. 'Or that they were the victims. Often they were drug addicts who needed fifty dollars to buy their drugs.'

Realising the police could make them safer, the street workers increasingly shared information with the Special Duties crew. Ron remembers the prostitutes telling him about a man who was standing over them, forcing them to turn tricks to line his own pockets. 'Many complained that he was violent and some prostitutes made statements that they were paying him money,' Ron says. 'So we had enough evidence to charge him with an offence called living off the earnings of prostitution.'

Aware that the man was staying in a cheap motel in Fitzroy Street, Ron, Hatton and Caulfield went to see him. It was a hot day so the pimp was lying on the bed with the door open. 'We all went in and he was informed he was under arrest for living off prostitutes' earnings,' Ron says. 'He became upset and violent, and in the process he punched Paul, which cut his eyebrow.'

'Ron basically said to him, "The police run this town now. You're not a required person here and it might be time for you to go",' Hatton adds.

Back at the cop shop, two further charges – police assault and resisting arrest – were added to the charge sheet. The pimp was bailed to appear at St Kilda Court; when he failed to turn up, a warrant was issued for his arrest. 'And to this day he's never been seen,' says Ron, unsure whether his words of warning prompted the pimp to disappear.

Hatton suspects that's precisely why he took off. 'He realised we were incorruptible and that he'd be in strife if he stayed,' he says.

*

Ron was achieving great results, but in a crime hotspot like St Kilda, it meant putting himself – a man with a family, like so many other police – in danger every shift. 'Policing was dangerous back then but Colleen accepted it,' he says. 'You just hoped nothing happened to you. If you constantly thought about it, you wouldn't leave the police station.'

One night Ron's commitment to the job almost cost him his life.

At 3 am one morning in 1984, he and another officer discovered three men sitting in a car in a dimly lit side street. It looked suspicious. 'I got them out and told them to stand beside the car,' he recalls. 'As they did, one of them dropped a gun on the ground.' He took off and Ron's colleague went in pursuit.

'Then the second bloke swung round and I grabbed hold of him,' Ron continues. 'He reached down and grabbed the butt of the gun in my holster and at the same time pushed me over a small fence.' Ron's assailant would not let go of the gun. The strap was still holding it in place, but for how long? 'I thought, *If he gets it out of the holster, I'm just waiting for the bang.*'

Ron had to think fast in this fight-or-flight situation. 'As I went over the fence, I pulled him over with me,' he says. That way, Ron figured, the crook wasn't pulling back on the gun so there was less chance he could get hold of it. Ron's instincts were right, and within moments he had overpowered his attacker and was on top of him, slapping on the cuffs. He got on the radio and called it in. 'I've got an armed man,' he panted, bleeding from wounds to his face and body.

It turned out Ron's assailant was a prison escapee from New South Wales. Ron was lucky to be alive, and he knew it.

After a doctor stitched him up, Ron phoned Colleen. Her immediate instinct was to go to the police station to be by her husband's side. 'But he said, "No, don't come down",' she recalls. 'I didn't know the severity of it. I was really upset that he didn't want to tell me. I wasn't made of cotton wool.'

Ron had not wanted to excessively worry his wife, so he played it down. 'It was the early hours of the morning and I knew she'd been asleep,' he says. But there was more to it than that and it revolved around the culture of the times.

'Back then it wasn't the done thing [to have a spouse come to your aid at the station].'

Colleen was mortified when she finally saw her bruised and battered husband, but realised why he'd left her in the dark about the extent of his injuries. 'Ron always took things on himself,' she says. 'He thought if he shouldered everything, he wouldn't have to worry anyone else. But I think I beat that out of him over the years!'

These days Ron rarely thinks about the night he almost came a cropper, 'But if I do,' he says, 'I know how close I came to being shot, and that's quite scary.'

*

Ron's results at St Kilda spoke for themselves. The renowned thief catcher quadrupled St Kilda's arrest rate. 'We went on to become the detectives we were because of Ron,' Hatton remarks. 'He taught me how to collect evidence and how to interview people. Both Mark [Caulfield] and I had a natural ability, but to temper our investigative skills with someone like Ron was fantastic. The wealth of knowledge he had!'

'Every three months we were arresting 180 people,' Ron says of his team, who rotated every three months. 'The arrests were mainly for offences such as stolen property, burglary, street prostitution and for substantial amounts of drugs.'

Ron was one of a new breed of sergeants at St Kilda Police Station. 'There had always been issues over members being charged with dishonesty and assault, and some who had ultimately been suspended and let go,' he says. But the new, younger group of sergeants – Ron included – all had a common purpose: to run an efficient police station without the whiff of corruption that had fouled the hallways before they arrived. 'The new breed was more accountable,' Ron says, acknowledging his strong senior sergeants for reinstating discipline at the station. 'There had been a time when some of the officers had thought they were Starsky and Hutch,' he says. 'They didn't even wear uniforms when they were meant to – they'd go out in the marked divvy van and get around in big jumpers.'

Ron remembers the first time he worked night shift at the St Kilda watch-house. 'The divvy van crew came back at three o'clock in the morning and it became apparent to me that they'd been drinking alcohol,' he says. 'I instructed that they weren't allowed to go out of the police station again and that they were to stay there until the end of their shift at seven o'clock.' It came as a shock to the divvy-van crew because they'd been used to a more laissez-faire approach in the past. 'I think sometimes members wanted to test the boundaries and test their sergeants,' Ron posits. 'But we were all committed to changing the culture.'

Still, the resistance mounted.

Ron recalls an occasion in which an expensive watch, which was meant to have been logged in the lost-property book, turned up in a young officer's locker. 'The junior member was charged with theft,' Ron recollects. Yet other officers maligned the sergeant who'd charged him. 'There was a lot of pressure put on that new sergeant because the attitude was, "How dare you put pressure on another police officer!"'

The theft was small fry compared with what was to come. 'One night at about two-thirty, the back of the police station caught fire and burnt to the ground,' Ron says. At the back of the station were two demountables that housed the officers' lockers, in which they kept all their notes and court briefs. At the time, the famous television journalist Mike Willesee was making a documentary about the challenges of city policing, so when he returned to Channel Nine in Sydney, he was armed with unexpectedly dramatic footage.

From the outset, there was talk the blaze had been started by a rat within the ranks. 'The investigation by the fire brigade showed it had started internally,' Ron says, adding that there was no evidence anyone had jumped the back fence to set the buildings alight. 'While it was never proven, there was considerable suspicion that a police officer had caused the fire, possibly someone sending a message: "Don't play with us".'

St Kilda Police Station was a hotbed in more ways than one and the hierarchy wasn't tolerating it. About six months later, after a workplace review, most of the detectives were sent to Russell Street's Criminal Investigation section. 'It was a clean-out,' Ron says. 'About a dozen temporary staff were put in, again to try to change the culture. St Kilda was a work in progress but over the three years I was there, changes did occur.'

Some of the changes stuck, but years later the bustling station was back in the news again for all the wrong reasons: in 2000, a stash of firearms was found in the police station's roof, followed by another stash – although fake – fifteen years after that. Who put them there, and when, remains a mystery, but it speaks yet again of St Kilda's murky past – a time in which five of Ron's colleagues ended up in jail or 'on the other side of the fence'.

'Many careers were shaped at St Kilda,' Ron adds, 'and some careers were ruined there.'

10

SAVING LOUISE

'Heroin was engulfing the streets of St Kilda, and trying to help a young addict was my attempt at rehabilitation. I was naive thinking you could just provide support and some basic needs. I soon learnt the desire to give up drugs had to come from within, only when they had hit rock bottom.'
– Ron Iddles

In much the same way he'd spotted cars that were out of place in Collingwood, Ron recognised that Louise Burke, who wore designer clothes and spoke with rounded vowels, wasn't born and bred under the glow of a red light. The first night she met Ron, the eighteen-year-old was on a fast track to trouble.

Louise Burke grew up with a loving mum and a success-oriented dad, an 'oil tycoon', as she puts it, whose sizeable income meant that, materially, she wanted for nothing. Her father John's career took the family overseas and by her teens Burke had lived in three different countries. Yet even though she was interested in the world around her, the constant upheaval unsettled her. She found it difficult to form lasting friendships and felt that she didn't belong.

While living in Thailand in the 1970s, Burke also found herself troubled by the Cambodian War. 'I saw a man's head blown off, and another with his guts eaten out and his eyeballs extending from his head,' she says. She believes now that what she witnessed led to undiagnosed post-traumatic stress disorder.

When she was fifteen, the family returned to Melbourne, where her parents enrolled her in a prestigious Church of England girls' school. But no sooner had Burke arrived than she became the target of teenage xenophobes, who bullied her for having lived in Asia.

'When I came back I was going, "What about the war?" But no one had heard of it,' Burke says. 'So I just left school and went to business college and became a fully qualified business secretary.'

Straightaway, the intelligent, statuesque blonde scored a job as an executive secretary for a leading advertising agency in South Melbourne. 'They had big plans for me,' she says. 'But then I got led astray a bit.'

Burke was 'led astray' by a charismatic Moroccan-born man named Mick who was ten years her senior. Beneath a haze of cannabis smoke, she lost any ambition she'd once had, and despite her employers' protests, she quit her job to squander her days with Mick on the streets of St Kilda. Mick introduced his impressionable girlfriend to heroin. 'It was in Fitzroy Street and he was looking for a bit of pot,' Burke remembers. 'He spoke to this guy who was the scummiest person I'd ever met, who said, "We've only got scag [heroin], man". Mick turned to me and said, "You wanna try that?" I thought, *This doesn't feel right and I don't want to be a part of it.* But he dragged me into it. He even showed me how to do it, like my personal heroin trainer. I did it just to fit in. I thought I was in love with him.'

Burke is the first to admit that love can make people do crazy things, but when heroin is added to the mix, all reason disappears. Under Mick's powerful spell, and with the lure of as many opioid rushes as she could imagine, Burke followed Mick to Sydney's Kings Cross. Soon, the former private schoolgirl was turning tricks to support their habits. Then, as quickly as Mick had entered her life, he left.

'No bloke was going to look after me so I had to look after myself,' Burke recalls. 'I looked after four other girls as well and cooked for them. Just to keep them off the street because they were underage.' It wasn't the kind of life Burke would have chosen for herself, but heroin had her in its grip.

A short while later, as Burke can best remember, she met a new 'street partner', Gus, a gentle drifter about her age. 'Gus had a good heart but he was not a strong soul,' she remarks. Nevertheless, the two began a relationship and moved back to St Kilda.

It wasn't long after that that Burke – on the nod and with drug paraphernalia in her handbag – first encountered Ron, working undercover, in a secluded laneway.

'We were working in Fitzroy Lane at the back of Fitzroy Street when we came across her,' Ron remembers. 'We asked her what she was doing and searched her handbag. Inside we found a syringe and a cap of heroin, and we had a look at her arm and could see a bruise mark.'

She was irked to have been arrested, but came to realise that this perfect stranger – a policeman at that – had her best interests at heart. Not only did he keep phoning her parents to make sure she wasn't using, but through regular pep talks, Ron encouraged Burke to lead a fulfilling, drug-free life. The way Ron saw it, Louise Burke was not a hopeless case, and with a loving family to support her, she might be able to get off heroin for good. 'I guess I thought I could save her,' he says.

When Burke appeared in court about six weeks later, flanked by her family and Gus, she told the magistrate she would never use heroin again. After the judge placed her on a good behaviour bond, Burke reassured her parents and Ron she had genuinely turned over a new leaf.

Ron's welfare checks seemed to make a difference because, for a while, it looked as though Burke had indeed turned her back on drugs. 'I walked into the police station at St Kilda in torn jeans and with a guitar to say thank you,' she recalls. 'The cops kind of ribbed me a bit. "Oh, you're gonna play us a tune, are you?" "No," I said, "I want to see Ron Iddles".'

Just six weeks later, she was back on smack and was again busted for drug use. 'Two divvy wagons had me cornered in an alleyway,' she says. She told the police officers her name was Elizabeth Montgomery, after the actress who played Samantha in the television series *Bewitched*.

Moments later, a third police car arrived, and out stepped Ron Iddles.

'She got charged again and I got the sob story – "You don't understand, no one helps heroin addicts, and now we've got nowhere to live!"' Ron remembers her saying.

Ron racked his brain for what he could do to help the

young woman this time, because his well-meaning gestures clearly weren't enough. As it happened, he'd been asked to speak about the effects of drugs at a Lions Club meeting. *Perhaps Louise might learn something from that?* he thought.

'So I asked her to come along, and she did,' Ron recalls, adding that he also asked her to tell the group about her own experiences. 'She was nervous about speaking but she did, and in the end, she even sang a song.' Fittingly, it was Neil Young's song about the perils of heroin use, 'The Needle and the Damage Done'.

Ron even took Burke on a family outing to the famous Hanging Rock in the Macedon Ranges. 'It was about resetting her environment,' he explains.

Keen to bring stability back to her life, Ron enlisted the help of a St Kilda charity to find her and Gus somewhere to live. The couple had been sleeping rough and bunking down with other junkies, which Ron knew would only lead to temptation. 'So we found them a flat in East St Kilda and set them up in it,' Ron says.

This was not something policemen did for drug users every day, and Ron's good deeds didn't stop there. Gus was trying to find work and had been complaining he needed a car to drive to job interviews, so Ron held a fundraiser. 'We got enough money so I bought them a 1966 grey-and-white Holden HR sedan,' he says.

On a roll, Ron then found Gus a job as a garbage collector. 'I arranged for him to get a job with Cleanaway,' Ron recalls. 'He was very appreciative because now he had a car, a flat and a job.'

It could have been the start of a happy, healthy new life, but Gus didn't share Ron's work ethic. 'He turned up on day one for the job, but not on day two,' Ron says. 'So on day three, I rang him at four in the morning and got him out of bed to make sure he turned up.' Gus did, but not for much longer. 'I think he lasted all of about eight days because he couldn't commit,' Ron says.

A couple of weeks later, Ron went to visit them at home and noticed the car he'd bought them was missing. 'I found out Gus had taken the car to a wrecking yard and got fifty dollars for it, which was the equivalent of a cap of heroin,' Ron says. 'I felt very disappointed in him but it showed me that, while I could help them, they had to want to help themselves.'

Even more worryingly, about three months later, the couple moved out of the flat Ron had set them up in. 'I was in contact with Louise's parents who said she was off the rails and involved in prostitution,' Ron says.

'I was homeless in Melbourne,' Burke says, remembering how she lost contact with those who cared about her and struggled to survive. 'I was on a park bench with my eyes frozen. And then I lived in a cupboard for three months.'

Soon afterwards, she moved back to Sydney, although what happened there is largely a blur due to her heavy drug use. What is known is that Burke overdosed time and time again. She would literally die on the street, only to be revived by ambulance officers wielding life-saving shots of Narcan.

'She'd ring from time to time, mostly off her face,' Ron remembers. Yet she desperately wanted to get clean and periodically checked herself into rehabilitation clinics. Then one day in 1994, she phoned Ron with momentous news: she'd given birth to a baby girl called Bonnie and wanted Ron to be her godfather. 'I always believed you only had one set of parents but if I could be a father figure then that was fine,' Ron says.

It would come to that, because years later, when Bonnie grew into a teenager, she went through a rebellious phase of her own. By that time, Burke's parents John and Jenny had moved into a Gold Coast penthouse where they had been looking after Bonnie until their daughter was able to move to Queensland herself. It came as a shock to everyone when Bonnie – who'd seemed so happy and settled – ran away from home and stopped attending school. It was shades of her mother all over again.

The way the Burkes saw it, there was only one person who could save Bonnie: Ron. Upon hearing the worrying news, he immediately flew to the Gold Coast to counsel his goddaughter. 'I gave her the big dad story,' Ron says. 'I said, "School's the place for you. Your grandmother and grandfather are looking after you and you don't want to end up like your mother."'

Fortunately, Bonnie heeded her godfather's advice and settled back into a peaceful life with her grandparents. She finished high school and enrolled in a graphic arts course, in which she thrived. Burke knows she has Ron to thank. 'He stepped up to the plate,' she says. 'I already thought he was an awesome bloke but he's the bomb. He needs to be cloned.'

Louise Burke finally gave up heroin three decades later and has been clean since. 'The trick,' she says, 'is to say no.'

It was Ron's influence that eventually helped her to do so. 'The reason I got through all that crap is because of the compassion of one man. Without him, I wouldn't be here now,' she adds.

'Without him, she'd be dead,' her mother Jenny agrees, adding that Ron's guidance gave Burke the strength to go on. 'He didn't have to do what he did for us; he was under no obligation to do so. It's embarrassing how much he's done for us. Our whole family holds him in the highest regard.'

Since leaving her dark days behind, Burke has begun studying psychology at university to help others battling addictions. She even invites the homeless and hungry to stay in her apartment, as another way of giving back to the community. She acknowledges that she couldn't have helped herself – let alone anyone else – without Ron, and credits him with teaching her the value of random acts of kindness. 'He's the most beautiful person on the face of the earth,' she says. 'I know we will remain friends forever.'

And whilst Ron acknowledges that 'Louise was an experiment at the time', he came across many Louises during his time in the job. Young people who, for whatever reason, had succumbed to the temptation of drugs and become hooked. He had learnt that he could not save every one, but there was something he could do. 'I could always be there with a listening ear,' he says.

11

THE ORIGINAL MR SIN

*'This was just fascinating. It was the first major joint
investigation for the National Crime Authority. It was
around one of Sydney's best known business people.
It involved a lot of intrigue and connections to
government. It took me into a totally different world.'*
– Ron Iddles

The highly secretive National Crime Authority was set
up in 1984 by the Federal Government in the wake of
the Royal Commission on the Activities of the Federated
Ship Painters and Dockers Union. The Commission, headed
by Frank Costigan QC, initially examined illegal activities
involving the Painters and Dockers, but later looked at other
forms of organised crime, including complex tax-evasion
schemes. While the Commission had its critics, it illuminated
the fact that organised crime in Australia was rife, and that a
new, national law enforcement agency was needed to fight it.

'The NCA was initially going to be something like the FBI
and sit above the AFP,' Ron explains. 'It was set up to be a
sophisticated organised-crime-fighting unit.'

The Victorian branch of the NCA was headed by Chief Investigator Carl Mengler, who was empowered to select police for his team from Western Australia, South Australia, Tasmania and New South Wales. The Northern Territory and the Australian Capital Territory were too small to spare any officers for the specialist unit, and Mengler didn't want anyone from the Queensland Police Force due to allegations of police misconduct, later exposed during the Fitzgerald Inquiry. And while Mengler ultimately employed police from New South Wales, he had to choose wisely. 'There were a lot of good cops in New South Wales but there were a lot of bad cops too, and they were very high in numbers in those days,' he says.

At the time, Victoria Police had 12,000 members, and it wasn't until Ron applied for a sergeant's position at the NCA that he and Mengler met. 'I interviewed him and he impressed me,' Mengler says. 'I selected Ron and I never regretted it in any way.'

Among the other Victorians to join the team were an inspector, Peter Halloran; a senior sergeant, Bob Ryan; and a senior constable, Ken Collins. The team, spread over three levels of a multi-storey building in Queen Street, Melbourne, was complemented by staff from other government agencies, as well as solicitors who gave legal advice and conducted hearings, and accountants able to provide forensic financial analysis. 'The investigators mixed with all the other workers and it was a good multi-functional team environment,' Ron says.

Ron was expected to crack his first case the moment he walked in the door. 'The first thing I ran was an investigation into an allegation of major drug trafficking in South Australia as a result of the Costigan Royal Commission,' he says. 'I spent six months investigating the allegation and ended up charging the person who made the complaint with cultivating a crop of marijuana.'

The unusual result prompted Mengler to ask Ron to go to Sydney with Bob Ryan and a senior constable from Western Australia, Jim Milligan, on another considerable mission: to investigate the affairs of shady businessman Abe Saffron. Nicknamed 'Mr Sin', the city's very own godfather, Saffron was a notorious nightclub owner and property developer, and Sydney's king of sleaze. Between the 1960s and early 1980s, Saffron reigned supreme over Kings Cross and the nightclubs and strip joints he owned there.

Inspired, it's believed, by mobsters he met in Las Vegas, Saffron knew how to make moolah out of sex, booze and a good floorshow. Yet these earthly delights came at a price New South Wales could ill afford, and Saffron's reputation became increasingly tainted with allegations of bribery, corruption, violence and even murder.

'The national head of the NCA was Justice James Stewart and he wanted us to look at Abe Saffron in relation to tax evasion, Juanita Nielsen's disappearance in 1975, the development in the early seventies of Victoria Point in Kings Cross, and aspects of the Luna Park fire in 1979,' Ron says.

'Everyone in Sydney knew who Abe Saffron was,' he continues. But Saffron wasn't quite as notorious interstate. 'He'd been mentioned in Bureau of Criminal Intelligence reports in Melbourne, but other than that I didn't know him as much more than a very successful businessman who was well connected and had a lot of influential friends.'

Among those influential friends were hardened criminals, politicians and senior police, so for the next few months, Ron and his fellow investigators would have to tread carefully.

*

As Ron familiarised himself with Abe Saffron's affairs, he had to familiarise himself with Sydney too, where he'd be spending the next few months living out of a suitcase in serviced rooms in the CBD and Potts Point, a cosmopolitan suburb which backs on to the Cross. The NCA expected it to be a complex investigation, taking between six to twelve months.

'Sometimes I'd go for three weeks without seeing my family,' Ron recalls. 'But I'd fly Colleen and Joanne up for the odd weekend, and other times I'd fly home late on Friday night then fly back again on a Sunday night. It was a lot tougher for Colleen, having to work and look after Joanne all on her own, but we both accepted there would be periods when I'd be away from home, even before I was selected by the NCA.'

The only other time Ron had been to Sydney was on his honeymoon, and he found it very different from the southern mainland capital he knew so well.

Kings Cross, Ron observed, was even seamier than St Kilda, with cockney spruikers lining Victoria Street outside neon-lit strip joints and peep shows, and street prostitutes with kohl-rimmed eyes touting for business. Like St Kilda, there were male prostitutes too.

'There was "The Wall", where young boys were picked up,' Ron remembers. 'And there were lots of other problems. There were massive amounts of drugs, and seedy rooming houses. There were also unscrupulous club operators and police corruption. It was one massive cocktail.'

Yet visitors to Sydney were invariably drawn to the seedy spectacle. 'Everyone who went to Sydney had to go to Kings Cross, even if it was for a look,' Ron says. Even Colleen and Joanne, on a visit to Sydney, went on a scenic tour. 'We drove through there so that Colleen could have a look,' Ron says. 'She was always so fascinated with the people.'

Ron got to know his new surroundings well, and was quick to find out who was who in town – with the help of key insiders on Saffron's own payroll. Among those offering assistance was one of Saffron's most intimidating cronies, James McCartney Anderson, better known as Jim Anderson, but sometimes called Big Jim. A Scottish-born hardman, Anderson was overseer of Saffron's Kings Cross nightclubs including the Carousel, where anti-development campaigner Juanita Nielsen was last seen alive in July 1975.

Nielsen – heiress to Mark Foy's department-store fortune and publisher of the community newspaper, *NOW* – had lived in Kings Cross where she'd vigorously opposed the construction of a $40-million apartment block. The building was to be called Victoria Point and had been proposed by wealthy property developer Frank Theeman, an associate of Saffron's. While the NCA was never able to gather enough evidence to prove who was responsible for Nielsen's disappearance and presumed murder, the investigators believed they knew. 'To this day, Saffron and McCartney Anderson are believed to have been behind her disappearance,' Ron says.

Yet while he fervently denied any involvement in Nielsen's disappearance, Anderson did admit to being involved in

Saffron's dirty business dealings and approached the NCA, offering to tell all. 'Part of his decision to come forward might have been to do with self-preservation and getting ahead of the pack,' Ron suggests, recalling the first time he and Bob Ryan met their powerful new informer in a hotel room. 'We knew he was a very influential person in Sydney,' Ron says. 'He'd been Abe Saffron's right-hand man for ten to fifteen years. He was also politically well connected, with strong connections to the Labor Party.'

Anderson, Ron knew, was also dangerous, having fatally shot a violent standover man known as Donny 'The Glove' Smith in 1970. (Donny 'The Glove' was so named because he wore a leather glove lined with lead to inflict extra damage on his victims. In the end, it was a good thing The Glove was so fond of lead, because Anderson filled him with it after The Glove broke his jaw. Big Jim Anderson was never indicted, but that's another story.)

The NCA was gathering evidence from others who knew Saffron, but Anderson made their job much easier. 'He provided us with important background information about how Abe Saffron operated his clubs,' Ron says. And it was immediately clear that Saffron was a fan of creative accounting. 'James McCartney Anderson presented us with two sets of books,' Ron remembers. 'One showed figures of what the clubs actually made. The other set of books were made for the purpose of defrauding the tax department.' They were known variously as the 'black' books and the 'white' books.

It had been a successful scam, just one of several Saffron had been running since the Vietnam War. And Anderson – whose job it was to count the cash – told the investigators Saffron always skimmed the profits and took advantage of his patrons. 'If you went into one of his clubs and asked for a Jack Daniels, for example, you didn't get Jack Daniels, you got a pretty generic brand,' Ron says. 'Then, as the night went on and people got drunk, the bartenders would just put their finger in some scotch and run it around the rim of the glass, which was just a glass of Coke. Anderson explained how they made massive profits just by doing that.'

Anderson didn't stop there, showing Ron and Ryan more dubious entries in Saffron's books, including one that pointed directly to the bent local constabulary. 'There was always, on the expense side of the ledger, a donation to the Police Boys Club,' Ron says. 'But as James explained it, that wasn't where that donation went. It was put in a brown envelope – and on a set pay day once a week – detectives came around to collect it. It was in return for police allowing the clubs to stay open and have prostitutes on the premises, and had been going on for years.'

Not only did Anderson tell the NCA how the scams were conducted, he also named the book-keepers allegedly in on it. 'At least three were female book-keepers, and two of them lived in New Zealand,' Ron says, recalling how he and Ryan subsequently flew to New Zealand at least five times to collect statements. They also tracked down bouncers in New Zealand who'd worked in Saffron's Sydney clubs and got a firm hold on how Saffron's business operated.

As the pieces of the puzzle kept falling into place, the investigators discovered another man who would become another important informant. 'He had previously worked for Abe Saffron for many years,' Ron says. 'During that time he became very close to Saffron and his wife, and would often be at their house in Vaucluse.'

Suspecting that the man – to be known here as Mick Long – might have intimate knowledge of Saffron's business affairs, Ron and Jim Milligan paid him a visit. 'I knocked on the door and Mick opened it. When we told him where we were from, he invited us in,' Ron recalls. Long's response came as a surprise. 'He said, "Where have you bloody well been? I've been waiting for you for a long time".'

'I let them know I was glad they came because I was toying with the idea – out of horrible obligation – to do something about the things that were going on because I was disgusted,' Long reveals. 'I was privy to a lot of things that were going on and nothing was being done to address it. Blind eyes were being turned to everything and I felt useless.'

Long knew he couldn't take his information to the New South Wales Police – it was too risky. 'I knew how corrupt the local police were and I couldn't have approached them,' he says. 'And the people about whom I had these concerns were well in with them. I was in quite an insidious position.'

It was a relief to learn the NCA investigators on his doorstep were from interstate. 'He said, "I'm glad one of you is from Victoria and one of you is from Western Australia, and I hope the NCA is serious about organised crime",' Ron recalls.

Long invited the investigators to come back two hours later, and he began to tell all – besides the how, where and when, he knew the addresses and phone numbers of key players in Saffron's empire. 'I was well organised and had an excellent memory and could tell them all these things,' he says. 'I think they realised they were on a goldmine.'

When Long first met Saffron, he had no idea of the scope of the small, well-tailored businessman's illegal dealings. 'Saffron was a true enigma. He really was. At our first meeting I found him very calm, very polite and very reassuring with no pretension of power or wealth,' he says, adding that in the many years he worked for him, Saffron was always softly spoken and did not swear. 'He was totally incapable of getting flustered.'

Others like Anderson got flustered on Saffron's behalf, employing brutal standover tactics to maximise cash flow and keep mouths shut. 'To what extent Saffron was aware of these goings-on, I don't know,' Long says, recalling how he'd wanted to get away from the underworld but had been in too deep to make sudden moves. 'It was very hard for me to be among them because I was never of the same mind-set of those people and I had to disguise that. It was peer group pressure; you had to be like them. But Saffron was different, he wasn't like them. He was civilised compared to them.'

But appearances can be deceptive. Aware at least that Saffron was involved in fraud, Long told the NCA all he knew about his former boss's bad bookwork. 'He quickly became an integral part of the investigation and his version of events corroborated James McCartney Anderson's,' Ron says.

Yet Long had been around long enough to know that a whistle-blower's existence is a precarious one. *What if Saffron and his henchmen found out Mick Long was no longer staying staunch?*

'That was no easy task, I'll tell you – to uncover all the things that were going on,' Long says. 'I had to fraternise with those people at night. All the while I was conscious that I could have been watched and something could have happened to me.'

Long became so suspicious of those around him that he even had reservations about some NCA members. 'The only thing that enabled me to continue in this way [being an informant] was my utmost faith in Ron and Jim,' he says. 'They were a formidable team. I had nothing but the highest regard for both of them.'

In Ron, Long noticed a calm, matter-of-fact demeanour, and he was impressed by the way 'he didn't embellish or make promises'.

'He was such a reliable confidante,' Long says. 'I knew if I told him something he wouldn't get it wrong or mix it up or mention something he shouldn't. I knew he was very astute.'

So when Long suggested he tell part but not all of what he knew, Ron was straight with him. 'He said, "No, I can't do that". Not only would he not break the law, he wouldn't even bend it just a touch,' Long says. 'Such was his character.'

Thanks to their informants and the vast intelligence they'd gathered, the NCA was now in possession of crucial evidence about Saffron's illegal business dealings, and knew they had a case against him. Armed with a warrant, they searched his home and turned up at his bottle shop, Crown Street Liquor, to see if he'd cooked his books there too.

'We wanted to see if there were any other documents relating to Les Girls [the drag nightclub] and about six other businesses he operated, because we wanted to be thorough,' Ron says, recalling how he was particularly eager to search a storeroom that he knew to be below the shop.

When Ron and Ryan turned up, the 'short, black-haired and always immaculately dressed' Saffron was there to greet them, the keys to his storeroom at the ready. 'It was like a cellar,' Ron says of the room. 'The walls would have been forty-five centimetres thick.'

Yet even though Saffron was obliging, there was something disarming about him. 'He opened the door to the storeroom and Bob Ryan and I walked in. There were no windows in there. In fact, there was nothing in there at all. He'd obviously cleared it out so we couldn't find anything on him in there.'

As Saffron stood outside the enormous storeroom watching the detectives, Ron became nervous. 'I looked at Abe who had a big smile on his face and thought, *If you want to lock us in here, no one will ever find us*,' he recalls. 'He was in a position of power because no one would have heard of us again.'

In the end, after an investigation that ran for around seven months and involving six personnel, the NCA had enough dirt to lock Saffron up. But much like the American mobster Al Capone, who was suspected of countless serious crimes, all the authorities could pin on Saffron were tax offences. 'Ultimately Saffron was done for defrauding the tax department of $10 million, due to the fact that we found out he was operating two sets of books,' Ron says, acknowledging the pivotal information given by Anderson and Long.

Saffron's arrest was often talked about in NCA circles later. Mengler, who coordinated the operation from NCA headquarters, remembers it well. 'The arresting officer said to me, "That's the first time I've arrested someone wearing $50 silk socks and a $5000 suit. They're usually wearing trackie dacks!"' he laughs.

After several unsuccessful appeals, Saffron served seventeen months behind bars, trading in his sharp, designer suits for prison-issue tracksuits. But it was only a temporary comedown. After his release, Saffron went on to live a long, prosperous and dapper life, passing away in 2006, aged eighty-six.

*

After Saffron was charged, Ron and his colleagues started investigating the suspicious 1979 ghost train fire at Sydney's Luna Park. Seven people – six of them children – had perished in the blaze, which Saffron was suspected of arranging, but the NCA could not prove it. 'We had information that Saffron wanted Luna Park burnt down so he could obtain the land to build apartments,' Ron says. 'The plan was to put petrol through and ignite it and it would have burnt the ghost train and the whole place down. No one knew there would be people in it, but there were several people killed.'

Simultaneously, Ron delved into other cases involving the members of the underworld. 'Everything I did in the seven months I was in Sydney was straight out of *Blue Murder*,' he says, referring to the 1995 ABC mini-series about the controversial detective Roger Rogerson and the violent criminal Arthur 'Neddy' Smith. *Blue Murder* dramatised Rogerson's 1981 shooting of Neddy Smith's standover man and drug dealer Warren Lanfranchi. Rogerson claimed it was self-defence and the New South Wales Police later awarded him a bravery medal.

In early 1986, an inmate at Sydney's Long Bay jail offered Ron a different version of the events surrounding Lanfranchi's death. 'He claimed to have an eight-millimetre movie of the shooting but said it was locked away,' Ron says.

What the prisoner told Ron about the content of the film cannot be revealed for legal reasons. For the first time, however, Ron can share this: 'The prisoner said there was only one other person who knew of the movie's existence and that was Sallie-Anne Huckstepp.' Huckstepp was Lanfranchi's girlfriend, a drug-addicted prostitute who became a whistle-blower after he was shot.

What Ron says next makes him shudder. 'About a week after the prisoner gave me that information, Sallie-Anne Huckstepp was found in Centennial Park, dead in the lake.' The thirty-one-year-old had been strangled and drowned. Ron doesn't know if her death had something to do with the information the inmate had just given him. 'It may have been a coincidence, or it may have had something to do with the person I spoke to in jail,' he says. Whatever the reason, he found it deeply unsettling.

*

Even though he'd worked as a homicide investigator, nothing could have prepared Ron for the uneasy world of organised crime in which life was cheap and dangerous secrets were a currency to be traded. 'At the time, there were a lot of underworld killings in New South Wales that the NCA was investigating,' Ron says. 'So all of a sudden we were in the middle of a heavy criminal element.'

It was when Ron started to investigate the unlawful activities of other police that he started to fear for his own safety. 'It got dangerous,' he admits, 'because of some of the people we spoke to about high-level corruption within New South

Wales Police. We became a bit of a target because back then it was frowned upon, I suppose, to report police corruption. It got to the point here we had to move from our accommodation every seven or eight days. It was really an insurance policy, to keep moving.'

Despite the pressures of the job, Ron continued to impress Mengler, who was later appointed Victoria's deputy commissioner. During his own esteemed career, Mengler identified the attributes of a top investigator and says Ron possessed them all, and more. 'The first attribute is honesty and high moral values,' he says. 'The second is a belief in what you do and the third is the ability to deal with facts and not supposition.' The fourth attribute is the desire to achieve, and the fifth is having enough energy for the job. Mengler says a top investigator also needs compassion and isn't afraid to show their emotions. 'You also need a sense of urgency – you can't put off until tomorrow what you can do today because you can lose evidence,' he adds.

'Quite simply,' Mengler concludes, 'Ron is an outstanding detective. One of the most outstanding detectives in the last thirty years.'

But after seven months at the NCA coalface, Ron was ready to go home, and asked if he could return to Melbourne to be with his family. He'd been away for a long time. 'But I needed to get away from that environment of the underworld too, in which people were constantly talking about police involvement in crime and corruption. It was information we had to pass on, but back then the attitude among police was, "Do not hit the beehive with a stick or you will be stung".'

So before he got stung, Ron packed his bags. 'Sydney was a

fascinating place to work and I met many underworld figures,' he says. 'I learnt from being up there that everyone has a secret. There is always a skeleton in the cupboard and if you approached people the right way, they were often happy to tell their story. It was all about listening and understanding.'

And Ron says that's why, decades later, Mick Long still rings him every year to wish him a merry Christmas.

12

THE MARAFIOTE MURDERS

*'I was privileged to be asked to reinvestigate
the disappearance and suspected murder
of Dominic Marafiote.'*
– Ron Iddles

Rumours of bent cops continued to abound during Ron's time at the NCA, especially during Queensland's Fitzgerald Inquiry, which began in 1987 and investigated police misconduct. During that time, Ron arranged to travel to the Gold Coast to meet a whistle-blower, who called in a panic a couple of days later to cancel. 'I'd made a time to meet him and when I rang to confirm he said, "Don't come, I've had a call from a very senior police officer. He threatened me and told me not to speak to you. If I do, I'll be signing my own death warrant".' Ron left him alone.

While the NCA continued to delve into police corruption, Ron turned his attention to one final drug case before returning to the Victoria Police Crime Department. It had dawned on him that the new breed of drug dealer had become as dangerous as the crooked police he'd been investigating.

Dealers had started using the drugs they were peddling, which made their behaviour unpredictable. 'You never knew how they were going to react when you caught them,' Ron says.

At least with old-school crooks, a copper knew where he stood. 'There was a mutual respect between police officers and old-style crooks,' he says. 'Old-school crooks would tell you that in those days, there was honour among thieves. They'd tell you there's no honour among thieves these days.'

They were eye-opening times and, after his final drug case at the NCA – over which Ron charged a man with possession of four kilos of heroin – he accepted a post as a detective sergeant at the Drug Squad.

But within three months he was back where he really belonged – on secondment to a special taskforce investigating a suspected homicide. The Crime Department needed him to work on a case that involved all the criminal elements he'd come to know so much about at the NCA: drugs, secrets, murder and fear.

It was known as the Marafiote murders.

*

Billy Lees was once a petty criminal who'd be the first to tell you that for someone who's never had a driver's licence, he's stolen an awful lot of cars. Yet, for a small-time crook, there was an honesty about him; his peers might even have said he was old-school. For Billy, car theft was one thing, but murder was a whole other game. So when he found out about the murders of Dominic Marafiote and his parents, Carmelo and Rosa, he didn't hesitate to tell the police.

On 18 July 1985, Mildura greengrocer Dominic Marafiote went missing and no one could find him. 'His truck was found on Sixth Street, Merbein,' Ron says, 'and that led to the property of a man called Sandy MacRae. Police spoke to Sandy MacRae about it in the early days, but he denied any knowledge of Dominic Marafiote's disappearance.'

The day after Dominic disappeared, his brother found their parents' bodies in their Adelaide home. They had been shot, execution style. The gunman's identity was a mystery until two years later, when Lees turned up.

'It was decided a small group of police should look into his claims,' Ron says. They quickly realised just how far Lees was prepared to go to help them. 'He made a statement to us and became a witness, not an informer,' Ron says. There's an important difference: 'Informers do not like their names to be known, whereas Billy was prepared to stand up and be counted, and ultimately, give his evidence in court.

'Billy Lees said Sandy MacRae had killed Dominic Marafiote, then went to Adelaide to kill his parents,' Ron continues. 'When we asked him how he knew that, he said, "Sandy told me".'

Lees also appeared to have inside knowledge about Rosa Marafiote's murder. 'He told us a pillow had been put in front of the muzzle of the gun to muffle it, but when it went off, the hammer of the revolver got caught in the pillow-case,' Ron says. 'Billy said, "That's what Sandy MacRae told me".'

Ron and a colleague, Detective Senior Constable Brendon Murphy, flew to Adelaide where forensic scientists told them they had found a grease mark on the pillowcase but hadn't yet been able to explain how it got there. 'We had it forensically tested and it showed that the killer had put a pillow at the end of the revolver, but that the revolver had got caught on the pillowslip, leaving the grease stain. So the first time the killer fired, the gun didn't go off.'

It confirmed to Ron and Murphy that Lees indeed had special knowledge of the murders. 'And that gave us two options to consider: was Billy Lees telling the truth as told to him by Sandy MacRae? Or was Billy Lees the killer? This information could only have been known to the killer or someone present, as it had never been presented to the media,' Ron says.

With thirteen years of policing behind him, Ron's gut told him Lees was no killer. 'When you meet people, you make an assessment,' he explains. 'Billy had some criminal history, but I was of the opinion he was telling the truth.'

Ron was right, and Lees offered the police further pivotal information. 'Billy Lees was of the opinion that Dominic Marafiote was buried on Sandy MacRae's property,' Ron says. 'So we all went up there, a team of forty police, to search for his remains. We executed a search warrant at five in the morning, which took MacRae and his girlfriend, Judy Ip, by surprise.'

Judy Ip was a petite woman whose ex-husband was a partner in Melbourne's Flower Drum, the city's most famous fine-dining Chinese restaurant. Her comfortable life changed dramatically after her marriage ended, and she embarked on a relationship with MacRae. It was a deadly partnership because MacRae would eventually force her to become an accessory to murder. 'She broke down and told me the whole story,' Ron says. 'She said, "I made a mistake in my life and that was to answer an ad in the *Weekly Times*".'

Alistair 'Sandy' MacRae had placed the ad in the rural newspaper, seeking a live-in housekeeper and offering attractive benefits. 'He'd said it was a great environment and that there was water-skiing and wine,' Ron says. 'So Judy went up to Merbein, near Mildura, packed up her things in Melbourne, and went and lived in.'

After two bottles of champagne, Ip didn't clock on as MacRae's housekeeper, but became his live-in lover. 'He was a charmer,' she says in her first ever interview. 'He could have sold ice to an Eskimo.' MacRae's apparent devotion to his family also appealed to Ip, who took her young son with her to Merbein. 'His [MacRae's] mother and father and aunty and two sons lived with him on the property too. It was the perfect family life.'

But not for long. No sooner had Ip settled in than her dreams of a happy family, life came crashing down. MacRae let her know who was boss, a bashing or a pistol-whipping his way of keeping her in her place.

'If I talked back I'd get a belting,' she reveals. 'If I was five minutes late coming back from the newsagent's, it'd be, "You're late", *whack!* That was how it was. He even said to me, "If you leave me, I know where your parents live.'

She didn't leave.

Ron wasn't the first detective to ask the diminutive Ip to dish the dirt. South Australian police had already asked for her side of the story, but she didn't like their tone. 'I'd like to help you but I know nothing,' she kept saying.

Ip maintained her line for hours. 'And then Ron strolls in,'

she says. 'Just his way and approach, he knew I was an innocent party, so to speak. I just felt I could trust him. And I
asked if I could see my son and he arranged that.'

Ron sensed that Ip had something to confess and, if treated
respectfully, would probably do so. He could see she was a
physical and emotional wreck. 'She was a small, fragile lady
who had been living in fear,' he explains.

Ron's straight-up, humane approach quickly yielded a
result. 'Sharpen your pencil, here we go!' Ip said to Ron. 'And
I gave him a minute-by-minute account of what happened.'

*

Judy Ip told Ron that MacRae had befriended Dominic
Marafiote, and had talked the forty-two-year-old into buying
a large amount of marijuana from him. It promised to be a
money-spinner because Marafiote could sell the marijuana at
a tidy profit. The only thing was, the dope didn't exist; MacRae
barely had a couple of wilting plants. 'He [MacRae] gave him
a sample which he took to someone he knew in Shepparton
and [after that] he said, "We'll have twenty tonnes",' Ip says.

The pair settled on a price and Marafiote agreed to go to
MacRae's property one night to buy the non-existent marijuana. 'I said, "But you haven't got anything [to give him]",' Ip
reveals. For that she got a whack in the mouth. On the day of
the bogus deal MacRae started digging up the yard beneath
the chicken shed. It was a sign the night was not going to end
well for Dominic Marafiote. MacRae's strategy, as police later
found out, was to lure Marafiote to his property, kill him and
steal the drug money.

But things didn't quite go to plan.

When Marafiote arrived in his truck to collect the crop, he spoke to Ip in the kitchen. Then at some stage Marafiote told MacRae he didn't have the money, which infuriated MacRae. According to Ip, MacRae said, "Dominic, come out and I'll show you the shit". He took Marafiote out the back and I thought, *What's he gonna show him?*'

Ip wished she could have warned Marafiote that MacRae was dangerous, but they only had a moment alone together. 'I was even going to say to him, "Get out of here, it's not good".' But she knew Marafiote considered MacRae his friend. 'He'd say, "But why, what do you mean?" I didn't have time to be questioned. I only had ten seconds, if anything. I just froze.'

What happened next would change Ip's life forever – and end Marafiote's. 'As I walked out the back I heard a bang and that was it. It was Dominic.'

Ip told Ron the whole, terrible story. 'Sandy then made Judy take Dominic to the chook yard and bury him,' he says. Afterwards, MacRae parked Marafiote's truck on the road to make it look like he'd decided to disappear.

Ip also told Ron that Marafiote had worn a gold chain and crucifix, which she removed after he'd been killed. In a way, it seemed like the right thing to do. 'When she was confessing to me, Judy said she still had the crucifix and the ring and that they were in her wardrobe, in a coat pocket,' Ron remembers. 'We later went back to her home and found the jewellery. There was even an inscription from his wife on the wedding ring, *To Dominic with love from Rose.*'

Even though Marafiote didn't have the money, his parents Carmelo and Rosa Marafiote did. Marafiote had planned to drive four hours to the Adelaide suburb of Woodville North to give them the marijuana and they were going to pay him on arrival.

Only it wasn't Marafiote who turned up on his parents' doorstep that night. 'Sandy and Judy had an old station wagon which they drove to Adelaide and got there at two or three in the morning,' Ron says. 'Carmelo and Rosa were still up as they were expecting to receive the truckload of marijuana from Dominic.'

When MacRae and Ip arrived, MacRae told the Marafiotes that Marafiote was on his way in the truck and that he had come for the money instead. 'Carmelo wasn't happy with that, so Sandy insisted they go for a drive, during which they'd see Dominic on the road,' Ron says. 'Sandy said, "Once you see the marijuana in the truck, you can pay me", but of course they didn't see Dominic because he was already dead.

'On the way back to the Marafiotes' house, Judy was driving, Sandy was in the front passenger seat, and sixty-nine-year-old Carmelo was in the back,' Ron continues. 'Sandy said, "I've looked in the rear vision mirror and Dominic's behind us now". Then, just as Carmelo turned around, Sandy shot him in the back of the head.'

When they pulled into the Marafiotes' driveway, MacRae left Carmelo slumped in the car. Once inside, he demanded the money from seventy-year-old Rosa. 'Sandy made Rosa kneel down on the floor,' Ron says. 'She said, "I don't have any money", which was when MacRae got the pillow, and on the second attempt, managed to shoot her through it.'

With no sign of the money in the house, MacRae decided to hit the road. But first there was the business of the body in the back seat. 'Sandy made Judy go out to the car,' Ron says. 'They brought Carmelo in and left him in the house.'

The pair arrived back in Merbein at around 7 am. 'Sometime later that day, the bodies of Carmelo and Rosa were found and Dominic's truck was found near Sandy MacRae's,' Ron says. The drug money even turned up when the forensic pathologist found $28,000 sewn into the hem of Rosa's blood-spattered nightdress.

It was a truly cold-blooded crime and the only way Ip could deal with the part she was made to play was by operating on 'automatic', and with the help of prescription drugs. 'After the Marafiotes' [murder] I came home and got up the next morning as if nothing had happened,' she says. 'If he [MacRae] said, "Get up, go and pick the grapes", that was it.'

Initially, police had thought Marafiote had left his truck on the side of the road in order to stage his own disappearance, just as MacRae had hoped. They also figured that for some unknown reason he'd travelled to Adelaide to murder his parents. 'But then Judy told us the real story and she took me to the chicken shed to show me where the body was buried.'

Still, Ron had to be certain the body beneath the shed belonged to Marafiote. He could not be identified through fingerprints, and with no DNA in those days, Ron had to find another way. 'The body had a curvature of the spine so we managed to get an X-ray of Dominic's spine from Mildura Hospital,' he says. 'The pathologist was then able to match the X-ray to the spine, so we knew for sure it was Dominic Marafiote.

'We charged Sandy MacRae with the murder of Dominic Marafiote and South Australian Police charged him with the murder of Carmelo and Rosa in Adelaide, and we charged

Judy Ip with accessory to murder,' Ron continues, adding that Ip agreed to plead guilty and give evidence against her former lover.

'After we'd charged them, I said to Brendon Murphy, "Let's doorknock all the homes in Sixth Street in Merbein again",' Ron recalls. It was a smart decision, because even though they'd canvassed the neighbours before, the detectives turned up a new witness. 'One of the houses we doorknocked was a nearby farmhouse and the husband told us he saw Dominic's truck go into MacRae's residence then come out, but he'd always been fearful of MacRae so he hadn't wanted to say anything.'

It helped police establish their timeline of events, and informed the way Ron would guide his teams in future. 'I'd say, "After you've charged someone, go back to the area where you doorknocked or where the suspect lived, because you could turn up more evidence.'

When Ron interviewed MacRae, he found him unlike any murderer he'd met before, and he'd met some shockers. 'There was something about him,' Ron says. 'I've always had the view that most people aren't born bad but they make bad choices, but there was something in his eyes that I thought was creepy and evil. I'd say of all the people I've dealt with he's the sort of person that'd come looking for the person who charged him.'

And that became a very real fear for Ron when he found out MacRae had escaped from Pentridge Prison while on remand. 'I can remember thinking, *I wonder why he's escaped*,' Ron says. 'Here was a guy facing three murder charges, so he had nothing to lose. I thought that he might think, *If I get rid of the people who charged me, I might get off.*'

But that wasn't the case. 'He was found in Moonee Ponds sitting on a verandah,' Ron says. 'He wanted to say goodbye to his father.'

*

While Ron was preparing his brief for the Marafiote murders, something wonderful happened. On Mothers' Day in 1988, Colleen gave birth to the couple's second child, a boy they named Matthew. 'I'd been trying from when Joanne was eighteen months old,' Colleen says. 'So when I found out I was pregnant I was really stoked. I couldn't believe it after twelve years.'

Ron couldn't believe it either when he first laid eyes on his son.

'He was thrilled,' Colleen recalls. 'The moment he looked at Matthew I think he ran out and told everyone in the hospital including the cleaner and everyone not related to us!'

'I was very excited because we'd hoped for another baby for so long,' Ron says. 'And then to have a son was fantastic.'

But almost immediately, work beckoned. 'The day Matthew came home from hospital, I flew to France on the Marafiote murder investigation,' Ron says. 'In the back of my mind I thought, *I'm doing the wrong thing by not staying at home*. On the other hand, it was an opportunity to go overseas to complete an investigation and solve three murders.' And even though he didn't want to leave his wife and newborn baby, he knew Colleen would cope. 'She's always been very strong and capable,' he says. 'Sometimes it's about balance, but other times it's about finishing a job you'd started.'

And even though France sounded like a glamorous trip, it was a necessary part of the investigation because Dominic Marafiote's wife, Rose, was living there. 'So I went to Avignon in France where I met Rose Marafiote and she identified the ring and the gold chain and crucifix,' Ron says.

*

Before he left, however, Judy Ip told Ron about another murder. 'She said Sandy had always been about money and was always scheming, and had killed another man,' Ron says.

Fifty-nine-year-old Merbein man, Albert O'Hara, known to his friends as Bert, had been hoping to start a boat-building company and, in December 1984, agreed to buy marijuana from Sandy MacRae. If O'Hara sold it on at a good price, perhaps he could open his business ahead of schedule.

But MacRae had other plans. It was like a test run for Marafiote's murder seven months later. 'Sandy MacRae lured Albert O'Hara to his property, where he shot and killed him,' Ron says. MacRae then stole the $10,000 Bert O'Hara had brought with him for the drugs. Ip pointed the police towards where she thought Bert had been buried, but they couldn't find him.

Ip had yet more to get off her chest. 'Brendon Murphy had to drive Judy to Fairlea Women's Prison and on the way she said, "I want to take you somewhere else".' Ip asked Murphy to go to a house she'd driven past once with MacRae in Epsom Road, Kensington. 'There was a front-end loader digging up the footpath and Judy said, "I hope they don't dig up the back-yard",' Ron says.

Ip then explained there was a body buried in the backyard and alleged it was more of MacRae's murderous handiwork. When asked later, MacRae told the police he knew the body was there and even drew a map of where to find it. 'A body was dug up from Epsom Road and it was believed to belong to a prostitute,' Ron says. But MacRae denied having anything to do with the woman's murder and subsequent investigations failed to prove he'd killed her.

But there was a development in the murder of Bert O'Hara. 'Sometime later, police got further information about Albert O'Hara and went back to Merbein and located his body,' Ron says. 'It was about a hundred metres from where we'd dug. MacRae got charged with that murder.

'In the end,' Ron adds, 'everything that Judy Ip told us was true, and police suspect there were more murders MacRae was involved in – up to seven. But had it not been for the help of Judy Ip and Billy Lees, the Marafiote murders mightn't have been solved. Ultimately, Sandy MacRae was convicted of the murders of the Marafiotes as well as the murder of Albert O'Hara. He was sentenced to thirty-six years but wanted life. He said something to the judge like, "I never want to get out. I'll be eighty-five when I'm released, I'll have nothing to live for out there",' Ron says. 'But in jail at least, he went on to run the music radio station.'

After serving ten months in prison, Judy Ip was released on twelve months' probation. But Ip would have been happy to stay behind bars because she was no longer being abused. 'I was happy in there,' she admits. 'I could've spent the rest of my life in there because I resolved myself to it.'

These days, Ip's adult son and her work keep her going,

but the memories are as vivid as ever. 'I thought of going to a priest and confessing, but it was too horrific,' she says. 'So I just lived with it. I still live with it.'

And Ip – who says MacRae once tried to take out a contract on her life from prison – still lives in fear. 'I'm still waiting for the hit to come,' she says. 'I never thought a person could be possessed by the devil, but he is.'

13

THE SEVENTEEN-YEAR ITCH

'I know it sounds strange but I just needed to do something different. It's quite normal for operational police to feel like that, even if they've been passionate about policing.'
– Ron Iddles

The way Ron sees it, drug work suits some detectives but he didn't want to make a career of it. 'In the end, you were rarely dealing with people. You were dealing with a product rather than a victim or a victim's family, and that didn't suit me.'

In late 1988 Ron was promoted to the rank of detective senior sergeant and filled a short-term vacancy at the Licensing, Gaming and Vice Unit where he carried out administrative duties. 'I wasn't there for longer than six weeks when I went back to Homicide,' Ron says.

Returning as a senior sergeant of thirty-four meant that Ron was now running investigations and leading his own crew. One of the men in his charge was his former lecturer and mentor from Detective Training School, John Hill, who was a detective sergeant. Ron says, 'It was a bit daunting.

John Hill was someone I'd always looked up to and now I'd arrived and was his senior sergeant.'

Ron recalls the first call-out they attended together at a house in Murrumbeena, in Melbourne's south-east. Upon entering the house, they saw a dead woman sitting in a lounge chair. 'I remember John asking me what I thought, and at that time he was probably far more experienced at homicide investigation than I was,' Ron admits. 'In the end we both came to the consensus it was an overdose, not a murder. There was no sign of forced entry and the blood from her mouth was not bright red, which indicated it could have come from her stomach, suggesting an overdose.' Forensic tests supported the detectives' theory.

'Usually it's the senior sergeant's decision how to actually handle a case, but I think John respected me as a hard worker and someone who had made their own reputation, so we had a mutual respect for each other,' Ron adds.

Yet even though Ron was finally leading a team at Homicide, something he had always longed to do, something else was playing on his mind. Something he didn't see coming.

*

'I'd been back at Homicide for only three months when I became restless,' Ron says. 'Often police officers with around seven to eight years' experience think about career changes and leave the police force. I don't think there are many officers who have not thought about it during their career at some time, but it is a big decision to walk away from such a secure job.'

Even though he'd landed his 'dream job', he had been an operational police officer since the early 1970s. *What would it be like to do something else?* he wondered. It was a niggling thought that just wouldn't go away. 'In hindsight, I wouldn't say I was burnt out but I'd never taken any time off from operational work,' he explains. 'Others, when they're promoted, take on a project or something at the Police Academy, but I'd always worked in busy areas.'

These days, Victorian police officers can take twelve months without pay and still keep their jobs, but that wasn't an option in 1989. 'Looking back, if that had been available then I would have done that to test the water, to work out whether I really wanted to leave for good,' Ron says. 'Decisions are based on the facts at the time and you can always look back and question it. Hindsight is a wonderful thing and deciding to leave was probably not my best decision, but later I became a better police officer for having done something different.'

With the decision made to try something new, Ron had to work out what he wanted to do. Truck driving came to mind. 'So I started looking into the possibility of becoming an owner–driver because I'd always had a love of machinery,' he says. 'And I'd always done something part-time. I'd driven tractors and at one stage I'd delivered meat. So I was looking for a job where I could work on my own as a driver.'

Soon, he heard about a job at Debco, a company that manufactured potting mix. 'I had an interview with the manager, a bloke called Chris Drysdale, and he said, "Buy yourself a truck and you can start!"'

Colleen found Ron's decision to change careers sudden and perplexing, given how much he'd thrived on being a detective.

'She was probably apprehensive that I was going to leave a secure job I loved, but she didn't say don't do it,' Ron says.

'It did surprise me at the start but then he explained how he felt,' Colleen says. 'I just wanted him to be happy. And that meant doing whatever he wanted to do.'

With two children to feed, Ron was also attracted by an increase in income. 'The pay rates were very good for an owner–driver,' he says. 'You could earn $140,000 a year.'

Drysdale suggested Ron do a two-day trial and hire a twelve-ton truck to deliver potting mix to see how he liked it. There were forty bags to a pallet, which Ron had to unload and stack in nurseries.

'On my first day I worked around the Melbourne metropolitan area,' Ron says. 'On the second day, I delivered potting mix to Yea and Mansfield, out in the country.' And as hackneyed as the saying might be, you can take the boy out of the country but you can't take the country out of the boy. 'I thought, *How good is this! I'm out in the country, meeting good people. There's no stress and no pressure – this is not bad!*'

Ron's next step was to buy a truck of his own. 'I went to Woods and Reeves [a truck dealership] and bought myself a 1982 T-Line 2670 International truck, a prime mover,' he says. 'They had to get the chassis extended and a tray put on it, so all up it cost $60,000.'

Now he had to settle on a start date with Debco. At first, he couldn't wait but in the month while the truck was being built, he started having second thoughts. 'I thought, *Here I am, about to borrow $60,000. What if I broke my leg and couldn't drive? What if the truck breaks down? There's no holiday pay and no sick leave. In the police force I got paid reasonably well,* *there was six weeks holiday leave a year as well as long service and sick leave. What am I doing?'*

To allay his fears, Ron asked other truck owners about their experiences. 'Fortunately they all said I was well and truly going to get a good return on my investment,' Ron recalls.

But there was still the matter of handing in his resignation at the Homicide Squad. 'I came in one day at 5 am and put a note on everyone's desk. I'd personally addressed them to every member, telling them I'd finally made a decision to resign, effective from a particular date.'

To a person, his colleagues were stunned. 'By eight o'clock when everyone got in they couldn't believe it,' Ron says. 'Then, when they found out I was going to drive a truck, they said I was mad.'

Some even assumed Ron had decided to leave because he'd been subpoenaed to give evidence at a police-board hearing investigating his former Detective Training School classmate, Denis Tanner. Tanner had been suspected of leaking information from Operation Mint, an amphetamine job Ron had worked on while he was at the Drug Squad. Tanner was cleared of any wrongdoing. 'My decision to leave had nothing to do with that whatsoever,' Ron says. 'It was just a rumour that some people latched on to.'

A supervisor promptly tried to talk Ron out of his decision. After all, he was regarded as one of the force's top detectives. 'But I was committed financially,' Ron says. 'The only way out at that point was to sell the truck. I'd made my decision and I stuck by it.'

*

On Ron's first day as a full-time driver, he met two amiable fellow drivers whom he talked to about the job. But there's no time for idle chatter in the trucking game. 'You won't earn money that way,' one of the truckies warned. 'Get that forklift, put twelve pallets on it and off you go.'

Ron delivered the potting mix to nurseries around town, where he unloaded it by hand. He was such a fast worker that he was soon earning $2500 a week.

Regulation truckie wear might have been shorts and a t-shirt, but Ron maintained his own functional sense of style. He'd come from Homicide after all, which other units referred to as the Gucci Squad because they dressed so well. 'I was the first driver they'd ever seen with a briefcase, in brown leather, with a street directory in it. The other blokes used to laugh at me for having it,' Ron says.

But no one laughed at Ron's organisational skills when he started saving the company time and money by streamlining its deliveries. 'I divided the Melbourne metropolitan deliveries into areas, which I put onto a sheet on the wall,' he says. It wasn't like analysing the timeline of a murder, but it required careful consideration nonetheless.

The more Ron learnt about the trucking business, the more he realised there were 'two sides to the ledger'. While he had plenty of money coming in, there was plenty going out too. 'I spent $1200 a week on diesel,' he recalls. 'And the truck had a 300-horsepower Cummins diesel motor which needed a big electrical charge to run. So if the truck didn't start, you'd have to "Holler for a Marshall" [call a battery company], and buy a battery that cost $650.'

Ron also had to replace his tyres regularly because his

truck carried a whopping twenty tons of potting mix at a time. 'Tyres were $320 each,' he says. He had ten of them.

And even though Ron was enjoying working by himself, at times it was a struggle. 'I'd even have to go to work with the flu,' he says. 'If the wheels didn't turn, I didn't get paid. That's when I started to realise how good a job Victoria Police was.'

Sometimes, Ron still had to attend court cases, which meant time off work, so he looked for another way to keep the wheels turning. 'I found a driver who I thought was reliable and paid him a small wage to keep the truck on the road,' he says.

Ron liked working for Debco but was all ears when a man named Peter Wilson phoned, having heard Ron had left the force. Peter owned a company called Coringle Furniture which manufactured and distributed pine furniture to shops around Melbourne. Before Ron accepted the job at Debco, he'd had a chat about the trucking business with Peter. 'Peter Wilson was an astute businessman and we really hit it off,' says Ron. 'When he called he said, "There's a driver leaving. If you want to come here, here are the conditions".'

At Debco, Ron was paid in accordance with how much work he did. Coringle Furniture, on the other hand, paid by the hour. That didn't make sense to Ron. 'I said, "There's no incentive. I could go and park under a tree",' Ron recalls. 'He said, "That's the way it is, but I'll guarantee you five days work".'

Ron had to admit it was a good offer. Attracted by the stability, he sold his prime mover and bought a brand new Isuzu truck. 'It carried fifty cubic metres of furniture,' Ron says, always happy to talk makes and models.

It was hard yakka, but Ron was up for it. 'We'd start loading the truck at seven in the morning,' he says. 'In the end I could load the truck in an hour.'

Ron got so fast at loading and unloading that he invariably ended up back at the depot hours earlier than his workmates. 'What are you doing back here?' his boss would ask. 'I'm finished,' Ron replied. 'So from then on they reckoned I could sometimes do two loads a day and I did,' he adds. It got to the point that a record amount of furniture was hitting shop floors, and within a year of Ron starting work, the company expanded. 'So I got the option to buy a second truck and I employed a driver for the second truck,' he says.

It was late 1990, and Ron's first time as an employer. Unfortunately, his second driver wasn't up to scratch. 'One morning I came in and there were cuts and bruises all over his face and I thought he was still affected by alcohol,' Ron says. 'I said, "Mate, you aren't working today". It was a busy time, so I kept him on, but he only lasted two months.'

From then on, Ron decided it would be smarter to trial potential drivers before offering them a permanent job. But that plan also went awry. 'I got a young bloke who I took out with me on a trial run and he was atrocious,' Ron remembers. 'He'd said he'd worked for a big trucking company but he was continually hitting the kerb.' After suggesting to the young man that he'd never driven a truck before, Ron paid him for the day's trial and told him not to come back.

A week later Ron received a letter, summoning him to the Industrial Relations Commission. 'The driver I'd terminated got up before the commission and said, "I thought it was a permanent position and I gave up a job to do it",' Ron says.

He couldn't believe his ears when, after he explained he was trialling the young man, he was told there was no such thing as a trial. 'So we went to conciliation and the young bloke wanted two weeks' pay.' Ron gave it to him, keen to put the incident behind him and get his truck back on the road.

It was a steep learning curve. 'I learnt that employing people is not that easy,' Ron says. 'At that time I had no idea about industrial relations or workplace contracts.'

*

On 2 July 1991, during Ron's truck-driving stint, he and Colleen welcomed another baby girl. They gave her an Irish name, Shae. 'We often went to Merimbula in our caravan for holidays and stayed beside a couple who had three young girls,' Ron says. One of them was called Shae. 'Colleen fell in love with the name.'

Joanne, who was fifteen at the time, was present at the birth. But there was something in it, besides a baby sister, for three-year-old Matthew too. 'We purchased a large toy truck for Matthew so he did not feel out of it,' Ron says with a smile.

Over the years, the family moved from Launching Place to the outer Melbourne suburb of Boronia, then to Wantirna, twenty-four kilometres from the city. There, they lived in a red brick house with timber frames which gave the impression of an oversized cottage. The day they moved in, Ron began to renovate, tearing down the outdated wallpaper, before installing a new kitchen, a new bathroom and laying fresh carpet.

By this stage Joanne was well into her teenage years, and Matthew had grown into an inquisitive little boy interested in machinery, just like his dad.

'My earliest memories are probably of Dad as a truck driver,' Matthew says. 'I do remember going on journeys with him. To keep me entertained he'd let me operate the high beam and dip the lights and what-not.'

Matt particularly remembers the overnight chicken runs. 'I carried a box or two but he was probably just giving me light boxes to make me feel like I was doing something,' he figures. 'It was probably while I was in grade one or two, and he paid me a dollar an hour.'

Not surprisingly, Ron developed a reputation as one of the best owner–drivers in town. Added to his six-day-a-week driving schedule was maintenance work on his truck on Saturday nights or Sundays. It didn't leave much time for home and family, but Ron never lost his hardworking, farm-boy attitude.

While he was at Homicide, Ron mightn't have talked about murder to his three kids, but growing up, Joanne, Matthew and Shae couldn't help noticing their dad wasn't like their friends' fathers. Yet there were times when the reality of their father's job registered. 'I guess I was exposed to photos and videos,' Matt says. 'Not intentionally, but if Dad was reading books on the table I'd flick through and see things. I was privy to some crime scene photos and stuff. I had some nightmares.'

Like Joanne, Matt also remembers his dad taking phone calls in the middle of the night when there had been a murder. 'He'd be arranging for photographers, forensic analysis and calling the rest of his crew,' he says. Sometimes, when Ron was spending a day at the office, Matt would get a lift to school with him. When he picked up other detectives on the way, Matt couldn't help but overhear them discussing the latest case. 'But that was my life and that was just normal to me.'

Shae also remembers being woken during the night. 'You'd hear Dad pacing up and down the corridor,' she says. 'You'd hear Mum asking what was going on and then she'd be laying out his clothes and helping him get ready.'

Even though Shae knew what her father did for a living, as a young child, she didn't dwell on it. 'I often forgot the severity of his job,' she says, 'that he'd often just come home from seeing a dead body.' In an echo of Matthew's memories, she adds, 'To us kids, he always kept on the down-low about it.'

During Melbourne's gangland wars, which erupted while Shae was in high school, her father was even more secretive than usual. 'We couldn't know his location for a whole year,' she recalls. 'We did see him but we didn't know where his office was. It was something to do with the underworld.' At times like that, Shae realised her dad's job was extremely dangerous.

By the time she was a teenager, Joanne had two much younger siblings, and it fell to her, as the eldest, to help her mum around the house. 'It was pretty tough,' Colleen says, recalling the demands of caring for a baby and a toddler at the same time, and working at a psychiatric hospital some nights. 'Joanne was into parties and boys and gatherings, but she helped me out a lot.'

'When I was eighteen I had a car, so I'd often do the kinder pick-up or the drop-off at school, or I'd look after Matthew and Shae,' Jo remembers. She didn't really mind because she knew how hard her parents were working to support the family.

She also noticed how they kept a keen eye on her welfare. Whenever she went out with friends, her dad would always drive her safely home. 'He never let me catch a taxi. He always dropped me off and picked me up, no matter what time it was,' Jo says. 'Looking back, I'm so grateful.'

Colleen always understood why her husband was so protective. 'He'd seen so much on the streets and didn't want Joanne to become a victim,' she explains.

Ron agrees that he worried about the risks that young women, including his eldest daughter, faced at night. 'Everything that I dealt with work-wise was negative, so in the end you build a fence around your family,' he says. 'But you can become over-strict. It took me a long time to realise not everyone out there is bad.'

Jo says that during the Homicide years, when her dad usually left home at five in the morning and didn't get home until eleven at night, her parents were like ships in the night. Yet they were still a formidable team. 'She really gets him,' Jo says of her mum. 'She knows when he's had a hard week. They were just amazing parents together.'

Ron would have liked to have spent more time with his kids, but he did his best. 'Colleen used to say that I'd build the sandpit but wouldn't play in it,' he says. 'But I always took an interest in what the children did at school. I was always on the school council and involved in working bees.'

Yet having a dad who was as meticulous as Ron could be a challenge, especially when it came to schoolwork. If Jo ever complained about a sub-standard result in an essay or a test, Ron would announce, 'You've got to get back to the six Ps, Joanne! Proper preparation prevents piss-poor performance!' At the time she detested the six Ps; now the concept amuses her.

When it came to boyfriends, Ron was always going to regard them with suspicion. 'He was such a policeman at that stage,' Jo says. It didn't help that her first love – a taciturn seventeen-year-old named Marcus Zammit – always turned up looking casual and brandishing a Slurpee. 'My initial thoughts about Marcus were mixed,' Ron says. 'He was a young guy who wore his baseball cap backwards.' *What sort of guy does that? Is he good enough for my daughter?*

A couple of years later the young couple started talking about marriage. 'Colleen and I were both saying, "Hang on a minute, you're only nineteen or twenty"', Ron says. 'Then we thought, *Hang on, Colleen was eighteen and I was nineteen and we survived.* But it was probably a different era.'

Even though Jo and Marcus had started making wedding plans, there was no way Ron was going to let them share a room; Marcus had to stay in the bungalow out the back if he was visiting. 'Dad would never let us sleep in the same room even when we were twenty,' Jo recalls. On one occasion, he used his detective skills to accuse her of breaking the rules. 'Joanne, come inside now!' he bellowed. She did as she was told. 'He was determined that I had been in the bungalow with Marcus all night,' she says. Colleen weighed in, as she knew her daughter was innocent, but there was no convincing him.

'Feel Joanne's bed!' he exclaimed. 'It's cold!'

They can laugh about it now.

The following year, at twenty-one, Jo graduated from Deakin University with a degree in primary-school teaching. It was all she had ever wanted to do.

'As a kid, she'd sit her dolls in a chair and act as if she was a teacher,' Ron remembers. Watching the graduation ceremony, he felt incredibly proud of his little girl – who, at 171 centimetres tall, was not so little anymore.

With her university days behind her, Jo and Marcus set a date. Ron remembers riding to the chapel in the hire car with his daughter. 'It was about a thirty-minute drive, so we just chatted and I wished her all the best in her married life,' he says.

Relieved to know that her father had accepted her fiancé, Jo's only concern now was the weather. 'It was March but we had hail, thunderstorms, the works,' she says. But, 'The minute I got out of the car and was standing with Dad, ready to go inside, a beam of sunshine literally shone on my dad and me. It came right through my veil. I don't know if it meant something . . .'

Moments later, with the sun still shining, Ron walked his daughter down the aisle. 'It was a very proud moment and she looked stunning,' he says. In an unconventional twist, Colleen joined her husband and daughter at the altar. 'We'd decided when the celebrant said, "Who gives this woman away?" instead of me saying, "I do", we said, "We do",' Ron recalls.

Having realised Marcus was worthy of his daughter, Ron welcomed him into the fold. 'It is easy to stereotype,' Ron admits. 'Over the years our relationship has grown. We ride bikes together, we go on family holidays together and are all very close,' he says.

'I think as Dad got older he let his guard down a little bit,' Jo remarks. 'Soon they had a great relationship and they like sharing a red wine together.'

Ron is now granddad to Keenan, Ella, and Darcy, whose middle name is Ronald, just like his granddad. 'We often watch Poppy on TV,' Jo says. 'He gets so excited!'

'He has always made time for us,' Shae, says. 'Even though he was on-call in his job, he was on-call all the time for us. You could call him and go, "I don't know what to do about this situation", and he'd say, "I'll sort it out and call you back". And he'd fix it.'

'I think I was the sneakiest out of the three of us. I probably did play up a bit,' Shae, who's now a marketing manager, admits. Aged sixteen, Shae would tell her parents she wanted to go out on Friday or Saturday nights.

'I'd say, "What's the function?" She'd say, "Just a gathering,"' Ron recalls. 'In the end I realised she was conning us. A gathering was a party.' And at parties, Shae wanted to drink. 'We were not overly strict,' Ron remembers. 'I told her she could have two Vodka cruisers.' Shae did not, however, stick to the two-drinks rule. 'Colleen was cleaning her room one day and found two twenty-six-ounce Vodka bottles,' Ron reveals. 'Along with the liquor was a bra and two plastic ziplock bags. Ever the detective, Ron suspected Shae had been concealing the vodka in the plastic bags and stuffing them in her bra before she went out. It gave a whole new meaning to being in your cups.

And while Ron's parenting style mellowed as his two younger children grew older, Jo didn't mind that he'd been strict with her. 'He was brought up with a lot of good values and I think

JUSTINE FORD

he tried to follow that through. He was very different to what he is now,' she says, adding that his firmness came from love. 'He's got the biggest heart of anyone,' she says.

And if ever his adult children were feeling down, Ron would email them, telling them he was thinking of them.

'He's very touching like that,' Shae says. He doesn't say a lot, but when he does he really melts your heart.'

Matt, today a Qantas pilot, agrees. 'I know he loves us all. He's probably not very verbose in expressing that, but you know through his actions how much he cares about you.'

And that, Matt adds, is mutual.

14

HOMICIDE – TAKE TWO

'After four-and-a-half years I never thought I would return to Victoria Police, let alone the Homicide Squad. It was an exceptional feeling to be sought after and supported by senior police and return to Homicide. I was apprehensive at first, not wanting to get ahead of myself, but once I was back there and with a few jobs under my belt, it was fantastic, and I owe that all to Geoff O'Loughlin.'
– Ron Iddles

The police force wanted Ron Iddles back. Inspector Geoff O'Loughlin had first met Ron during the investigation into the Marafiote murders when he was a senior sergeant helping coordinate the three jurisdictions involved. It came as quite a shock to O'Loughlin when he heard a few years earlier that Ron had left the police force. 'I remember thinking at that time, what a loss to the department.'

O'Loughlin was running the sergeants' course at the Police Academy but had also spent around twenty years on the force's recruit and reappointee boards. 'As a result of being on this panel I was always aware of getting talented applicants to rejoin and I knew Ron would be a great asset if he came back,' O'Loughlin says.

By the early 1990s, Victoria Police needed more experienced leaders within its ranks and, for O'Loughlin, Ron was an obvious choice. He recalled how, during the investigation into the Marafiote murders, a South Australian officer had spent several hours trying to wear down Judy Ip, when Ron calmly asked if he could interview her. Even though he was granted permission to speak to Ip, O'Loughlin still had to stop the South Australian detective from re-entering the interview room. 'I think he was concerned Ron could achieve what he couldn't,' says O'Loughlin. He was right.

'After about an hour Ron came out and said to me, "The body is buried in the chook shed at the farm",' O'Loughlin says. Ron continued interviewing Ip while O'Loughlin arranged the subsequent search. 'After they [the crime scene investigators] dug down about two feet I said to Ron, "They haven't found anything". He just said, "Keep digging". They did, and the body was eventually located, much to everybody's jubilation – except the killer's!'

O'Loughlin attributes most of the operation's success to Ron. 'I was extremely impressed with Ron's demeanour during that investigation: down to earth, industrious, dedicated and very competent,' he reflects. 'We went our separate ways but I watched his progress in the force with interest.'

When O'Loughlin was at the academy, he was determined to appoint a lecturer who could elevate the level of crime-scene investigation training. The person he chose would have to be the cream of the crop, the detective's detective. The only problem was that that person was now driving trucks for a living.

O'Loughlin pondered how to persuade Ron to return. 'Thinking it would be best to get Colleen onside, I asked if she thought Ron would be interested in lecturing the students,' he recalls.

But Colleen found the phone call rather peculiar. She had never met O'Loughlin, yet here he was, sounding her out. Colleen remembers O'Loughlin asking how Ron was going and if he was enjoying being a truck driver. 'Then he said, "Do you think Ron would like to come back to the police force?"' Convinced her husband was content, Colleen decided on his behalf, saying, 'He's made up his mind and he's fine doing what he's doing.' She even decided not to tell Ron about the inspector's call, assuming he wouldn't be interested.

But something in Ron was changing. 'As the weeks went by I sensed something was going on in his head,' Colleen reveals. Busy with the children, she didn't ask what, and he didn't volunteer any information either.

Not one to give up, O'Loughlin phoned Colleen again three months later. 'Once more he said he really wanted experienced police officers in the force and would really like Ron to come back,' Colleen says.

O'Loughlin – who was later awarded, among other distinctions, the Australian Police Medal – knew the importance of the follow-up call. 'After chatting for a while I realised Ron still had an interest in the job,' he says. 'Colleen even said to me, "Ron talks to the TV when a homicide is being reported, saying, 'I bet they haven't done such and such!'"' he laughs.

Colleen knew she had to tell Ron about this latest exchange, and was surprised by his response. 'He said, "I was thinking of going back anyway".'

The family had seen a great deal more of Ron while he was driving trucks. Generally he didn't work on weekends, so they were able to go on outings together, and having him home at dinnertime still felt like a novelty. But as Colleen thought more about her husband's recent pensive moods, it all made sense.

'Deep down I felt he missed it and probably didn't feel complete in himself,' she says. 'I think he needed to have a break from all the stressors of the job, so this enabled him to go back refreshed, with total commitment to the job, and further his career.'

Unfortunately for O'Loughlin, the Police Academy was not about to benefit. Instead, Victoria Police offered Ron a position back at the Homicide Squad. If he hadn't fully made up his mind before, this was the clincher. It was, after all, the only place he'd ever really wanted to be since he'd watched *Homicide* in short pants.

'So in the end I sold the truck and went back,' Ron says with a smile.

'I was happy for him once he'd made his decision,' Colleen adds. 'I was always supportive of what he did and I was also glad he got his old police number back.'

And Victoria Police, according to O'Loughlin, was already better for it.

*

By April 1994 Ron was recharged and ready to get back into the job he'd loved. First, he had to complete a refresher course at the academy as a thirty-nine-year-old. 'As I recall, he quietly told the staff some of their training notes were wrong!' O'Loughlin says.

Talented as he was, even Ron couldn't avoid the force's red tape. So even though he'd left as a senior sergeant, he had to return as a constable and work his way back up. 'Initially it was a bit daunting because some people didn't like reappointees,' Ron explains. 'Their attitude was, "How is it this bloke can just walk back in?" The mentality was, "He's a retread".'

Ron let the comments wash over him and, with the promise he would be fast-tracked to his previous rank within two years, he never acted above his station. 'I never tried to be anything but a constable,' he says. 'I didn't come over the top and say, "That's a crap idea". I did the work at that level.' The work included helping fellow officers at crime scenes and taking statements 'to get back into the swing of it'.

Ron noticed there had been significant changes since he left the squad. 'One of the biggest was that we now had 286 word processors,' he remembers. 'They were very basic, but when I left we only had typewriters.'

It was the dawning of a new era.

*

Ron's first brief after his reappointment was the murder in late 1994 of nursery owner Ann Taylor at Churchill in Gippsland. 'She'd been stabbed three or four times at her nursery,' Ron says. 'Someone had tried to find her and hadn't been able to, so they went inside and found her dead behind the counter.

A knife was then found on the roof, which turned out to be the murder weapon.'

Ron remembers the crime scene so vividly it's as if he's still standing in it. 'The cash register was open and the phone was off the hook,' he says. 'It gave the appearance that Ann had been standing behind the counter when someone had gone in demanding money. It looked like she'd then picked up the phone to call for help and was murdered.'

Ron noticed a stick at the front of the shop. 'It was a very green branch, about 4.5 foot [1.37 metres] long,' he says. 'It had been whittled by a knife so it was now just a clean stick.' What was its significance? 'It was something that was foreign to the nursery,' he says. 'It hadn't come from any of the plants and it just looked odd.'

Ron and another detective looked around the neighbourhood to see what else was out of place. In the meantime, news of Taylor's murder had spread and a motorist had come forward. 'He said he'd seen a young boy aged about thirteen or fourteen hanging around a bridge about one kilometre from the nursery,' Ron says. 'He saw the young person hide as he drove over the bridge.'

When Ron and his colleague investigated the creek bank beneath the bridge, 'There were some bushes there and their branches matched the stick in the nursery,' Ron says.

Already, Ron was back thinking like a homicide investigator. 'Sometimes homicides are about trying to collect facts. That's called induction,' he explains. 'Then you try to use the logical facts to work out what happened.' That, he says, is deduction.

'Our view was that whoever was responsible lived in Churchill,' he says. Someone who knew Ann Taylor would be alone in her quiet nursery and, for some reason, took their time fashioning a branch from a nearby bush into a stick. He couldn't help but wonder if the boy beneath the bridge had something to do with it.

It started to look more that way when the detectives door-knocked the houses near the nursery. 'Someone said they'd seen a young boy from a troubled background in the local newsagency on the day of the murder,' Ron recalls. 'The boy had cash, which he didn't normally have. He bought four or five packets of AFL football player cards. That was at about eleven in the morning.'

Immediately, Ron wanted to know why the disadvantaged boy was suddenly cashed up. Could he have stolen the money from Taylor and killed her in the process? There was only one way to find out and that was to identify the boy.

Ron and his offsider hotfooted it to the newsagency, hoping the proprietor knew the boy's name. They were in luck. 'He told us his name and said that he had been into the shop,' Ron says. 'The newsagent confirmed that the boy – who was thirteen years old – had cash on him and had bought some football cards.' He also said the youth was a student at the local high school.

'So our next port of call was to the school principal,' Ron says. 'We found out that they always did rollcalls and that the boy wasn't at school at 8.30 but there when the roll was called in the afternoon.' The detectives also learnt that the teenager had taken the AFL cards to school to swap with his classmates.

Now convinced the uncharacteristically well-off truant had likely robbed and stabbed Taylor, the investigators went to the housing commission home he shared with his mother and siblings. 'His mum said there was no way he could have done it as he was at school,' Ron says. But Ron knew differently.

The investigators asked the boy some preliminary questions while his mum sat and listened. 'From there we took him to Morwell Police Station, where we got a bail justice to sit in on the interview as an independent third person, rather than his mother, who agreed to the process,' Ron says.

At first, the boy said he didn't do it. 'So I said a person of similar description had been seen at the bridge around 8.30, not far from the nursery,' Ron says. 'Then he confessed.'

It wasn't like any homicide Ron had ever dealt with before. He wanted to know what could possibly drive a thirteen-year-old boy – *a child* – to kill. 'Later he went on to explain that things were really hard at home financially,' Ron recalls. 'Every now and then he'd do a paper round, but he felt like he wasn't included at school because other kids could afford to buy AFL cards or something from the tuckshop.'

So the penniless boy hatched a devious plan to obtain some money. 'He decided to wag school, and while he was sitting at the bridge that morning he began whittling a stick with a knife,' Ron says. 'He knew the nursery opened at 9.30, so he went there and saw Ann watering plants outside. The way he saw it, that was his opportunity to go in and rat [rob] the till.'

But what began as a robbery ended tragically. 'He didn't see Ann come back into the office,' Ron says. 'She surprised him while he was taking money from the till and she picked up the phone, he assumed to call the police.' But the boy had a knife. 'He said he panicked and took the phone off her,' Ron continues. 'He said he didn't know why but he stabbed her two or three times. He then left her there and threw the knife on the roof, and didn't tell anyone what he'd done.'

The teenager returned to school, where he washed Taylor's blood off his hands. 'Then he went and bought the AFL cards and put the balance of the money he'd stolen from the nursery in a tin in his bedroom,' Ron says. 'He felt that by going back to school with football cards he'd be accepted in the community.'

He wasn't. Instead, Ron charged him with murder and he was sent to a boys' home while he awaited trial. 'I can remember seeing Ann Taylor's husband, David, and he just couldn't believe the senselessness of the whole thing,' Ron says.

Ultimately, the boy was found guilty of manslaughter, not murder. 'The maximum he could get because of his age was three years, and he got the maximum, three years,' Ron says.

He credits old-school detective work with the result. 'We solved the case by doorknocking half the town. That's what they taught us at Detective Training School: get out and pound the pavement. Make your own luck. Talk to people. They're highly effective techniques that are sometimes neglected in the modern era.

'It was good to solve the case, but I could never get over the fact that a thirteen-year-old could feel so displaced in his own environment that it could lead to this,' Ron continues. 'He came from a broken home. He didn't dress as well as the other kids, and even though his mum worked, he didn't have the money for football cards. The crux of this whole tragic case was that he didn't fit in.'

Still, it was hard for Ron to comprehend. 'I said to him, "Why'd you take a knife?"' Ron recalls.

'I just took it,' the boy replied. 'Just in case.'

15

THE MONSTER INSIDE

'This case proved the value of CCTV and to my knowledge was the first time in Australia that a murder had been captured on closed-circuit TV.'
– Ron Iddles

By 1996, Ron was once more a senior sergeant, leading his own team at Homicide. In the two years it took for him to move back up through the ranks, he proved he was no mere 'retread'. His colleagues came to realise he was a man worthy of their respect, an experienced detective who could raise the standard of every investigation. It wasn't long before his crew members were calling themselves his 'loyal soldiers'.

But Ron still liked driving trucks. 'Any kind of machinery, really,' he says. So when his best mate, Ray Relf – who owned a poultry delivery business – asked Ron to give him a hand, the homicide investigator couldn't resist. Ray needed some time off, as he'd been working seven days a week, and he knew how much Ron liked getting behind the wheel. 'So I put in a request to do a second job but it was knocked back because it was in the transport industry,' Ron says. It was considered a conflict of interest because police enforced the law on those employed in that industry, including taxi, tow-truck and truck drivers.

Ron saw it differently. 'I argued it was the food distribution industry and that the mode of distribution was a truck,' he says. He was pushing his luck, but even his superiors had to admit there was some logic to his argument. 'In the end, I was called up to the assistant commissioner, who said my request was approved.' And while the assistant commissioner felt satisfied that Ron wouldn't break the road rules, he didn't want him breaking food safety rules either. 'He said, "I don't want you delivering chickens to a refrigerator that says ten degrees when it's meant to be four degrees",' Ron adds.

Soon, however, what began as a favour for a mate turned into a regular job when three other drivers asked Ron to fill in for them too. Ron drove the truck on his days off and the hours were gruelling (1 am to 10.30 am), yet, in a way, it felt like a hobby.

He liked it even more when he started doing runs to the bush. 'I'd pick the truck up at the yard in Lilydale at about 12.30 am with five tonnes of chicken in tubs,' Ron says, 'then I'd make my way to Yea, then drive across to Seymour. Seymour Coles was the first drop at about 2.30, 2.45 am.' After that he headed to Shepparton, then to small towns like Numurkah, Tatura, Kyabram and Nagambie. 'I'd end up back at Lilydale at midday. So it was an eleven-and-a-half-hour shift, a round trip of 560 kilometres.'

It would seem eccentric to most – a little crazy even – that a busy homicide cop would want to drive a truck full of chooks through the night, let alone do the heavy lifting required of a delivery man, but Ron took great pleasure from the turn of the wheel, the open road and the fresh country air. Admittedly the chooks weren't much company, but that's how he liked it.

*

One summer's morning, after driving the poultry truck all night, Homicide head Detective Inspector Paul Sheridan called as Ron was making his way back to the depot. Two men had been murdered and a woman was critically injured in the iconic Century Building in Melbourne's gem-trading district. Sheridan knew Ron was on leave, but could he come in? Ron went home and had a shower, and was back at Homicide by 2.30 pm.

Designed by the renowned Australian architect Marcus Barlow, the white Art Deco Century Building in Swanston Street was considered one of the most secure buildings in the city, with cumbersome doors, security intercoms and surveillance cameras keeping the resident jewellers safe inside. But on Wednesday, 4 December 1996, the security was shattered when someone gunned down three people in an eighth-floor suite. The victims were Lean Thoeun Pin, 52, his wife Siv Eng Pin, 44, and their son, Virayuth Pin, 23. Both father and son were dead, and Siv Eng, who'd also been shot, was in hospital, clinging to life.

The Pins – as Ron's team discovered – were model citizens. While working as a tram conductor, Lean Thoeun had operated a gem wholesaling business from home, hoping to open a jewellery store one day. In 1995, his dream came true when he used his life savings to open the doors of Pin Gems in Swanston Street. The family felt optimistic about the future, having fled Cambodia twelve years earlier for Australia, a peaceful country where they could feel safe.

News of the shootings reverberated around the CBD. For some city workers, the incident was reminiscent of another multiple shooting in 1978, just a few doors down in the even more magnificent neo-gothic Manchester Unity building. On that occasion, three male gem traders were shot to death and eight precious diamonds stolen.

Sheridan told Ron there was a witness to the murders – a jeweller named Manuel Adajian, who occupied an office on the building's fourth floor and had been in the Pins' office during the entire ordeal. Adajian was at Homicide waiting to speak to Ron.

Ron recalls meeting the jumpy forty-one-year-old. 'Manuel told me he'd gone up to see the Pins because he'd borrowed a diamond ring from them,' he says. 'He said he'd needed to take it back and there was a dispute over money.'

Adajian told Ron that while he was with the Pin family, someone pinched a nerve in his shoulder and he blacked out. When he regained consciousness, he couldn't believe what he was seeing – the whole family, shot. 'He said he then heard the police at the door and was very grateful he'd been rescued from this incident,' Ron says.

But Ron wasn't a mere student of human behaviour, he was a master of it, and there was something troubling about Adajian's story and demeanour. 'To me that story didn't ring true,' he says. 'And I spoke to another member who'd driven Manuel back [to St Kilda Road]. He said he'd had eighteen hundred dollars in his pocket.' *Really?* Ron thought. *Where did he get that?*

The whole story about waking up in the same room as three people who'd been shot sounded fanciful to Ron. 'I said, "I don't believe him. I want to do a formal interview",' he recalls. 'He's potentially the killer.'

During the videotaped interview Adajian repeated the same story. 'He said he'd gone there, they'd had a cup of tea, then he'd hurt his shoulder,' Ron says. 'When he'd come to, they were all dead.'

A short time later, there was a break in the case. 'I got a call from the crime scene examiners at the wholesalers' office to say, "You won't believe it, it's all captured on video",' Ron recalls. He arranged for a copy of the video to be brought down to St Kilda Road. At first, Ron saw Adajian entering the office, sitting down and the hospitable Pins making him a cup of tea, just as he'd said. 'You then saw him jump up and pull a gun from the back of his pants,' Ron says. 'He was fairly flustered and uncoordinated and he grabbed hold of Mr Pin's jacket but he managed to break free.'

The Pins' son, Virayuth, who was sitting at the desk, hit a silent alarm under the table. It alerted a security company and in turn, the police. 'Manuel went back to the table, finished the cup of tea, then got Mr Pin Senior and Junior [to stand] in front and fired three shots into each,' Ron continues. 'He then turned around and shot Mrs Pin twice.'

While the murder video gave Ron a clear insight into how the events unfolded, it was nevertheless confronting. 'Life is very precious,' he reflects, 'and in the space of two seconds two lives were lost and a third destroyed.'

The video then showed Adajian going to the safe, from

which he started removing all the diamonds. 'He then saw Mrs Pin was still alive so he pistol-whipped her with the butt of the gun,' Ron says. 'She was rendered totally unconscious given she'd already been shot twice to the skull.'

After that, Adajian took off his jacket, put the diamonds in it and slung it over his shoulder like a swag. He also took Lean Thoeun's wallet and counted its contents. *Surprise surprise*, thought Ron. *He's counted eighteen hundred dollars, the same amount of money that was in his pocket.*

Adajian tried to open the door to make his getaway but it was locked. The building's high security was designed to keep dangerous individuals out, but now it was keeping one in. The killer started to panic. 'He was looking for some type of button to release the door so he could leave,' Ron says. But he couldn't get out and the cops would arrive any minute.

'You could just about see his thought process kick in. It was as if he realised, *I'm done*,' Ron continues. 'Then he went into the mode of being a witness, wiping down the gun so there were no prints, making sure there were no diamonds on him, and that the only thing in his pocket was the eighteen hundred dollars, which he later claimed was his personal money. He left the diamonds, however, tied up in his coat beside the front door. In total, he'd loaded up $1.5 million worth of diamonds in his coat.'

Responding to the alarm, the police barged through the door to be confronted by the terrible, bloody scene. According to Ron, Adajian said something like, 'Thank God, you've saved my life! This is horrific!' After that he was taken to Homicide as a potential witness.

'So after I'd seen the video I interviewed him again,' Ron

says. 'Could you have done this and don't remember?' he asked the dark-haired man shifting in his seat. 'He said absolutely not.

'So I got the video and said, "I want you to watch this and tell me what happens",' Ron continues. Adajian quietly watched the video of himself having a cup of tea. But when he saw himself stand up and shoot the Pins, he appeared shocked and horrified. 'He said, "Oh no, oh no! There must be a monster inside me!"' Ron says.

Ron asked him how long this monster had been inside him. 'He said "Only today". I said, "How do you explain it?" He didn't know how to explain it . . ."It's me but it's not me".'

The only way to understand the man with the monster inside was to delve into his background and find a motive for murder. 'It turned out he was a heroin addict who was married with two children and he owed money all over the place,' Ron says. Significantly, Adajian had told various associates on the day of the murders that he was going to come into money. 'He said he was going to get an inheritance and be able to pay his debt,' Ron says. 'He telegraphed to people that was the day it was going to happen.'

When Adajian faced court for the murders of Lean Thoeun Pin and Virayuth Pin, and the attempted murder of Siv Eng Pin, Ron still had a hurdle to overcome. 'The question was, was he sane or insane?' he says. 'So I needed to prove he knew what he was doing, and if that was the case, that he knew it was wrong.'

For advice, Ron turned to the distinguished forensic psychiatrist, Professor Paul Mullen, who'd assessed the Port Arthur mass murderer, Martin Bryant. 'He said Manuel Adajian was sane because if he was insane he would not be socially in tune with people, and there he was in the video, having a cup of tea and interacting,' Ron says. The professor also pointed to the way Adajian counted the money and knew exactly how much he had. 'He said, "In my professional opinion, he's sane".'

In the end, Ron scored a conviction. 'Manuel Adajian ended up pleading guilty and is now doing thirty-five years,' he says.

And while Siv Eng Pin ultimately survived the ordeal, she is living out her days with severe brain damage in a nursing home.

16

JANE THURGOOD-DOVE

'There were many twists and turns with this high-profile case.'
– Ron Iddles

Ladies Day at the races is when women from all over Australia dress in their finest florals for the third day of the Melbourne Cup Carnival. It's a fun day, unless you guzzle too much bubbly, back a loser, or you're a horse.

On this day in 1997 – 6 November – Ron, who was working the afternoon shift, was called out to a house in Melbourne's north-west to investigate the shooting of a woman named Jane Thurgood-Dove. Ron was told the thirty-five-year-old had been taken to Royal Melbourne Hospital, where she was fighting for her life.

Jane, a bright-eyed, neatly presented mother of three, had spent the day much like any other: taking two of her children to school and another to playgroup, then catching up on the gossip with a neighbour in the street.

Why shoot this suburban mum? Ron wondered. Was it a domestic dispute? Or was there more to Jane Thurgood-Dove than met the eye?

According to Ron, 'This is one of those homicides that galvanised the public and created massive amounts of media. Everyone wondered why an attractive woman would be gunned down in the driveway of her own home.' The case would consume him for almost fourteen years.

*

Ron hadn't been expecting a murder that day. He'd always found Ladies Day (officially called Oaks Day), a 'fairly relaxed' time. 'When I found out about the shooting I was sitting at Homicide in air-conditioned comfort,' he recalls. 'An hour later I was standing over a body.'

On the way to the Thurgood-Dove house in Muriel Street, Niddrie, Ron received a call from police headquarters to say there was already a development: a burnt-out car had turned up in Ryder Street, Niddrie, about 1.5 kilometres from the crime scene. Police suspected it had been used in the shooting.

But first things first: the victim. Ron wanted to know if Thurgood-Dove was going to survive and, aware that doctors could receive patient updates faster than the police, he asked a forensic pathologist to call Royal Melbourne Hospital and find out. 'Hospitals have very strict protocols around privacy, so if you get a pathologist – who's a doctor – to ring, you get a better sense of the condition of the patient,' Ron explains.

As the pathologist set about calling the hospital, Ron arrived at the crime scene, which was swarming with uniformed police and buzzing with static from their radios. There was a primary school two doors down, so SUV-driving mums doing afternoon pick-ups – some still in their race-day best – craned their necks to peer past the police tape.

At least two people, including a schoolgirl and a woman who lived nearby, had witnessed the shooting, so the first uniformed officer at the scene was able to give Ron a reasonably detailed briefing. 'He said apparently Jane had driven into the driveway in her early-model Toyota Landcruiser with her three kids in the car – Scott, who was eleven, Ashley, who was six, and Holly, aged three.' A split second later, another car pulled up behind them. 'A Holden Commodore then drove into the driveway and the passenger got out,' Ron continues. 'He was wearing sunglasses and a beanie, was scruffy and slightly overweight.'

It looked as though Thurgood-Dove knew instantly she was in grave danger. 'She yelled out, "Oh no, oh no!"' Ron says. 'So the question for the police was, *Did Jane know that person? Or did she see a weapon?*' She started running frantically around her car, circling it at least twice until she fell over. Her pursuer – who was indeed armed – had her cornered. 'At that point the gunman fired two shots into the back of her head. He then ran back to the car, which sped off.'

Jane Thurgood-Dove's children saw everything.

*

Immediately after the briefing, the uniformed officer took Ron over to her car, where he saw she hadn't been taken to hospital after all. 'Jane's body was still lying there,' he remembers. 'I said, "How can that happen when I was told she was taken to hospital?" They said, "No, she died here at the scene". Ron was unimpressed but acknowledged that detectives didn't always receive accurate information at the start of an investigation as events were still unfolding. He made a mental note to get it right for the rest of the job.

Ron asked the uniformed officer where the Thurgood-Dove children were and was told they were at the milkbar. 'So about ten minutes later I was able to have a conversation with Scott,' Ron says. 'He briefly told me what had happened. He said he'd seen his mum get shot.'

Scott possessed an emotional intelligence beyond his years and, unable to save his mum, had tried to shield his siblings. 'Even though he was young, he had the foresight to take his younger siblings to the corner shop three doors down,' Ron says. 'I said, "Where's your father?" expecting him to say, "We don't live with our dad". My brain was ticking over and I was thinking, *Is this a domestic?* 'He said his dad – Mark Thurgood-Dove – was at Styrapak [a polystyrene factory] at Campbellfield. I then asked him when he last saw his dad and he said he left for work this morning.'

Straightaway, Ron sent a colleague to the factory where Mark Thurgood-Dove worked as a foreman. 'One, to see if Mark was at work,' Ron says, 'and two, to find out – if he was there – if he'd had the opportunity to leave.' He quickly learnt that Thurgood-Dove had been at work all day. 'So sadly, one of my detectives had to tell him that Jane had been shot.' It is a job every police officer dreads.

Police at the Niddrie house began to process the scene, taking photos and video, and collecting exhibits. Ron remembers one clue that stood out to him. 'There was a big powder burn at the back of Jane's head and there were particles on the weatherboard of the house,' he says. 'It indicated it was an older-style gun and possibly self-loaded. In ballistics terms, it was unusual.'

Portly gunman, outdated firearm.

Perhaps, Ron thought, *the abandoned, burnt-out car down the road might tell us something.* 'From the numberplate we were able to establish it had been stolen from outside the Carlton Football Club at Princes Park on the Monday of that week,' he reveals. He arranged for the car to be more thoroughly examined.

About three or four hours into the investigation, Ron visited Thurgood-Dove's parents, John and Helen Magill, who lived nearby. Standing in the driveway of the Magills' house, Ron had to tell the distressed father the hard facts of a homicide investigation. 'I said, "You know what, John? You're equally a suspect. The way I work is, I try to eliminate the family first – including Mark – and then I work my way out".'

By this time, the confused children were in their grandparents' care. Ron will never forget how the youngest was acting. 'I went inside and Holly was running around and asking where her mum was,' he says. 'The police helicopter was up and even though she was only about three, I think she associated the helicopter with her mum's death.'

A short while later, Mark Thurgood-Dove arrived, giving Ron the opportunity to talk to him too. 'He was very quiet and reserved but emotional, and had the children around him,' Ron remembers. 'He told me he would ring Jane from work every day to see how she was going, but that day, he didn't call.

They'd had an argument the day before over a personal issue and he'd decided he wouldn't ring.' Ron says as a detective he would normally have found that odd but he and his colleagues were satisfied because he had been at work all day and could not have pulled the trigger. 'But,' he adds, 'we weren't satisfied at that stage that he hadn't contracted someone else to do it.'

Around midnight, Ron and his crew returned to the office, the scene of many late-night brainstorms. Detective Inspector Paul Sheridan asked Ron how the investigation was progressing. 'Terribly,' the weary senior sergeant told his boss, recognising this was not a domestic murder he could solve quickly. 'Jane and Mark were classified as schoolyard sweethearts by Jane's parents,' he said, 'and from all accounts there were no issues within the marriage.'

When homicide detectives don't find a breakthrough within forty-eight hours, they can face long, drawn-out investigations, as he knew all too well from the Maria James case. At least there were witnesses, Ron reasoned, and that helped. But who would want to kill Jane Thurgood-Dove who, by all accounts, was a warm, gracious woman, devoted to her family?

'If you don't have a motive, you're going to struggle,' Ron explains. 'And twelve hours in, we had no motive and had a gut feeling we were in for the long haul.'

*

From the outset, the media was fascinated by the murder of Jane Thurgood-Dove, perhaps because she was a mum, an innocent victim, or a well-presented woman in her prime. Whatever the reason for the heightened interest, the Homicide

Squad was going to make the most of it, knowing that someone in the community had information about the murder. 'We put out a FACE* image of the driver from the witness descriptions,' Ron says. 'And we tried to manage the large volume of interest in the case.'

Every morning after Thurgood-Dove was killed, Ron started work at 5 am. He wanted to sift through information that came in from Crime Stoppers overnight so that, by 7 am, he could allocate appropriate tasks to his detectives. They were long, intense days for the whole team. 'After spending the day finding out anything we could, we'd regroup as late as nine or ten at night and talk about what we'd achieved and where we were going from there,' he recalls.

From a forensic point of view, the stolen car was of interest. In it, the crime scene examiners had discovered a second-hand Apollo brand battery that had 'Good. 2.11.97' marked on it. That indicated someone had purchased the second-hand battery on 2 November 1997. Not by the owner of the car, though – before his car was stolen, he'd had a brand new Dunlop Dynapak battery in it.

In the back of the car, police found a fire-damaged men's jacket that didn't belong to the car's owner either. The Homicide Squad asked the media to publish pictures of the battery and the jacket and it yielded a result. A man phoned to say the jacket was his and that it had been in the back of his VN Commodore, which had been stolen from Flemington Racecourse. 'His car was recovered in Myross Avenue in Ascot

*FACE (or Facial Automated Composition and Editing), is a database of sketched facial features that functions like a digital Identikit. It was created by a former officer of Victoria Police, and is now used in more than 40 countries.

Vale with the jacket and a pair of sunglasses missing, as well as the car battery,' Ron says. 'The batteries were taken from both VN Commodores, which we could now link because the jacket from the first car wound up in the second car, which was used in the murder.' It was all very strange.

Ron thought if he could find out where the battery from the murder car had been purchased and by whom it might lead him to the killer. 'We checked nearly every wrecking yard in Melbourne,' he says. His crew found two car yards that may have sold the battery but couldn't confirm it either way. 'We could never work out who purchased that battery or satisfy ourselves it came from a particular wrecking yard.'

But why steal two cars and replace their batteries in the first place? What did it mean? 'All it shows is a connection between two stolen cars, and for whatever reason they stole the battery out of each car,' Ron says.

Even he was baffled.

*

Getting inside the mind of a murderer is difficult when you don't know who they are or their motive. In an effort to find out more about Thurgood-Dove's life, the detectives continued speaking to those closest to her, including her sisters, Susan and Sandra. That's when the case started hotting up. 'Susan said that about ten days before the murder, she visited Jane, who was somewhat stressed,' Ron says. 'She asked what was wrong but Jane said, "I can't tell you". When Susan asked why, Jane said, "If I told you, you'd never ever understand".'

So Jane Thurgood-Dove had a secret. *One she couldn't tell her sister, who was close to her,* Ron thought.

Rummaging through Thurgood-Dove's handbag, the investigators found a clue. 'In Jane's handbag was a card from a police officer,' Ron recalls. 'It had his name on it and he worked at an inner Melbourne police station.'

A member of Ron's crew paid the policeman a visit and asked how he knew Thurgood-Dove. It turned out that he was a good friend of the family and had lived with Jane's sister Susan for two years. Jane had also cleaned the policeman's house to make ends meet. 'But there was more to the relationship than that,' Ron says. 'The police officer told us he had been in a sexual relationship with Jane, and that her husband Mark didn't know anything about it. He said the relationship was over but that Jane still cleaned his house.' *No wonder Jane couldn't tell Susan her secret,* Ron thought.

Ron says the policeman made a written statement saying he'd last spoken to Thurgood-Dove about a week before her murder. He'd phoned her while he was on night shift and she was cleaning his house. 'He said he spoke to her for about a minute, but he was tired and didn't want to keep talking,' Ron recalls. 'But when we checked the phone records we found out that the call went for a lot longer than that.' This gave Ron new questions to ponder: *Was the police officer simply mistaken, or not being open with the facts?*

While the investigators looked more closely at the chatty policeman, Ron arranged an extensive canvass of Niddrie. Ever-conscious that a good old-fashioned doorknock was the best way to turn up leads, he and his team rapped on around eight hundred doors, asking residents if they'd seen anything unusual around the time of Jane's murder. 'We found out the car that had been used on the day of the murder had been seen in the street on the weekend before the murder, at around 12.30 on the Tuesday morning,' Ron says. That was two days before Jane was gunned down. 'The passenger had scraggly hair and was smoking a cigarette.'

Locals had also seen the car outside the children's school. 'Another witness also saw the car in Keilor Road in Niddrie,' Ron says. 'The witness noticed the numberplate with the letters *DKU* and remembered it because she'd thought, *That was the university I went to overseas*.' And yet another witness saw the car on the day of the murder. 'At about 6 am it was parked opposite Muriel Street,' Ron says. 'When Mark went to work it was there, directly opposite in a side street. Quite clearly someone was watching Jane's movements.'

Another witness, who lived in Ryder Street, Niddrie, where the getaway car was later found burnt out, told the detectives he'd seen the vehicle there around 10.30 am on the day of Thurgood-Dove's murder. 'No one was in it,' Ron says, 'and it moved sometime after two o'clock. So we basically had the movements of the car from when it was stolen to when it was burnt out.' He adds that sometimes when the car was seen there were two men in it, at other times, just one.

But who were they? And what was this all about?

*

Ron had a saying, 'The answer's in the file'.

He meant that the key to an investigation – and sometimes, the murderer's name – could be found in the original police file, in the information collected early on. Ron went back and looked closely at every detail gathered in the immediate wake of Thurgood-Dove's murder.

'The first information report suggested Jane's murder could have been a case of mistaken identity,' he says, that the bullets might have been meant for another resident of Muriel Street, who lived further down the street with her husband. 'The husband was known to the police and in the years prior to 1997 he had defrauded a man,' Ron says. 'That man subsequently wanted to kill him and engaged a hitman to do so.' But the plan had backfired. 'The hitman he hired was actually an undercover cop and the man who tried to hire him was ultimately charged with incitement to murder and did a short time in prison. *Could this have been meant as a payback for incitement to murder?* When questioned, he told police he knew nothing about the murder.

However, this did set Ron to considering the similarities between the women, and he realised a gunman could indeed have mistaken them. 'They both lived three driveways from a corner,' Ron remarks, adding that the shooter could possibly have gone to the wrong house. Not only that, but both women were around the same age and had fair hair. 'So we went and saw her husband and said, "Was it possible this was meant for you or your wife?"' Ron recalls. 'He was very polite and told us to get fucked.'

Ron went back to the drawing board.

The doorknock also revealed that a young man had heard a fiery argument at the Thurgood-Doves' place. 'He was about nineteen and he lived in a caravan in his mum's backyard, and the fence adjoined the Thurgood-Doves,' Ron explains.

'On the Saturday prior to her murder, around 31 October, he heard a big argument in their backyard.' He recognised Mark's voice. 'He didn't know what it was about but he knew it was heated,' Ron continues, adding that the young man hadn't come forward earlier because he didn't know what the argument was about.

'Now we had a situation,' Ron says. 'Mark had had an argument with Jane on the Saturday, he didn't call her on the day she died, she had a secret she couldn't share with anyone, and there was a policeman who'd either not been truthful or was mistaken about the time he spoke to Jane.'

Ron decided it was time to take the investigation to the next level. 'I made the decision that both Mark and the police officer would have to be interviewed formally because I felt that was the proper process.' But after Ron phoned the policeman, the senior constable's solicitor intervened. Ron explained he wanted to interview the officer because the Homicide Squad had uncovered concerning information. The interview was arranged, but it was of no help to the investigation. 'The police officer adopted his right to silence,' Ron says. 'On advice, he made no comment. He also refused to participate in a line-up and refused to give his DNA for the purposes of elimination.'

But as Ron knew, there are other ways to uncover information. 'While the policeman was at the Homicide Squad I took out a warrant to search his house,' Ron says, adding that he decided to look around himself. What he saw startled him. 'The mantelpiece was virtually a shrine to Jane,' he reveals. 'Also, the code to his mobile phone, which we took possession of, was Jane's date of birth.' It was a similar situation with his computer. 'Not only that, but he had changed his will and wanted to be buried beside her.'

There was no doubt in Ron's mind that Jane Thurgood-Dove was still more than a household cleaner to this man. 'From that point on, he remained a suspect and we worked hard to eliminate him,' he says. He found out that on the days the two men had been seen in the car, the policeman was not rostered on at work. 'And on the day just one man was seen in the car, he was working.'

Ron paid the officer's mother a visit. She told him her son had been fascinated by her ex-husband – a well-known criminal, and used to go to the State Library to research him. But there was no crime in that and it did not shed any light on the gunman's identity.

However, as it happened, there *was* someone who claimed to know the killer's real identity – and he was ready to talk.

'I got a phone call from a very well-known underworld figure, Des "Tuppence" Moran,' Ron says. 'Des and I had, I guess, a mutual respect for each other. He said, "I would never normally do this but that was an innocent lady that was shot dead",' Ron recalls.

Moran told Ron he was at a coffee shop in Ascot Vale when one man passed a gun to another, who fitted the description of Thurgood-Dove's killer. Two days later, the man who'd borrowed the firearm returned it and the men had words. 'You shot that lady,' the gun's owner had accused the other man. Moran also told Ron the word on the street was that the hit had been arranged by someone Thurgood-Dove knew. Ron investigated but he could not build a case on rumours.

Even though it seemed incongruous for the underworld

to be talking about Thurgood-Dove's murder, it kept Ron open to all manner of possibilities. There had to be *some* reason why this picture-perfect mum was shot down outside her home in Niddrie, an ordinary suburb that rarely, if ever, made the news.

As the cogwheels of Ron's mind turned, the phone rang.

'Out of the blue I got a call from the policeman saying, "I want to see you".'

Ron could tell he'd been struggling. 'The policeman told me he'd been having an affair with Jane for about three years,' Ron says. 'That it had continued probably right up until three or four months before her murder. That he actually loved her and felt aggrieved that no one considered his feelings.' The officer told Ron he was now prepared to participate in the investigation, and was subsequently interviewed by Detective Sergeant Gordon Hynd. 'The policeman explained how their relationship started, but denied any involvement in her death,' Ron says. It was helpful to hear about the policeman's relationship with Thurgood-Dove, but it didn't progress the investigation.

A while later, Ron decided to interview the policeman and Mark Thurgood-Dove again, arranging for them to both come into Homicide on the same day. 'The purpose of that was to offer them a polygraph test,' he says. It would be the first time Australian police would allow a lie detector test to be conducted and even though Ron knew the results could not be presented in court, he believed it was a helpful investigative tool. 'Polygraphs are good to eliminate the innocent,' he says.

Ron explained to both men they did not have to sit the test, which would be conducted by former Victoria Police detective

Steve Van Aperen, better known as The Human Lie Detector. 'I explained to them it was a win–win situation: if you pass the test, you'll never hear from me again, and if you fail, it isn't admissible in court.'

Mark Thurgood-Dove took the test first. He passed.

Not so the police officer.

Both men were told of the results and, according to Ron, the policeman took it badly. 'He was very shaken. He spoke to some people about taking a second test – he could not believe it.' But as Ron points out, even though he believes polygraphs can help eliminate the innocent, those who are not guilty sometimes fail. 'Polygraphs are believed to have an accuracy of around 92 per cent, so there is some small room for error,' he says.

The policeman did not want to appear in a lineup so Ron decided to devise another way for the witnesses to get a good look at the him. So, without him knowing, Ron surreptitiously arranged for the officer to go to a public place where the girl and the woman who'd witnessed Jane Thurgood-Dove's murder could clearly see him. 'At the end of the process they were both asked if they had seen anyone in the last two hours who looked like the gunman.' Both said they had not.

Even though information constantly came to hand, the solution to Jane Thurgood-Dove's murder was no clearer. Ron found it frustrating. 'Understandably, there was a lot of pressure to solve the case from a community point of view,' he says. 'It kept generating media attention and was a case that the public followed.' Ron worked on it for six weeks in a row without a day off, until Colleen ordered him to have a day's rest. But still, his mind ticked. 'The team was overloaded with information and it was about keeping on top of it and steering the ship.' Ron tried to narrow down the facts.

'So this was the situation: we knew that the policeman had not been up front about the length of his phone call, he was in love with Jane, he'd been in a relationship with her, he had no alibi on the day of the murder and he failed the polygraph.'

'Even though there were facts to support that the police officer was involved, my gut said he wasn't,' Ron says. 'On a whiteboard we had reasons why it could have been him, but looking at it rationally, why would he get someone else to do it? Why not do it on his own? If he was in a relationship with her, why not do it while she was cleaning his house?' And then there was the question: if he loved Thurgood-Dove so much, why would he want to do it at all?

'So about two to three years into the investigation I undertook a covert operation in the hope of getting new evidence against the police officer or proving his innocence,' Ron says. He cannot go into the detail, as it would reveal police methodology, but it certainly did not point to the police officer's involvement in any way.

Even though the case was proving one of the toughest of Ron's career he had no plans to give up. He recalled one of the mantras on the whiteboard at Detective Training School: 'Failure is not an option'.

He knew, however, that sometimes cases remained unsolved, no matter how much time and effort police put into investigating them. The Homicide Squad was boasting a 93 per cent success rate – but would this be one of them?

Fortunately, Ron was leading a team of five of the Squad's best detectives. 'I think the culture was very good as we were all passionate, dedicated officers who were focus driven,' he says. Ron saw it as his responsibility to set the bar high and his troops never let him down. Not only did they work skilfully and relentlessly on the case, but they lived up to Ron's ethical standards. 'Trust was never an issue,' he says. 'There was always a goal which was to achieve a result.' Ron never encountered any political pressure but the media increasingly hounded him for answers. 'It was about learning to work with the media and not against them,' he explains. 'It was sometimes a challenge, but I hoped in the long run it would be worth it.'

As a way of taking advantage of the media's unfailing interest, Ron and his colleagues held more than thirty media conferences, imploring the public to come forward if they knew anything, no matter how small, about the Thurgood-Dove murder. Ultimately police received more than 1300 pieces of information. It was encouraging but would it be enough?

*

Years went by and Ron was unable to crack the Jane Thurgood-Dove case, but not for want of trying. Then in 2003, Police Commissioner Christine Nixon announced a $1 million reward for information about her murder. Her parents, John and Helen Magill, had long been advocates of an increased reward, which had previously been set at $100,000.

On the day the seven-figure sum was announced, Ron received a phone call at Homicide from a man who said, 'I've only ever met you once. I know what happened. I'm not going to be greedy. I only want $100,000.'

In what sounded like a conversation from a TV drama, the caller told Ron where to meet him. 'He said, "I'll be wearing a balaclava. You give me the hundred thousand in a paper bag, I'll give you the information, and you'll never see me again". I said, "It doesn't work that way. It's paid on results".' Reward money was paid only when someone's information led to the arrest and conviction of those responsible.

Ron knew this might finally be his chance to find out who had murdered Thurgood-Dove, so he sought his superiors' advice. 'After an hour-and-a-half of negotiation it was agreed we'd pay him an initial deposit while we checked his information to see if it was correct,' Ron says. 'We'd pay the balance on an agreed date but it certainly wouldn't be $100,000.'

The meeting place was a carpark near the beach at Geelong. 'The condition was that I had to go alone to meet him,' Ron says. But this seasoned detective wasn't stupid and he knew, from the time he was attacked in St Kilda, what it felt like to wonder if he was going to live or die. 'There were security measures put in place,' he acknowledges.

The men had arranged to meet at 10.30, and Ron arrived on time. As he waited in his car, the informer called Ron on his mobile to check if he was there. 'I said I was, and would see him soon.' Ron's plan – should he need one – was to get out of the car quickly if he were threatened. 'Action will always beat reaction,' he says, recalling another of his favourite sayings. 'I figured if he jumped in the car with a gun, I was going to jump out the driver's door.'

Ron expected the man be five to ten minutes away – enough time to psych himself up for a potentially dangerous encounter and ensure his colleagues were on high alert. But he didn't even have time to call them. 'Before I'd even dialled, this person was sitting beside me in the passenger side of the car,' Ron recalls. 'He'd jumped straight in the car. I shat myself!'

The mysterious informer opened a packet of cigarettes. Ron, who'd taught himself to smoke so he could fit in with crooks and make them feel relaxed, puffed on a couple too, even though he hated the taste. Beneath the haze of smoke and promising to be honest, the man dropped a bombshell. 'He said, "The actual gunman is dead. He cocked it up. He shot the wrong person and was never paid for the job",' Ron says. 'He said, "I'll give you his name but I'm telling you, he's dead".'

The informer told Ron the gunman's name was Stephen Mordy, who was connected to a bikie gang in Geelong. He also inferred that a man named Jamie Reynolds – who was also connected to Geelong bikies – had helped steal the cars. He only had a nickname for the getaway driver. Ron said he would look into the information and speak to the informer again in a few weeks. He then gave him the money in a brown envelope.

*

Back at Homicide, the detectives scrutinised the new information and found that Stephen Mordy was indeed dead. 'We also discovered that Stephen Mordy looked like the FACE image of the gunman,' Ron says. The detectives also identified the alleged car thief, Jamie Reynolds.

Ron's next step was to speak to a contact from Geelong – an 'old-style crook' in his sixties who had spent time in jail and knew who was who in the criminal underworld. 'He confessed to me that Jane's murder was a case of mistaken identity, that it was meant as payback for a man who lived in Muriel Street who had a criminal record,' Ron says. 'He indicated it was meant for the criminal's wife.'

As the pieces of the puzzle finally appeared to fall into place, the Homicide Squad was at its busiest ever, investigating Melbourne's now infamous gangland war. It meant that Ron couldn't use the technical and specialist resources normally available to him because they were being monopolised by Taskforce Purana, set up to investigate a string of underworld murders. Ron wanted to kick-start another investigation around the alleged car thief, Jamie Reynolds, and find out the getaway driver's real name. But he was stymied. 'While the investigation was on hold, Jamie Reynolds drowned in 2004 in a boating accident,' Ron says. He wouldn't be getting anything out of him.

The situation disgusted Thurgood-Dove's dad, John Magill, who challenged senior executives at Victoria Police. 'He was upset that more resources were going into finding out who had killed criminals rather than his daughter, who had never been in trouble with police,' Ron says.

As time went by, Ron was able to identify a man he thought might have been the driver, but there was not enough evidence to lay any charges. Then, about ten years into the investigation, came another promise of a breakthrough. 'One night at midnight I got a phone call from a criminal and he said, "There's a man who knows exactly what happened to Jane Thurgood-Dove",' Ron recalls.

The criminal said the man with the information wanted

to meet him. Ron said Friday was best. 'No,' the crook said, 'if you don't meet him tonight, you don't get the information!'

Just what I need, thought Ron, *another cloak-and-dagger rendezvous*. But he realised if he didn't speak with this latest mystery man, he might miss out on a significant lead. 'So I rang Steve Sheahan, a detective I worked with and said, "We're going to meet someone but I don't know who it is",' Ron recalls. The meeting was to take place outside the old Melbourne Motor Inn at the top of Elizabeth Street near Flemington Road in the city.

Under the cover of night, Ron and Sheahan drove to the location and waited. Ron was never a nail-biter but not knowing who or what to expect from the impending meeting, this would have been a good time to take up the habit. Around 1.30 am, a four-wheel drive pulled up. Inside was a familiar face. 'Straightaway I saw it was the husband of the woman suspected of being the gunman's intended target,' Ron says. 'He said, "You and I are going for a walk". I said we aren't going anywhere, and invited him into the police car.'

They drove to a pub where they could talk.

The man told the detectives he didn't want to be rude but essentially, they were dumb. He said he had a tape-recorded murder confession and 'all the players in a fishbowl'. 'He said, "All you've got to do is bait the rod and you'll catch the fish",' Ron remembers.

It was late and Ron wasn't in the mood for metaphors, so he asked his would-be informer exactly what he wanted. 'He said he wanted $2 million and a public statement to say this was not a case of mistaken identity and it was not meant for his wife,' Ron recalls. 'And he said, "If you give me $2 million, I'll give it to charity".' The man's munificent intentions aside, Ron pointed out that the reward system did not work that way. 'I said, "How do I know what's on the tape is true?"'

The detectives called an end to the meeting, but over the next three months they met at least half a dozen times with the man, who didn't want to hand over the full recording without being paid. 'On one occasion he played me a part of a tape,' Ron recalls, 'but it didn't have a confession on it, it didn't identify anyone, and was of no use whatsoever.'

The man then engaged a solicitor. Ron told him the only way to progress the matter was for the police to obtain a copy of the tape, including a full transcript, so they could fully investigate it. 'The solicitor made an appointment to see the police commissioner, Christine Nixon, with the man, and the same demand was made: that Victoria Police pay $2 million for the tape.' When Ron was asked what he thought of the offer, his answer was to the point: 'No way.'

'Eventually,' Ron continues, 'we took a different course of action and the man was subpoenaed to a coercive hearing where he was compelled to answer questions about the information he alleged to have. Further investigation as a result of the hearing established the information was totally false and of no substance.'

*

Ron spent well over a decade investigating Jane Thurgood-Dove's murder but, much to his chagrin, he didn't crack the case. Had the investigation been adequately resourced throughout, the outcome might have been different, but Ron isn't one to speak in what-ifs.

He knows that none of those closest to Thurgood-Dove arranged for her to be killed. 'Her husband, Mark, passed the polygraph test, which indicated he was in no way involved,' Ron says. 'The police officer was also eliminated and, on the information I have, Mordy did it.'

So that makes the most likely scenario, according to Ron, that the murder *was* a case of mistaken identity but with key players dead, including the gunman, and no evidence of who arranged the hit, the case remains unsolved, and the $1 million reward still stands.

17

CRIME-BUSTING DRIVER

'Driving buses was my other world to escape into – it
was like a release of pressure, and for forty-eight
hours I was living another life.'
– Ron Iddles

The same year Ron began investigating Jane Thurgood-Dove's murder, detectives from the Homicide Squad, not content with catching killers, decided they wanted to raise money for charity. So in 1997, officers who felt up for a new challenge cycled 530 kilometres over three days from Mildura on the Murray River to Port Fairy on the Great Ocean Road, with proceeds being donated to a hospital. The event has taken place every year since, with the money now donated to other worthy organisations, including Beyond Blue.

It inspired in Ron a love of long-distance cycling although he didn't ride in the inaugural event. Instead, he drove a ten-seater support bus, which Firefly Coaches had donated for the three-day ride. The fundraiser created such a buzz that the following year more detectives wanted to take part, so Firefly upgraded them to a twenty-seater coach. Ron was impressed by the company's community spirit and when he met their director, Joe Bono, he openly admired his luxury coaches. He also told him he drove a poultry delivery truck part-time. Bono asked Ron what licence he had. A heavy vehicle licence, Ron replied.

'So I said to Ron, "Why don't you come and drive some big buses?" But it wasn't just the fact that Ron could drive heavy vehicles that led Joe to offer him a job. 'It was his presence,' Joe explains. 'The way he conducted himself when I first met him. I knew he was a true professional.' Joe kept at him until Ron said he'd consider it.

After all, driving buses was in his genes – his dad Bill used to drive the bus from Echuca to Melbourne before he was born. Ron had to resign from his poultry-delivery round, though. He felt it was time for a change and admits that coach driving was a lot cleaner and easier. Not only that, but behind the wheel of a Firefly Ron could step up his love of modern machinery. 'Their coaches were immaculate and the way they were looked after was the envy of other bus companies. I thought it was pretty special driving a coach worth $700,000 to Adelaide.'

Colleen, however, felt differently. She had always encouraged Ron to do the things he wanted, but she could not understand why he would accept another job that took him away from his family. 'I could honestly say his work was never a problem even when he worked forty, fifty, sixty hours straight or was away for two weeks at a time,' she says. 'But this did my head in.'

It took Ron a couple of trips to get into the swing of coach driving and to get the sleep he needed afterwards. He also learnt that the hour or so before dawn was the toughest for a night driver, but if he needed fresh air, he'd pull over and stretch his legs. Soon he felt even more certain that he'd made the right decision. He found long-haul driving relaxing. 'Some people liked fishing, some liked golf . . . this was about having an interest outside Victoria Police and the Homicide Squad,' he explains. 'It could be classed as an escape because it kept me balanced and all-rounded. Sometimes, going over to collect the coach, it was like the world would lift off my shoulders, and it released any work pressure or stress.'

Along with the more peaceful job, Ron also got a kick out of operating the coach's state-of-the-art features. He'd never driven a tractor or a truck that was this fancy. 'I'd sit in the driver's seat which was like a cockpit with many switches and gauges and lights. And everyone who came on board had total trust in me – that I would stay awake all night and get them to their destination safely.' And he did, every single time, with not one complaint.

*

A year later, Ron started making daylight trips to Adelaide and after that, Joe asked if he wanted to drive from Melbourne to Sydney. Ron was enjoying it, but soon found himself doing twenty-six runs a year, which meant that, for half a year, his family didn't see him on weekends.

'It got to the stage where Colleen was saying, "Why do you do it so much? Don't you want to be at home?" But I found it a way to totally switch off. When I crossed over the bridge to collect the coach at Maidstone, it was like the world of crime had left me. I used to listen to music – country music by Charlie Pride or Jim Reeves, sometimes Celine Dion, or ABC midnight talkback.'

Sometimes lonely passengers or those unable to sleep ambled down the front of the bus, hoping for a yarn. If they needed Ron's assistance he was there to help, but for safety reasons – and also because he relished his quiet time – he began to outlaw conversations at the start of every trip.

Ron noticed that a number of his passengers were backpackers who treated the journey as a cheap night's accommodation. Sometimes, in the days before discount airfares, more than a dozen coaches would carry football fans from Adelaide to Melbourne to watch a game. That was one night when Ron didn't mind a natter. 'They were good nights because you'd talk on a two-way radio to another driver,' he says. Ron also drove passengers from Melbourne to Sydney to watch the fireworks.

When he wasn't driving coaches, Ron was working full-time at Homicide and increasingly turning up on the TV news. His face was becoming familiar. He recalls a passenger engaging him in conversation during a rest stop at Tintinara Roadhouse in South Australia. 'I can't work you out,' he said to Ron. 'I know your voice, I know your face. I've either heard you on 3AW or I've seen you on a cooking show.' Ron suppressed a chuckle. 'I never divulged who I was,' he says. 'That was my private life.'

Ron met other interesting characters too. 'Another night before I left Adelaide there was a guy wearing all these gold chains and I knew he was a criminal,' he recalls. 'He came up and said, "You and I are on opposite sides. I know who you are".' Ron looked at him squarely and replied, 'Well, you won't have to worry then. I'll get you to Melbourne safely'. The crook slept soundly all the way home.

On another occasion, Ron drove the coach back from Adelaide to Melbourne then, after a four-hour sleep at the depot, went to see the most important witness in a murder trial due to start the following day. The witness's mum answered the door and was instantly taken aback. 'You just drove me from Adelaide to Melbourne!' she exclaimed. 'Well, I got you here safely,' Ron responded with a smirk. He liked that line.

*

Never one to completely switch off, Ron found coach driving a good way to solve murders. 'There were times when I'd be driving along and thinking about a murder investigation,' he says. 'I'd get to a truck stop for a meal break and write down some ideas on paper.' Sometimes, a member of his crew would ring him from the office. 'The sergeant would ring and say they had a job. So I'd quite often give advice from the driver's seat. That's where I had to be conscious I didn't talk too loudly.'

Then there was the night when Ron drove to Adelaide after an intense shift at Homicide. One of the other drivers had called in sick and Bono had phoned everyone he knew to find a replacement. 'We had no spare drivers,' Bono says. 'We even rang other companies to see if they could help out.' But no one could, so Bono decided to call Ron on the off-chance he could do a week-night shift. 'He said he had to lock up a criminal that evening,' Bono recalls, adding that Ron reluctantly agreed to do it on one condition – that he bring the coach to him so he could get some rest before departing.

It was Ron's most exhausting night behind the wheel, one he swore he would never do again. 'He's one out of the box,' Bono acknowledges, reflecting on what Ron did for him that night. 'I've never found another person like him. He's a beautiful man.'

*

A couple of years into the bus-driving job, Victoria Police tightened their policies around part-time jobs so Ron had to reapply to drive his beloved Fireflys. His application was immediately rejected on the basis that there was a potential conflict of interest because police had a regulatory authority over coach drivers. As with the chicken truck, Ron recognised this was a situation that demanded logic. 'I argued that it was really the same if I was pulled over driving a motor car,' he explains. 'I also said there was no conflict of interest because as a coach driver I was actually governed by three other organisations – the Taxi Directorate, Vic Roads and the Department of Infrastructure.' Once again, Ron's superiors couldn't argue.

And so, for years to come, between solving some of Australia's most shocking murders, coach captain Ron Iddles safely delivered thousands more passengers to their destination. For Ron, route timetables, big machines and all things mechanical were easily managed, ran more or less as expected, and when things broke down, were fixable – parts were easily replaced. The human mind and its motivations, by contrast, were far less predictable, and the solutions to crimes often not as straightforward or even logical. Long-distance driving helped Ron work on those questions, and occasionally, it even yielded some answers.

18

TALES FROM THE UNDERWORLD

'If you don't break your values and don't promise something you can't deliver, you can get trust in the criminal world, and people will talk to you. I think over a long period of time you build up a reputation, but that doesn't come overnight. And if you do anything to compromise it, you never get it back.'
– Ron Iddles

Organised criminals generally take an all-seasons approach to murder. Consider Melbourne's infamous gangland war back in the 1990s and early 2000s. The underworld in Australia's own Gotham City proved they could carry out killings on the most frostbitten of winter's nights, so long as they were armed with a handgun, a vaguely rational motive and a fleecy-lined hoodie.

It was just after 8.30 on one such winter's night – Friday, 15 June 2000 – when Ron took a call from D24. He should have knocked off, but typically was still at his desk, poring over evidence from the recent murder of underworld drug dealer, Richard Mladenich. 'You've got a job,' said the emergency communications officer, interrupting his train of thought. 'It's in Essendon. We're pretty sure Mark Moran's been shot.'

Richard 'The Lionheart' would have to wait.

*

Mark Moran was big news. The thirty-five-year-old was one of the highest profile underworld identities in the country. His mother was Judy Moran, Jason Moran was his half-brother, and his stepfather was Lewis Moran. Criminal royalty.

Ron recalls arriving at Moran's impressive house in Essendon, protected by a wrought-iron Federation-style fence with two large gates. Moran hadn't made it inside, but had been shot out the front while still in his white Holden ute. 'The driver's door was open and Mark was half out of the car, slumped,' Ron says. 'There was a large amount of blood around as two firearms had been used – a shotgun and a handgun.'

Even though police had responded rapidly and blocked off the street, people were appearing out of the shadows. Knowing there had been trouble, 'The underworld had already started to arrive – they probably had a better communication system than the police,' Ron explains. His mobile was also ringing hot. 'Criminals were calling me and saying, "Is it true? Is it true? Is Mark dead?"'

Mark's stepfather was among those at the scene and he did not want to engage with the police. 'That night I had a blue with Lewis Moran,' Ron remembers. He was hoping the Moran family elder would help him solve Mark's murder. 'Standing on the verandah, I said to him, "I know you don't have any respect for police. But you'll find out who killed

Mark before I do, so all I ask is that you get a solicitor to call me with the information".'

Lewis Moran regarded the detective with contempt. 'You can get fucked,' he replied. 'I'll look after this myself.'

Lewis's brother, Des 'Tuppence' Moran, was there too, and because of his good relationship with Ron, he tried to make peace, but it didn't work. 'We got no cooperation from the dad. Lewis was someone who just didn't talk to you. He just saw it as not right. But other criminals were prepared to sit down and have a coffee with me. They mightn't have told me anything helpful, but there was often that mutual respect. But Lewis Moran had a hatred for police.'

It was almost unheard of for members of the underworld to hate Ron even though he was investigating murders in which they might have been involved. 'It was because of that connection he has with people that others don't,' Ron's former crew member Tim Peck explains. 'You could go to any crime scene and a lot of investigators would have trouble putting aside what a person had done.' But Ron wasn't like that. 'Ron had the strength to talk to people and get that bond,' Peck adds. 'The number of offenders who confessed to him was unparalleled.'

Not only that, but some criminals even responded favourably when they saw him because they knew he had integrity. 'It's honest Ron, Uncle Ron,' they'd say. 'I can talk to him.'

*

Among the early suspects in the murder of Mark Moran were Dino Dibra and underworld kingpin Carl Williams. Dibra had a rock-solid alibi. 'When we got the call for the job, Dino Dibra was in our office,' Ron says of the twenty-five-year-old, who was bumped off four months later.

What had Williams been doing at the time of Moran's murder? Even though Ron had been working for twenty-two hours straight, he intended to find out. Accompanied by a crew member, he stormed Williams' place at around 4.30 am. In situations like this, he knew he was taking his life in his hands. 'You always prepare for the worst, some type of confrontation,' he says. 'Your heart's pumping and there's a massive dump of adrenaline because it's about going into the unknown. If you are not conscious of the fact something may go horribly wrong, then you will make mistakes. You need to ensure the forced entry is swift, to ensure the element of surprise.'

'I went straight to the front bedroom and found Carl and his wife Roberta there,' Ron continues. One of the couple's associates was in a room at the back of the house, too. Fortunately, no one made any trouble and Williams had a fully fleshed story for the police. 'Carl told me he wasn't involved in Mark Moran's murder and gave an explanation where he was that night,' Ron recalls. 'He said he'd driven to Gisborne to see somebody and that he'd stopped at a petrol station with a convenience store, and had bought some water.' Ron and his team looked into Williams' story and found CCTV footage of him buying water, just as he'd said. 'I later wrote a report which said Carl did have a motive to kill Mark Moran but on the fact that there was CCTV, it was highly unlikely that he was responsible, although he might have set it up.' (In 1999, Moran shot and wounded Williams, who had started to move into the drug trade, which had been dominated by the Morans.)

The Purana Taskforce eventually took over the investigation into Moran's murder and subsequently charged Williams with murder.

To Ron's surprise, he was subpoenaed to give evidence for Williams at the committal hearing. 'That was on the basis of my previous report and also around the fact that we'd checked the CCTV and confirmed the time he bought the water that night,' he says.

Ron did not think Williams had pulled the trigger and was not afraid to say so, even though it was in direct contravention to the case his Purana colleagues had built. 'Given the time of the murder it would have been impossible for Carl to drive to Gisborne unless he exceeded the speed limit and crashed every red light, but the Purana investigators were saying you could do it if you sped. Carl was committed for trial but ultimately that charge was withdrawn.'

Ron would have testified for the devil himself if it meant telling the truth. 'It came to me through Carl's legal team, but also through Roberta, that Carl was surprised I stood up and told the truth as I knew it,' he says. 'Carl thought I'd support the detectives from Purana and that my evidence would not conflict with the charge he was facing.' Ron had great respect for the Purana team, but had to tell it as he saw it.

He says that, from then on, Roberta Williams occasionally called him. 'There were times when she rang and said, "Carl will only trust you. Can you go and see him in Barwon Prison?"' Ron visited Williams there at least once. When he first arrived, he noticed Williams was 'a little bit apprehensive, but only on the basis that other prisoners want to know what police are seeing them for'. He adds, 'Other than that, he was fine and we chatted about the matters he wanted to discuss.'

But Ron didn't always go to see Williams when he was invited. 'That's because there was a view held by some that he might be trying to manipulate the process of justice by constantly asking for me,' Ron says. 'But again, I had the view, never close down the line of communication. I'd been around for a long time. I was always cautious and careful dealing with criminals, and I always documented it. But it was just a fact that there were times when people would tell me things they wouldn't tell others.'

As it turned out, after giving evidence for Williams, members of the underworld reached out to Ron in unprecedented numbers. 'Other criminals would ring me – some I'd never met before,' he says. 'One said, "I've been in jail for over twenty-five years, I'm out, and I'm told that you're trustworthy". I went and met him on several occasions and he ended up providing information that actually prevented homicides.'

Ron's association with the Williams family continued, and in November 2008 he was called out to a suspicious overdose at a unit in Moonee Ponds in Melbourne's north-west. It was Carl's mum, Barbara Williams. 'Roberta turned up at the home while I was there,' he recalls. 'I know that Roberta and Carl – even though he was in prison by that time – took some comfort in knowing that I was there.' Ron says there was speculation Barbara's death had been a murder, not a suicide. Either way he intended to get to the bottom of it. 'We wouldn't leave any stone unturned,' he says, adding that the cause of death soon became known. 'From examining the scene, looking at a note that was located, and CCTV from a shop opposite, it all showed that she had taken her own life, which is what the coroner found.'

*

Ron went to the scene of so many underworld hits from the mid-1990s into the next century, he has lost count. 'There was an escalation after Mark Moran was shot,' he says. 'We were up to about fifteen underworld killings in two years. Investigators started talking about who they thought would be next.'

Among the cases Ron was called out to was the death of Graham 'The Munster' Kinniburgh at home in Kew in December 2003, the shooting of Andrew 'Benji' Veniamin at a Carlton restaurant in March 2004 (Mick Gatto was charged but ultimately acquitted of murder on the grounds of self-defence), and the shooting of Lewis Caine in Brunswick two months later. 'Lewis Caine had no ID on him,' Ron remembers. 'But he had a mobile phone with two SIM cards in it. It was quite common for the underworld to have multiple SIM cards, so that, coupled with the fact that he'd been executed, told me he was part of the underworld.'

The murder on 31 March 2004 came as a shock: Lewis Moran was dead. 'I had a call from Tuppence – Des – to say, "Ron, you won't believe this. Lewis has been gunned down". I couldn't believe it.' He'd been shot at the Brunswick Club in a hit organised by Carl Williams. 'By the time Lewis was murdered, Mark Moran was dead, and Jason Moran had been shot too.'

Years later, in June 2009, Des Moran also ended up on the wrong side of a gun. It was just a few weeks after he'd told Ron he was worried because someone had opened fire on his car. 'He was shot at his favourite coffee shop in broad daylight,' says Ron. 'I was somewhat shocked, as he was not involved in the underworld as such but had a name that was. His death marked the end of an era and, to some extent, the end of the Moran name.'

And as history shows, in April 2010, the man widely considered to be the underworld's most powerful player, Carl Williams, was also killed – bashed to death in Barwon Prison by a fellow inmate.

So much wasted life – more than thirty in the end. And for what? All around greed, drugs and in-fighting. 'They turned on their own,' Ron says. 'Thankfully they've stopped, but will there be another era? I don't know.'

During these killings, which left many Melburnians, innocent and guilty, nervous, Colleen knew her husband was digging into the lives of some of Australia's most dangerous underworld criminals. Had she begun to consider the possibility that one night, her husband might get caught in the crossfire and not make it home?

'No,' she replies, 'that was his life. That was what he did. I always knew there was a risk but what could I do? I was a policeman's wife.'

*

One of Ron's greatest fans, curiously, was one of the underworld's most famous identities – Mark 'Chopper' Read. He'd heard through the criminal grapevine that Ron was a cop of his word.

Ron first met Chopper in 2002 when a Tasmanian detective phoned and said he wanted to interview the former standover man about a missing person case. Ron drove to Chopper's house in Collingwood to sound him out. 'He said something like, "I don't know you but I've heard a lot about you",' Ron recalls.

Chopper rang his solicitor for advice, then drove to the Homicide Squad office with his fiancée, Margaret Cassar, who remembers the day well. 'In the lift, Ron said, "I believe you guys are getting married. What date?"' She replied the ceremony would be on 19 January, adding, 'Nothing's going to get in the way of that!'

The Tasmanian detectives interviewed and released Chopper, who started calling Ron periodically. 'It might have been as simple as, "I want to go overseas but I've got a criminal history – can I get a passport?"' Ron remembers. Another time Chopper wanted advice about how to buy a car. 'Sometimes it was just around basic things, because he was someone who had spent a lot of time in prison. While he was street-wise, there were some things that he didn't know how to do.'

Not all cops are on good terms with career criminals but Ron maintains that, so long as the relationship is professional, they should be. 'I always had the view, never burn the lines of communication because one day those people might pick up the phone and give you information that might solve a crime,' he says. 'You should never close the door to those who reach out to you. In some cases there may be an ulterior motive, but detectives should always be prepared to listen.'

Sometimes Ron used to run into Chopper by accident. From time to time he and Colleen had dinner at an old corner pub called the Leinster Arms in Collingwood. It turned out to be Chopper's local. 'He was often there with his wife, Margaret, and their son Roy,' Ron says. 'If I was in the restaurant he'd leave the bar and come over. He'd always say, "How are you, Mr Iddles? How are things going?"'

For someone who'd spent so much time in Pentridge, Ron always thought Chopper's manners were impeccable.

Ron was always mindful to note in his diary any interactions he had with Chopper, or any other underworld identity. Gifts were out of the question. 'One night he offered me one of his paintings, which was hanging on the wall at the pub,' Ron recalls. 'His paintings were unique. In my view they wouldn't have won an artist's award!' Not that Chopper was trying to win any prizes. 'He said, "I just put a canvas up in my backyard and splash paint all over it. And people pay for it!"'

'But as he said, he had to do something,' Colleen remarks. 'Because who was going to give him a job? He had to do something, and at the end of the day he was a dad who wanted to provide for his family.'

At first Colleen was amazed her husband knew Chopper Read, but she quickly separated the man from the myth. 'When you actually knew him, he was gentle and kind. He was always interested in our kids and he always asked after them.'

Chopper's wife, now Margaret Read, took to Ron too. 'It's because he stood out from the rest and was honest,' she says. 'And when you meet him he doesn't talk down to you with a detective voice, like most of them. They made it clear, "We're the detectives and you're the wife of a high profile identity".' But Ron was never like that. 'He never, ever looked down on Mark or thought he was up to no good,' she says.

During their tete-a-tetes, Chopper used to tell Ron about

the books he'd written and his latest exploits, including the time he teamed up with notorious former Sydney detective Roger Rogerson and ex-AFL player Mark 'Jacko' Jackson to tour the comedy circuit, before deciding to perform on his own.

Ron also recalls how Chopper invited him to a book launch at a restaurant in upmarket Toorak. Even though Chopper phoned Ron regularly, he acknowledged it might not be appropriate for the high-profile homicide cop to attend. 'He said, "Look, I understand if you don't come because people will see it as a bit of a conflict",' Ron says. And while he didn't go to the launch, Colleen did, and found the evening fascinating. 'She told me that there were several senior prison officers there and they seemed to have a mutual respect,' Ron adds.

Similarly, it was because Chopper respected Ron that he used to ask him how to respond when other police called and asked for information. 'It might have been about something historical, or something that had happened in H Division,' Ron explains. 'He'd ring and say, "What do you think?" and I'd say, "Talk to them".'

Most significantly, Chopper credited Ron with helping him turn his back on crime forever. It was no coincidence that after they met, Chopper never again re-offended. 'I think Ron used to say, "Keep your head above water".' Margaret says. 'Mark would say, "Yeah, I'm definitely not going back to prison". Mark always did credit Ron for the big turnaround.'

As time went by, Chopper told Ron he was infected with hepatitis C, and that it was damaging his liver. 'He related the story of how he was in H Division at Pentridge and back then they were forced to share razorblades to shave,' Ron says. 'He believed that's how he probably contracted it.'

A while later, the hardman with the larrikin streak became gravely ill with liver cancer. Even though it was obvious he was in bad shape, it didn't stop members of the public from homing in on him. 'He said he went to a function on Grand Final Day and was coughing blood,' Ron says. 'He said he finished wiping his mouth and someone asked him for a photograph and to sign something.' Even Chopper Read – once considered one of Australia's most violent criminals – was shocked. 'He said, "Sometimes people talk to me about having no morals and no values, but sometimes there are people who are worse than me".'

'With a lot of people, with Mark, they didn't see the person,' Margaret continues. She acknowledges that her husband sometimes told the media tall tales to amuse himself, but his relationship with Ron and his family was firmly rooted in honesty. 'When you met Mark, he filled the room up,' she says. 'Mark could be the hardest person and also the softest.' Margaret believes Ron could see that. 'He's warm and sincere and he understands people. He recognised that Mark was no longer interested in or part of the criminal world. He meant that, and he never went back.'

Over more than a decade, Ron, Chopper and Margaret shared laughs – and in Chopper's case, information – over many cups of tea, and the Reads considered Ron their friend. Even so, Ron maintained his exemplary professional stand-ards. 'He's definitely by the book,' Margaret remarks. 'He's a man of integrity and rules.'

In Chopper's final months, he and Margaret became involved in the production of a documentary about his life. In it, Chopper wanted to tell viewers how Ron's guidance had prevented him from reoffending. Figuring there was a positive message in the film, Ron asked if he could take part, but Victoria Police told him to decline the request. 'They saw it as maybe not a good look, or a risk to the organisation,' Ron explains. Margaret understood but continued to invite Ron to events. 'He went straight to his superiors and if they said no, he did not attend,' she says.

Shortly before her husband passed away, Margaret called Ron to say that Chopper wanted to see him. 'Mark was highly fond of him,' Margaret says. 'He really loved him.' Ron and Colleen both went to Royal Melbourne Hospital. Chopper was listless. 'He looked terrible. He was totally yellow,' Ron remembers. Chopper talked about how he hoped he had provided adequately for Margaret and Roy. It was something he had spoken about to Ron before and it was clearly preying on his mind.

'I was really happy to go and see him and I wanted to thank him for being so nice over the years,' Colleen says. 'I thought it was just really nice that he wanted to see Ron before he died.'

Being a cop, Ron eventually turned the conversation to crime. 'I said, "I've got to ask you some things. Is there anything you want to confess, or any information I should know about?"' he asked. The dying man said no, but told Ron that an interview he'd done with a television current affairs program would give a different impression. 'He thought the story was about how he'd turned his life around, but the focus was on his past,' Ron explains. 'He said he got pissed off and indicated he'd been involved in two or three other murders.' Chopper even took the crew to an oval where he alleged one of the bodies was buried. 'He said, "In the end, Ron, they basically forced me, and what I said was basically shit".'

Three days after speaking to Ron, on 9 October 2013, Mark Brandon 'Chopper' Read died. He was fifty-eight.

Margaret invited Ron to the funeral but he thought it inappropriate to attend. 'Despite our mutual respect, people would have read something into it,' he acknowledges.

Ron's influence even rubbed off on Margaret and Chopper's son, Roy, who's wanted to be a policeman ever since he started school. 'He knows that Ron Iddles is the man,' Margaret laughs. 'If he sees a policeman, Roy will spark up a conversation with him.'

Ron says he feels honoured that Chopper held him responsible for giving up a life of crime, and he still keeps in contact with Margaret, just as Chopper would have wished.

*

Ron also inspired one-time murder suspect Glenn Heaton, who once rubbed shoulders with Melbourne's armed robbers.

Overwhelmingly strong, Heaton knew from an early age how to use his fists. In 1986, aged sixteen, he was the Australian Junior Middleweight boxing champion. It was his first fight. By the time he was 17, the young champion was punch-drunk, and started mixing with gangsters he met on the boxing circuit. Ten years later he found himself accused of an armed robbery at the Lower Plenty Hotel in Melbourne's north-east, during which a security guard, Alexander McGaffin, was shot dead while delivering money. Ron was the investigator assigned.

The first thing Heaton noticed when he met Ron was that the detective shook his hand. No police officer had done that before. The second thing was Ron's plain-talking style. 'He said to me at one point, "You'll find I never talk bullshit like some other coppers",' Heaton recalls. He found Ron's approach admirable: Ron was no pushover, but unlike other police Heaton had met, he used his brain, not the butt of his gun, as a weapon. 'When being investigated by police you shit your pants when Ron's on your case,' Heaton says. 'He is one of a handful of people who is not scared of me and the only person in the country I fear.'

Heaton was acquitted of all charges and after the trial Ron offered some sage advice. 'He said, "Now it's time to get on with your life, son. Don't screw it up",' Heaton recalls. 'Those words changed my life.'

Years went by and Heaton did his best to follow Ron's advice, but, needing the detective's counsel again, he called him out of the blue in 2008, and has remained in contact since. 'I have called Ron multiple times when feeling out of control, homicidal and psychotic. I can call Ron Iddles and dob myself in before I do anything stupid,' he says. 'With Ron's echo in my head I pull up before I go too far.'

He continues, 'Through boxing and crime everyone admired me for my violence. I now feel ashamed of such thinking.

'Ron Iddles has saved lives, mine included.'

*

When investigating one of Australia's most enduring missing persons mysteries, Ron met a well-known serial killer who, while he had no links to the underworld, was another high-profile criminal who appreciated the detective's honesty.

In 2010, Ron was looking into the disappearance from Kananook railway station of twenty-three-year-old Sarah

McDiarmid in July 1990. Coroner Iain West had ruled it was foul play, but the question remained: who was responsible?

Paul Denyer's name came up. In 1993, he had murdered eighteen-year-old Elizabeth Stevens, twenty-two-year-old Debbie Fream and seventeen-year-old Natalie Russell, and was dubbed 'The Frankston Serial Killer'. *Had he murdered Sarah McDiarmid too?* Ron wondered, and headed to Port Phillip Prison to find out.

'When I got there he said, "I'm not going to participate in a conversation with you unless you change the documentation to say Paula Denyer",' Ron recalls, explaining that the prisoner was transgender and identified as a woman. Ron amended the paperwork and Denyer agreed to see him. 'He had long hair and wore lipstick but had not had a sex change.'

Ron got down to the business of McDiarmid's disappearance. 'He said, "I'm sick of being accused of that murder,"' Ron recalls. 'He gave me sufficient details to form the view he wasn't involved and wanted it to be publicly known. He thought it didn't do justice to Sarah McDiarmid's family. I could see the point.'

Soon afterwards, someone leaked to the *Herald Sun* that Ron had visited Denyer in jail. 'I then gave some comments to the *Herald Sun* saying Paula was not involved,' Ron says. 'After that I got a letter from Paula thanking me for my honesty. And I probably got two or three other letters prior to leaving the Homicide Squad.'

A few years later, when Ron finally left the Homicide Squad, everything would change. Those who needed his help to fit back into society, or who wanted to give him crucial information, would still phone, but they all asked the same question: 'Who am I going to deal with now?'

Victoria **Police**

Oath

Police Regulation Act 1958—Second Schedule

I, ___Ronald William IDDLES___ Swear by Almighty God that I will well and truly serve our Sovereign Lady the Queen as a Member of the Police Force of Victoria in such capacity as I may be hereafter appointed, promoted, or reduced to without favour or affection malice or ill-will for the period of twelve calendar months from this date, and until I am legally discharged; that I will see and cause Her Majesty's peace to be kept and preserved; and that I will prevent to the best of my power all offences against the same, and that while I shall continue to be a member of the Police Force of Victoria I will to the best of my skill and knowledge discharge all the duties legally imposed upon me faithfully and according to law.

Sworn before me at Melbourne

on this ___twenty second___ day

of ___October___ 19 73

Signature _Ronald W Iddles_

Andrew A Ivy JP
Justice of the Peace

Taking an oath: In October 1973, Ron Iddles vowed to protect the people of Victoria. He has served the community ever since.

BRIGHT FUTURE FOR SENIOR DETECTIVE

A young man who was educated at the Lockington Consolidated School and the Echuca Technical School is now a Senior Detective with the Homicide Squad in the Victorian Police Force.

Twenty five year old Ron Iddles joined the police force 5 years ago. He was Dux of the complete Academy and was stationed at Collingwood where he completed his retention training and was also Dux of that course. Whilst there he received a commendation from the Chief Commissioner for the high standard of his overall work performance.

This was a rare distinction as there are seldom more than two of these awards issued each year.

He then joined the Criminal Investigation Branch and completed a detective training course of which he was Dux and joined the Homicide Squad.

When he was stationed at Fitzroy he served under Sgt Bernard Gaffney who was until recently the relieving Sergeant at the Rochester Police Station.

Senior Detective Ron Iddles is currently investigating the Ricketts Point murder case.

Local boy makes good: When Ron was twenty-five, the _Rochester Campaspe News_ recognised him as one of the Victorian Police Force's rising stars.

Early days at Homicide: (left to right) Detective Sergeant Jack Jacobs, Ron, a local policeman, Coroner Kevin Mason, Detective Senior Sergeant Brian McCarthy, Detective Sergeant Rowland Legg and Barry Bolton, clerk of the Coroners Court, in 1981.

Suspicious bones: (left to right) Brian McCarthy, Rowland Legg, Ron, two dingo trappers, Jack Jacobs and a local policeman. A dingo trapper found bones at Porepunkah near Bright in Victoria. It wasn't a murder; the bones turned out to belong to an animal.

TV times: Ron and his workmates met Mike Willesee when the journalist filmed at St Kilda Police Station. Mike returned to the office with a bigger story than any of them expected. (Left to right) Mike Willesee, Rod Porter, Ron, Vince Costanzo.

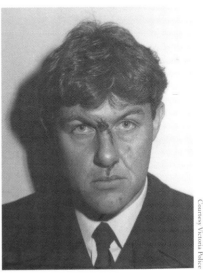

Crime scene: Photos from an armed robbery Ron foiled in 1984. The would-be robber punched Ron in the face and he needed stitches. Ron's attacker was found guilty of serious assault.

Brush with death: Some of the injuries that Ron sustained in the attack.

Taking note: Ron outside the Esquire Hotel in St Kilda, where underworld figure Richard Mladenich was shot dead in May 2000.

Door stop: Ron addressing the media in 2012 at the end of the trial of Shane Bond over the murder of Elisabeth Membrey. Bond was acquitted.

Peter Ward / Newspix

Ron and fellow detective Lee Cunningham at the funeral of criminal Victor Peirce in 2002. He wasn't there to mourn; he wanted to see who turned up. Often, he says, killers turn up at underworld funerals.

Norm Oorloff / Newspix

Integrity: Outside the Coroners Court in 2007, Ron shakes the hand of Peter Smith, a man he arrested for murder before proving he was innocent.

Courtesy Ron Iddles

No ordinary dip in the river: In 2003 Ron retrieved a body from the Goulburn River at Kialla near Shepparton. He told reporters it was a cow so they were not alarmed.

Fairfax / Penny Stephens / Fairfax Syndication

Compassion: Ron comforting the girlfriend of a man shot by police in South Melbourne in 2008.

Country crime scene: Ron coordinating the search for the body of drug dealer, Ricky Ganly. His body was found in a car submerged in water at a mine site in Avoca.

Fairfax Syndication

Fairfax / Jim Aldersley / Fairfax Syndication

Fire and ice: Ron investigates the 2013 ice-fuelled murder of William Stevenson, near Bendigo. Stevenson was bashed, stabbed, then burnt. Before leaving Homicide, Ron investigated seven ice murders in a row.

AAP Image / Dan Peled

Crucified: Ron explains why he showed a photo of murder victim Jill Meagher (for less than two seconds) at a fundraiser in 2013. His speech was about the investigation into Jill's murder and the need for people to look after each other. But a media storm hit and Ron bore the brunt.

Alex Coppel / Newspix

From cop to CEO: Since starting as Secretary of The Police Association of Victoria, Ron has put officers' health and welfare first.

The Great Man: After twenty-five years at Homicide, Ron is looking forward.

19

RIGHTING A WRONG

'During this investigation I was in turmoil and an emotional wreck. I always had a feeling deep down that the bloke I'd charged with murder hadn't done it.'
– Ron Iddles

Sometimes, even the most experienced cops get it wrong.

One night in 2002, Ron was called out to a popular wedding reception venue in Melbourne's south-east to find out who had murdered security guard Slawomir Tomczyk. The forty-four-year-old had been savagely beaten to death while on his late-night rounds.

Four months later, Ron charged a thirty-seven-year-old named Peter Smith over the murder. Almost straightaway, Ron had a niggling feeling he'd nabbed the wrong man, and would spend a year trying to prove it.

'It's never an easy decision to lock someone up,' Ron says. 'If you're going to deprive someone of their liberty, you've got to get it right. You never want to send an innocent person to jail.'

Not all cops would have the integrity to lobby for a man they'd locked up, but Ron was not motivated by ego. All that mattered was the truth – for Slawomir Tomczyk *and* Peter Smith – and Ron did everything in his power to find it.

*

Polish immigrant Slawomir Tomczyk, known to his family as Slawek, never wanted to be a security guard, but after being retrenched from his job as a jeweller, he was grateful for the work. Slawek was a peaceful man who helped support his elderly mother, Janina, who also lived in Australia. On weekends he enjoyed exploring his adopted country and hoped to meet someone special to share in his adventures. It was not to be.

On the night of Thursday, 21 February 2002, Slawek, who worked for a company called PSE Security, was conducting mobile patrols in Berwick, Narre Warren and Endeavour Hills. It was also his job to patrol the grounds of the Casablanca Reception Centre in Cranbourne, where he was required to make sure the doors were locked, four times during his shift.

His first visit to the reception centre that evening was just before 10 pm. As usual, he parked the security van in the driveway before ensuring the building was secure. When he returned to the van, Slawek noticed one of the front tyres had been slashed, so he called his boss, Sandy Sempel.

Sempel suggested Slawek replace the tyre then continue his other patrols. A few minutes later, a man walking his dog saw Slawek changing the tyre and asked if he needed any help. Slawek was grateful for the offer but turned it down.

At 12.20 am, Sempel's phone rang again. Slawek had not turned up at the McDonald's restaurant at Endeavour Hills, where he was due to conduct a routine check. It was unusual, because Slawek was reliable. Sempel decided to look for him.

Around 2 am, Sempel arrived at the Casablanca Reception Centre. 'In the driveway, there was blood and skid marks,' Ron says. 'At first his boss thought he had injured himself changing the tyre but when he went around the back of the reception centre he found Slawek's body.'

When Ron arrived at the scene, uniformed police directed him to a small wooden gate behind which Slawek had been dumped. 'He had been hogtied and dragged by his belt on his back,' Ron says with distaste. 'He had probably been attacked in the driveway, though, because there was blood spatter on the car jack.'

The security van was no longer at the reception centre. Police recovered it at six in the morning, abandoned at Clyde North. 'Bits and pieces from inside the van were scattered over a two-kilometre stretch of road,' Ron says. 'Various items had been thrown into the grass. I have no idea why.'

There were strange clues at the crime scene, too. 'We found a wheel brace and bolt, which looked like it had been ground to a point at one end,' Ron says. He did not know the significance of the bolt at the time, but kept it as hold-back information so that only police and those involved in the crime knew about it. He chose not to tell the media that Slawek had been tied up either.

When Ron's team spoke to Slawek's devastated family, they told him he had no enemies. 'So it looked like he was in the wrong place at the wrong time,' Ron says. The reception centre had not been broken into, so what was the point in murdering the security guard?

At 8 am, while Ron was still combing over the evidence at the crime scene, a man anonymously called the police and named who he believed was responsible. 'We located that man but he had an alibi which, at the time, appeared to have been corroborated,' Ron says.

About two months later, a used car salesman told police of a suspicious conversation he had overheard at his workplace, Cranbourne Auto Market on Sunday, 24 February, 2002. He said that two men – one young, and the other noticeably over-weight – had driven into the yard in a yellow Ford XD station wagon. A green Mitsubishi L300 van soon turned up and a man with dreadlocks spoke to the others.

According to the witness, the man with dreadlocks alleg-edly asked if they had found the bolt or nut. The overweight man reportedly said 'The jacks [police] must have it'. The man with dreadlocks then allegedly said: 'This will show them we mean business. We bashed him with a bar – you could hardly recognise his face. We bound the fucken cunt. He had it coming. That will teach them a lesson – we don't muck around.'

The conversation continued in this vein and the witness said he heard the dreadlocked man say that they'd dragged their victim around the back. 'The idea had been to make it look like he'd been bashed in the RSL carpark,' Ron says.

The salesman – who'd been working under a car during this disturbing exchange – ended up taking the man with dreadlocks for a test drive in a white Holden Statesman. Inexplicably, he drove to an address in Monahans Road in Cranbourne North.

The salesman said the same dreadlocked man returned a

week later, on Saturday 2 March, and took the car out for three hours. He wrote down his licence details and entered his name in the sign-out book: Peter Samuel Smith. 'And he later identified Peter Smith from a video identification tape,' Ron adds.

Ron was interested to hear that Smith had allegedly discussed the unpublicised bolt, which he now knew had been used to puncture the security van's tyre. 'It had probably been welded onto a square metal plate and had broken off and fallen to the ground,' he says. 'So the man talking about it must have either been at the reception centre when the murder was committed, or known someone who was.'

Ron mounted surveillance on Smith, but did not find any evidence he had been to the address in Monahans Road. The investigators did, however, find a length of blue nylon rope identical to what Slawek was bound with at Smith's house. With the Department of Public Prosecutions satisfied there was a case against him, Smith was arrested in June 2002, and charged with murder.

'There was enough evidence to charge him,' Ron explains. And while he accompanied the police when asked, Smith vehemently denied any involvement in the guard's murder. He said he had only been to the car yard once, on Saturday, 16 March 2002. He had even entered that information in his diary, which Ron noticed was meticulously kept.

Smith's vehemence bugged Ron. In his experience, murderers often 'go quietly' and fight the charge later in court. But Smith was outraged, unlike anyone he'd ever charged before. *Was it possible he really was innocent?* Ron wondered. 'When you tell someone they are charged with murder and they have done it, it is not new information,' Ron says. 'If they have not done it, there is a massive reaction.'

He knew he had to dig deeper.

*

During the committal hearing, Ron grew increasingly uneasy, especially when Smith was ordered to stand trial for murder. 'My emotions were mixed,' Ron says. 'If he stood trial and was convicted of something he hadn't done, that would weigh on me heavily. It really did play on my mind and after the committal I was mentally exhausted.'

As Ron's mind ticked over, something jumped out at him: he hadn't seen the car salesman's sign-out book himself. He had seen a faxed copy but not the original, so he arranged for the book to be forensically examined. 'After the examination, one of the scientists told me that the dates in the book had been changed,' Ron says. 'He could tell by the handwriting.' The fact was, Peter Smith had only been to the caryard once, on 16 March, just like he'd said.

Yet the alteration of the dates hadn't been a deliberately misleading act. 'The car salesman had somehow put two dates together and it resulted in a misidentification,' Ron explains. He says the salesman was an honest family man with no criminal history, yet his evidence about the sign-out book had proved unreliable. 'We shouldn't run this,' Ron said to the Director of Public Prosecutions, Paul Coghlan, QC. 'I don't reckon he's done it.'

Ron found other evidence to support his belief that the accused man was innocent. Among his discoveries, he learnt the rope found at Smith's house was *not* the rope used to tie up Slawek Tomczyk. 'I had it forensically tested,' Ron says. 'I'm glad I did that.'

As a result of Ron's digging, Smith was exonerated and set free after eleven months on remand. No one has ever been caught for Slawek's murder, but Ron could give an innocent man back his life. 'I couldn't let it go to trial and say, "This is just a matter for the jury",' he says. 'There would be some who would let it go to court and say, "If he beats it he beats it, let it run its course". But for me it was about being true to myself. If you've got strong values, why wouldn't you do something? I had to fix what was wrong, even though it wasn't my fault.'

*

In 2007 Ron told an inquest into the murder of Slawomir Tomczyk that he believed the car salesman had indeed over-heard the conversation between the men in the car yard but he had wrongly identified Smith as one of the people involved. Smith had taken a car for a test drive, but it was on the date in his own diary, not on the day the men had allegedly spoken of murder. 'I was able to show that the first time Peter Smith went to the car yard was way after the murder,' says Ron.

For a few moments during the inquest, knowing how close Smith had come to a lengthy jail term, Ron struggled to control his emotions. 'I couldn't hold myself together,' he admits. Coroner Peter White – who later commended Ron on his integrity and for acting 'in the best traditions of the force' – adjourned proceedings for five minutes while the detective regained his composure.

'The lesson is to never underestimate the power of a gut feeling,' Ron says. 'And my gut feeling told me, *He didn't do it*. Even though I'd charged him, I was able to turn around and prove it wasn't him. It was a massive relief.'

Outside the court, Smith said that despite being 'a bit bitter' about being wrongly imprisoned, 'I've got a hell of a lot of respect for Ron. He's done more than he could possibly do'.

20

MURDER AT THE MALL

*'If you do not get out and talk to people
you will never solve a crime.
Crimes are not solved sitting at your desk.'*
– Ron Iddles

I t wasn't just night patrol guards who had to watch their backs.

In the early to mid-2000s, there was a spate of terrifying hold-ups on armed vans owned by Armaguard, Brambles and Chubb. The hold-ups were highly planned and, during one, a security guard was shot in the stomach, but survived.

Chubb guard Erwin Kastenberger was not so lucky. He knew his job was dangerous but never expected to die. A conscientious worker who had migrated to Australia from Germany after being orphaned as a child, Kastenberger was a gentle and loving husband, father and brother, looking forward to the birth of his first grandchild.

On Tuesday, 8 March 2005, Kastenberger and another guard, Bob Crowe, were making a lunchtime delivery to the Commonwealth Bank at the bustling North Blackburn shopping centre in Melbourne's east. As stunned retailers and shoppers watched, they were ambushed by two bandits in ski-masks and fluorescent tops. Ordered to get on the ground, Kastenberger did as he was told and promptly surrendered the bag of cash containing $162,000.

Police say that's usually when an armed hold-up ends and the robbers flee with the money. This time, however, as fifty-eight-year-old Kastenberger huddled silently on the ground, making no attempting to pull out his gun, the taller of the bandits, clad in an orange vest, shot him in the shoulder. The bullet shattered Erwin's vital organs and the grandfather-to-be toppled over.

As the bandits took off with the cash, Erwin Kastenberger took his dying breaths.

*

When Ron was first alerted to the murder, he was giving evidence in a Geelong court, so he asked another of the Homicide Squad's crew leaders, Detective Senior Sergeant Jeff Maher, to accompany his crew to the crime scene. When Ron arrived at the shopping mall, which police had temporarily closed, he examined Kastenberger's body in situ, and viewed the shopping centre's surveillance footage. 'It showed Erwin basically on the ground, and then the suspect bent over and shot him,' Ron says.

He and the other investigators picked laboriously over the crime scene for clues and continued to speak to traumatised witnesses, including some school children. Meanwhile, Kastenberger's body was taken to the Coroner's Court.

Ron asked one of the shopping centre's cleaners if they could wash the guard's blood from the ground, but they said no. 'In the end, I went to the cleaner's room, got some disinfectant, a bucket and a mop, and cleaned it up myself. I thought, *I can have it done in twenty minutes and the shopping centre can reopen*,' he recalls. There was no point waiting for crime-scene cleaners because no one could decide who should foot the bill. It was a ghastly job. 'It hits home when you're mopping up a fellow human being's blood and you know it's happened right there,' he says.

Back at police headquarters, Ron met with detectives from the Armed Robbery Squad. Ron knew there had been a series of armed van robberies around Melbourne, which suggested a professional gang was at large. The Armed Robbery boys identified two men they suspected over similar heists.

'I said, "We're going to grab your suspects",' Ron recalls. The Armed Robbery detectives said they didn't want Homicide to arrest them, but Ron put his size thirteen foot down. 'I said, "No, that's not how we work".' He explains, 'It was about getting to them early, getting a commitment as to where they had been, to lock them into a story.'

The following morning, Ron and another detective arrested the suspects. 'But within about half an hour we'd eliminated them both because they were alibied,' he says. He asked the Armed Robbery Squad if they could nominate anyone else. They offered him a larger list of possible offenders. 'They came up with about twenty-two armed robbers and some were higher on the list than others,' Ron says. 'I said to my crew, "Within seven days, we need to have spoken to everyone on that list. If we haven't done it within that time, it will make things difficult, because people won't be able to remember what they did on that day".'

So the team split up and tracked down all the armed robbery merchants on the list. They were surprisingly cooperative. 'Some of those who had priors for armed robbery were more than happy to have a conversation,' Ron says. 'Some of them said to me, "Ron, I might do armed robberies but I don't kill anyone. This is a big shame on the profession".' Ron knew they were being honest. 'It's like a job to them,' he explains. 'Some of them take pride in what they do. They would not kill someone.'

Among those on the list were three men suspected of being part of a professional gang – Jerry Murphy,[*] Mark Dickson and a fifty-two-year-old named Hugo Rich, who had committed a series of armed robberies. Ron says Rich – who, curiously, had also worked as a stockbroker and a successful insurance salesman – was quite the snappy dresser. 'He did several armed robberies dressed in an overcoat,' he says, adding that he was born Olaf Dietrich in Germany but changed his name to Hugo Rich 'because he loved Hugo Boss suits and wanted to be rich'.

Next, Ron scrutinised every phone call that had hit the mobile-phone tower near the shopping centre around the time of Kastenberger's murder. 'Then we interviewed everyone to ask them why they were using their phones near the shopping centre,' he says. The detectives also managed to track down Mark Dickson – who shared a flat with Jerry Murphy – and asked where he was when the crime was committed. 'He said he and Jerry Murphy hired a car and went to Ballarat for the day and got back at around 4.30. Jerry then decided to go interstate to see his mum.'

[*]Name changed

The detectives asked Dickson to get his flatmate to call them when he returned to Melbourne. A day or so later, Murphy turned up at police headquarters. 'He said he had nothing to say and exercised his right,' Ron recalls.

They caught up with Hugo Rich, too. 'He said he was at work in Little Bourke Street all day,' Ron says. 'He claimed to work for a solicitor.'

In the meantime, Ron sent detectives to Ballarat to look for video footage of Murphy and Dickson that might corroborate their story. On 8 March, the cake shop's surveillance camera had captured images of Dickson, always on his own, but not Murphy. 'It shows Mark coming out and walking up a mall section in Ballarat,' Ron says. 'There is also other footage of Mark Dickson in a phone box in the mall around 12.30 that day. Other footage shows him back in the phone box around one o'clock.'

Ron was curious to know who Dickson had been calling from the phone box. 'He tried three times and on all occasions he rang two different mobile numbers,' Ron says. 'We discovered those mobile numbers were hitting the mobile-phone tower at the shopping centre.' It suggested to Ron that Dickson was phoning other gang members who were involved in the heist.

Ron's theory was confirmed when he and his team identified that the phones Dickson had been ringing were purchased from a small phone shop in the Melbourne CBD. 'We went there and the shopkeeper identified Murphy from a photo board as having purchased those two phones in false names,' Ron says. 'By now I was fairly confident Murphy was involved, confident that Dickson was providing an alibi for

Murphy and, more than likely, Hugo Rich had something to do with it because he was part of that crew.'

When Ron's team spoke to a man named Brett James, who worked for Rich on a casual basis and was on parole for armed robbery, he said Rich had not been at work at the time in question. 'He was pretty sure Hugo was involved in armed robberies and said the week before he indicated he was going to do a job which was going to be a dry run,' Ron says. 'And when we established his movements for 1 March, we were able to put him at North Blackburn.'

Brett James also told the police that a few days after the murder and armed robbery, Rich, aware that James had a knack for electronics, wanted him to produce a DVD that showed him and Rich in the office. 'He said Hugo was going to have a solicitor walk in [and appear on the footage], and have Brett stamp it to say 8 March at 12.40,' Ron says. Ultimately, Rich's workmate did not produce the falsified disc.

Meanwhile, Rich maintained he'd been at work that day and explained that at around 12.40 a solicitor came in and gave him some papers, which proved he hadn't been out of the office. 'So I went and saw the solicitor and we had a fairly robust discussion,' Ron says. 'Another team member took a statement from him in which he said he gave the documents to Hugo Rich around 12.40, then saw him again a couple of hours later,' Ron says. 'But at that time Hugo Rich was hiring a car in Werribee, which cast doubt on the solicitor's statement.

'I went and saw the solicitor and said, "I don't put any credit in that statement. You can't have seen Hugo Rich at that time because he was hiring a car. You might want to consider your position". By that time, he had the shakes.' A couple of hours later, '[The solicitor] came in and gave a statement to say he hadn't seen him and that Hugo Rich had basically prepared his statement for him,' Ron says, believing the solicitor had felt intimidated. 'So by now I'd confirmed that Hugo Rich, Mark Dickson and Jerry Murphy had been involved, and that Mark Dickson had provided an alibi.'

By intercepting the two new phones Murphy had purchased, the police discovered the gang was planning another armed robbery. Knowing the last job had escalated to murder, Ron urgently ramped up the investigation – he wasn't going to let another innocent person die.

'We then identified another bloke called Sean Hogan,' Ron says. 'He'd never been in trouble before. Then we identified his cousin, Chris Cullino, who'd never been in trouble before either.' In the meantime, Ron was running intense surveillance on Dickson. 'It got to the point, a few months after Erwin Kastenberger's murder, that we knew they were going to do an armed robbery in Dandenong,' Ron says.

On the day of the planned hold-up, the entire Homicide Squad was on edge. Ron, sleeves rolled up in his trademark style, led a forty-five-man operation from headquarters, where listening devices allowed him to eavesdrop on everything the robbers said inside their van. Aware the job was going down at Dandenong Plaza, it was up to Ron to 'call it' – in other words, decide when to send in armed officers to arrest the bandits.

'Then we heard someone in the van say something like, "Oh shit, the A-Team's here",' Ron remembers. That told him an Armaguard van was present: in armed robbers' parlance, 'A' stood for Armaguard, 'B' for Brambles and 'C' for Chubb. Yet even though the robbers had been looking for a Chubb

273

vehicle, Ron feared they might take the opportunity to hold up the Armaguard van instead. Ron urgently called Armaguard. 'I said, "Under no circumstances are your guards to get out of the vehicle because we reckon something's going to go down".'

Ron instructed the police at the scene to keep out of the armed robbers' sight. 'If we intercepted them at that stage, we might have been able to get them for a stolen car, say, or having a handgun, but we couldn't yet prove conspiracy to commit an armed robbery,' he explains. 'A situation like this is very tense. If you make the wrong call, if you let it go on for too long, they could do the armed robbery and someone could die.'

The would-be robbers left the scene, 'possibly because they were looking for the C-Team,' Ron posits. 'They went to the Bunnings carpark where they put on overalls, gloves, pulled their caps down, then headed back to Dandenong Plaza.'

It was do or die. 'I was convinced the job was on and said to pull them over,' Ron says. In a flash, Homicide and Armed Robbery detectives swooped, arresting the occupants of the van – Dickson and Hogan. 'Then someone said to a member of the surveillance team, "There's been a bloke sitting where the armed van should have come in",' Ron remembers. 'I realised he'd probably been waiting for the armed van and was the person known as The Eyes. He'd be the one who'd call and say, "The van's coming in". They arrested him too – that was Chris Cullino.'

Murphy, however, was not there. 'He was in the Supreme Court listening to the trial of Mick Gatto over the murder of Benji Veniamin,' Ron says, adding he did not believe Murphy knew either Gatto or Veniamin. It did not surprise Ron that Murphy was absent, because he'd worked out that not every member of the gang was present at every job, and that they generally recruited others to take part. He says each job 'belonged' to someone and that members of the gang used documentary evidence to prove they were elsewhere. On this occasion, Murphy had signed into the courthouse – proof he was not at Dandenong Plaza. Rich wasn't there either; he was serving time in jail for deception.

Hogan was relieved to be arrested. 'He said, "Thank God you've got me. I didn't want to do this",' Ron recalls. 'He also said something like, "I hope you blokes have had a listening device in my house or garage because I've been saying, 'Come and get me. Help me out of this position'".' Hogan could not have made it clearer that he hadn't wanted to be involved: 'He made full admissions and said he was also involved in the North Blackburn job,' Ron says. 'He was approached by Mark Dickson.'

Hogan told Ron that during the North Blackburn hold-up he was sitting outside the Commonwealth Bank in one van while Murphy and Rich were in another, at the back of the shopping centre. 'As soon as he saw the Chubb van come in, it was his job to make a call to Jerry to say, "Job's on",' Ron says.

Hogan didn't see what happened next but he did hear it because he and Murphy had kept the phone line open. 'He heard a bang,' Ron says. 'He took off in his van.'

Later that day, Hogan drove the van to Montmorency in Melbourne's north-east. 'He left it parked on the side of the road and put the phone down a drain,' Ron says. 'Then somehow he heard on the news that a security guard had been shot dead and thought, *Shit*. He caught up with Hugo and Jerry later that night and he and Jerry went and burnt the vans out.'

Eventually, Hogan returned home. 'He got $20,000 out of it but he just felt sick,' Ron says. 'Then he said Mark wanted him to do another job, the Dandenong Plaza job. But last time someone had died and he didn't want to be involved,' Ron explains, adding that Hogan was prepared to plead guilty and give evidence against Rich, Murphy and Dickson. 'Chris Cullino also made admissions about Dandenong,' he adds.

Murphy, however, was nowhere to be found. 'We did a lot of publicity about the fact I was looking for him and had a warrant for his arrest,' Ron says.

Murphy must have seen the news because soon after, around one in the morning, he phoned Ron. 'He said, "It's Jerry. I want to give myself up".' It was good news, just at a strange time of the day. 'He said, "You're following me". I said, "Jerry, I'm here in bed",' Ron recalls, acknowledging that no one really believes he sleeps. Jerry told him he wanted to go and see his girlfriend before handing himself in. Ron considered the request and said yes when Murphy gave him an undertaking he'd be at police headquarters at four o'clock. Not all police would be so trusting but Ron's gut feeling told him Murphy would stick to his word. The following afternoon, Murphy turned up at St Kilda Road as promised, where Ron and other detectives interviewed him over the murder and armed hold-up at North Blackburn. To Ron's surprise Murphy stayed staunch and told the investigators he had nothing to say.

'Afterwards I said, "Consider the possibility, Jerry, that if you go down for this you'll do twenty-five years for murder",' Ron recalls. He said he believed Rich had shot Kastenberger. 'I said, "You didn't pull the trigger. You might get ten years off". But he said he wasn't doing anything.'

After an intensive investigation, Ron ultimately charged Murphy, Dickson and Rich. 'I also charged Sean Hogan and Chris Cullino, who pleaded guilty to armed robbery, and were prepared to give evidence against the other three,' Ron says. 'We probably had about a hundred witnesses, all sorts of different people,' Ron says. 'They were committed for trial.'

Ron then received a call from a solicitor who said Murphy wanted to talk to him. 'He said he'd plead guilty to armed robberies and would give evidence,' Ron says. He spent about a week taking a detailed statement from him. 'He said it was the hardest decision he'd ever made, going from the dark side to the light side,' Ron says. 'He said he was going to be considered a dog but he wasn't going down for something he didn't do. Then Mark Dickson came along and I took a statement from him too. Both pleaded guilty to charges of armed robbery and conspiracy to commit armed robbery, which left Hugo Rich standing on his own.'

'I had a lot to do with Jerry Murphy, leading up to the trial,' Ron reflects. 'He had a brilliant mind, analytical. He became a brilliant witness. And he told the court that Hugo Rich had fired the fatal shot.' Ron says life is now very different for Murphy, who served his minimum six years in jail. 'He has totally turned his life around. He is a success story.'

*

The trial of Hugo Rich lasted almost five months and, in June 2009, a jury found him guilty of the murder of Erwin Kastenberger as well as one count of armed robbery. In sentencing Rich the following November, Justice Lex Lasry said, 'I am [equally] satisfied that you deliberately and cold bloodedly shot Mr Kastenberger . . . The unknown factor is why you did that . . . Both guards were armed but neither made any attempt to use their firearm to defend themselves or the money being carried.'

Turning to the victim impact statements, the judge said, 'Each of these victim impact statements highlights the phenomenal tragedy which was the murder of Erwin Kastenberger. Not only was his life extinguished but the lives of a number of people, including those close to him, have been forever affected. Each member of the family has described the extreme emotional and psychological effects of this tragedy. These statements also demonstrate that the time between 8 March 2005 and the present has been very difficult and the continuing legal process which has occurred during that time has, itself, been extremely difficult . . . Nothing that the Court can say in these proceedings can possibly assuage the loss and grief that this family obviously continue to feel.'

Justice Lasry sentenced Rich to life in prison for murder, and twenty years for armed robbery. He directed Rich to serve a minimum of thirty years without parole. Rich, however, considered by many to be 'the best bush lawyer in jail', appealed the decision. By 2014, aged sixty-one, he exhausted his appeals and continues to serve his life sentence.

'You could say that Erwin Kastenberger's family are serving a life sentence too,' Ron remarks. 'Their lives have never been the same since he was killed in the line of duty.'

21

DOUBLE MURDER AT SAND BAR NUMBER TWO

'You have to be prepared to lead your staff
even if it means stripping down to your jocks
to retrieve a body from the river.'
– Ron Iddles

What does a murderer look like? Ron learnt early in his career at Homicide that wherever there are humans, there are disagreements, grudges, jealousies and murder and neither geography nor any amount of fresh country air can change that.

'Sometimes the motive for murder is revenge, sometimes it is lust, sometimes it is broken relationships, sometimes it's over finances,' Ron says. 'But sometimes you can look deeply for a motive and it can be obscure or minor.' He harks back to the Christmas Day murders where everyday people slaughtered family members because they didn't like their presents. 'I've even investigated a murder that took place after an argument over the music being played on the CD,' he adds, shaking his head.

Once there was a time when people thought it was safe to live in the bush. But by the mid-2000s, crystal methamphetamine, or ice, had found its way to Australia. A decade later, its use had spread like a festering sore to the farthest reaches of the country, leaving people from Ballarat to Breadalbane looking sideways at their neighbours to see if they were sporting ice scabs.

But even before everyday Australians started breaking bad on methamphetamine, there was trouble in country towns, just like anywhere else. However, when those squabbles turn to murder, the ramifications run deeper in smaller regional towns than in larger cities.

On Sunday, 9 February 2003, the townsfolk of Shepparton in north-eastern Victoria learnt a canoeist paddling up the Goulburn River had found a man's battered naked body submerged in the water. By the time Ron and his crew arrived at Kialla, five minutes out of Shepparton, the lifeless man had been fished out of the water and was lying on the riverbank. Even though his identity was unknown, a seasoned homicide cop like Ron knew that dead men tell tales: 'He was of Caucasian appearance, in his late fifties to early sixties, and he appeared to have some type of head injury,' Ron says. 'It's often unclear, though, when a body has been in water, because they can sometimes have marks which look like they were homicide victims, when in fact the marks might have been the result of fish or yabbies eating the flesh.'

But yabbies didn't do this. Once the man's body was taken to the Coroner's Court in Melbourne for a post-mortem, the pathologist confirmed that Ron was investigating a murder.

'The man had died of blunt trauma to the head,' Ron says. 'He had a fractured skull caused by a piece of pipe, or similar.'

Solving a murder is generally impossible when you don't know the victim's name, so Ron held a media conference by the riverbank in the hope that someone who'd been camping or fishing there could identify the man. 'The other hope was that they might be able to tell us if they'd seen anything suspicious,' he adds.

As the media conference drew to a close, a journalist peering past Ron's shoulder and into the river, piped up. 'That looks like another body!' Ron turned around to look at the protuberance jutting out of the water and reassured the young reporter it was just a cow carcass. Satisfied, the journalists each recorded their pieces-to-camera along the riverbank, then headed off to file their reports.

Ron turned to his team of detectives. 'I think it is a body,' he admitted. He had suspected it from the moment he saw it, but hadn't wanted to startle the reporters. It was just as well, because Ron stripped off his shirt, tie, trousers and socks and said to his crew, 'Guess what? I'm going in.'

He knew that most detectives wouldn't be inclined to paddle out to a cadaver, but Ron wasn't most detectives. 'If you thought about everything you did as a policeman, you wouldn't survive,' he explains. 'It mightn't have followed all the protocols but it was about getting the job done.'

No one was going to stop him – he was the boss. But no one was going to join him either. 'One of the reasons I swam out is because there was a current and I didn't want it to take the body away,' he says. 'The other is that it would have taken quite a long time before we could get a police boat out there.'

Also, he had to know for sure that the body was human, not bovine. It turned out that he and the TV reporter were right – it was indeed another dead man, this time with no visible injuries.

With the likelihood that he was now investigating a double murder, Ron had to get both men identified, quickly. *Perhaps*, Ron thought, *if I can find out the identity of the second man, it will lead me to the identity of the first.* He made a snap decision, even though he knew it was unorthodox. 'We had a camera in the car,' he says, 'so I took a photo of the second man's face and, without consultation, decided I would release it on the six o'clock news in the media.' He was certain someone would recognise the man and call police straightaway. 'Again, it's about going with your gut instinct.'

At two minutes past six, Ron received a call from the boss, Detective Inspector Chris Enright, who had watched the news and asked Ron if he thought an artist's sketch of the man's face might have been more appropriate. 'In hindsight, maybe it was a mistake,' Ron concedes, 'because I think if you deal with death as a homicide investigator it isn't offensive. You forget there are a lot of people in the community who haven't seen a dead person, so they might well be confronted by an image on the news.'

Especially in a close-knit community like Shepparton, where locals might know the dead man. But it yielded a result, just as Ron had hoped. 'By 6.05 I had at least five phone calls identifying the man I'd pulled out of the river as Allen Raymond Thomas,' he says. The callers also revealed where the forty-six-year-old had lived. 'We went to that address, not really knowing what we'd find,' Ron remembers. 'There was evidence of some sort of disturbance in the kitchen and lounge room, but no one was home.'

The detectives doorknocked the neighbours' houses to see if they could shed any light on the matter. 'We established that two men were living there and from the description we gave, we established the identity of the second person in the river as sixty-year-old John Gordon MacKay.'

The dead men were housemates.

Thanks, in part, to the country-town grapevine, Ron quickly found a suspect – Daniel John Nuttal – a twenty-five-year-old from Shepparton who was acquainted with the older men. When Ron took him in for questioning two days after the bodies were found, it looked like he'd have a quick result. 'He made full admissions,' Ron says. 'He even did a re-enactment for us.'

Nuttal told them another man had been involved – thirty-two-year-old Jason Paul Guthrie, also from Shepparton. He and Daniel used to drink with Thomas and MacKay. At first, the police couldn't find him. 'I'd been back in Melbourne for a couple of days when I received a phone call to say he was at a farming property about thirty kilometres outside Shepparton, so I arranged for the Shepparton detectives to go and arrest him,' Ron recalls. Once the arrest had been made, Ron drove back to Shepparton to interview him. He, too, made admissions.

With both Nuttal and Guthrie charged with murder, Ron returned to Melbourne to prepare the brief.

*

Nuttal and Guthrie's night had begun with several alcoholic drinks and later a drive to Allen Thomas and John MacKay's house in Ashenden Street, Shepparton. They forced their way in through the front door, then MacKay was bundled into the back seat of the car and Thomas into the boot.

Nuttal then drove Guthrie to 'Sand Bar Number Two' on the banks of the Goulburn River, during which they discussed killing the men. Guthrie struck MacKay forcibly to the head and body with a metal car lock, inflicting grievous bodily harm. Nuttal maintained that he asked Guthrie to stop and had tried unsuccessfully to pull him away. Nuttal then helped him drag MacKay into the water and held him down until 'the bubbles stopped coming up'.

Nuttal said he'd agreed to help get Thomas out of the car boot as he was afraid Guthrie might hurt him too. In sentencing Nuttal, His Honour Justice Robert Osborn stated: 'Thomas struggled but Guthrie dragged him into the river and held him under the water for a period which you estimate at four to five minutes.'

After all the violence, Nuttal drove Guthrie back to Nuttal's mother's house where the men questioned what they had done. According to Nuttal, Guthrie apologised for involving him. The men then drove to nearby Broken River where they burnt the clothes they were wearing, afraid they might implicate them, before drinking more alcohol.

*

The trial began in November 2004, with the jury finding both Nuttal and Guthrie guilty of two counts of murder. During sentencing, Justice Osborn outlined the circumstances Ron had uncovered while investigating the case. For participating in 'the senseless and horrific destruction of two lives', Justice Osborn sentenced Nuttal to thirty years with a non-parole period of twenty-four years. He said he was not satisfied, on the balance of probabilities, that Nuttal had been coerced into his actions. Justice Osborn sentenced Guthrie to a total effective sentence of thirty-two years, with a non-parole period of twenty-six.

It was alleged in court that during a previous incident Guthrie had been angry with Allen Thomas who had accused him of spending his (Thomas') rent money, while he (Thomas) was in jail. So had a possible grudge led to murder? The judge said this in sentencing Guthrie: 'No sensible explanation for your conduct on the night of the killings was (however) advanced either to investigating police or at your trial other than you were "pretty pissed and off your head" and "just drunk and stupid".'

Regardless of motive, Ron says murder is ultimately about 'man's inhumanity to man'. It's that simple.

'I often get asked what does a murderer look like,' he says. 'I reply, "They look like you or me". But they've made a bad choice.'

THE ANSWER'S IN THE FILE

'This chapter is about my commitment to a dying father whose six-year-old had been raped and murdered. The lesson is the ABC of Homicide: Assume nothing, believe nothing, check everything, and ensure the facts guide you.'
– Ron Iddles

Ron's hard won maxim, 'The answer's in the file', was put to the test when he was appointed head of a new investigative team called the Homicide Cold Case Unit in 1999. It ran for three years and was set up to investigate unsolved historic cases. At the same time, the supercop continued investigating hot jobs as well.

One morning, as he was chipping away at yet another troubling case, the phone rang. At the other end was Denis Clarke, who'd read in a newspaper article that Ron had been put in charge of the new unit. Clarke told Ron that his daughter, Bonnie, had been raped and murdered when she was just six, back in 1982. Ron had heard of the case and found it deeply disturbing. Impressed by Ron's unparalleled clear-up rate, Clarke believed Ron was his last hope. 'I need you to do something about this,' he said to Ron. 'I'm dying of cancer.'

Solving a historic murder is no mean feat; in most cold cases, there was no fresh evidence and leads had dried up. So Ron knew better than to make promises, but he gave Clarke an undertaking he would look into it. He immediately started digging into the file with a brand new Homicide Squad investigator, Detective Senior Constable Tim Day. Ron and Day familiarised themselves with every detail of the murder, which had happened in the northern Melbourne suburb of Northcote. Bonnie, a happy, intelligent child, had lived in a house in Westbourne Grove with her mum, Marion Clarke (now Wishart), who was separated from Bonnie's dad. They'd been there for about two years.

Around eleven o'clock on the night of Monday, 20 December 1982, Marion checked on her daughter before going to bed herself. She saw that Bonnie was sleeping soundly with her much-loved poodle-chihuahua cross, Moomsie, dozing at the end of the bed.

The following morning, when she poked her head into Bonnie's room, Marion noticed she was still in bed, and unusually pale. When Marion drew back the covers she was horrified to discover that Bonnie was naked with a hole in her chest and bruising to her neck. There wasn't much blood, though; it looked as though someone had cleaned it up. Frantically, Marion dialled triple zero before running screaming into the street.

*

Around the time Ron and Day started picking the old file to pieces, they arranged for a story to be published in the *Herald Sun*. As a result, a school friend of Bonnie's, Kylie Ward, came forward. Kylie, who was also six at the time of the murder, expressed concerns about a boarder who had lived at the Clarkes' house. 'She used to go there after school and the boarder would look after them,' Ron says. 'He would have Bonnie on his knee and touch her.' Even as a child, Kylie found the boarder's behaviour unsettling, and remembered Bonnie telling her that he had once stood over her bed watching her.

Kylie wasn't the only one who'd found the boarder's behaviour unusual. As the detectives leafed through the old statements, they read that an adult visitor to the house had recalled the boarder saying he 'liked little children'. The boarder had also reportedly used the word 'attracted' when, after a bath, Bonnie had walked naked into the lounge room to dry off in front of the heater. Who was this mystery boarder? Ron and Tim set about trying to identify him.

They didn't ask Marion for the boarder's name because the original investigators had suspected her of murdering her daughter, and she had not yet been eliminated. 'The original investigators thought Marion wanted Bonnie out of her life and suspected the sexual assault was a throw-off, in other words, a secondary crime to make the police look for a male, not female offender,' Ron explains.

'I was questioned at length and accused within the first hour,' Marion recalls, adding that the detectives said she was 'not grieving properly'. The media was quick to get in on the act too, portraying Marion as a potential killer, after which members of the public wrote her vile, threatening letters.

Day soon identified the boarder as Malcolm Joseph Thomas Clarke, unrelated to his victim. Some people knew him as Mal, but others called him Joe. In 1982 the twenty-eight-year-old worked as an assistant film projectionist at three cinemas in the city. On the day of Bonnie's murder, he was on a rostered day off. In the early days of the investigation, police spoke to Clarke but did not consider him a suspect.

Ron and Tim put Malcolm Clarke under the microscope. They discovered that eight months after Bonnie's murder, in August 1983, Clarke had been arrested over the aggravated rape of a neighbour in Brunswick. He had used a knife during the terrifying attack. Not only that, but during the investigation, police found items in Clarke's unit relating to the mutilation killing of a twenty-two-year-old Prahran woman, Theresa Crowe, in June 1980. Clarke was finally found guilty of sexually assaulting the Brunswick woman and also the manslaughter of Theresa Crowe. He served eleven years behind bars and was released in 1994.

The way Ron saw it, the modus operandi in all the crimes, including Bonnie Clarke's murder, was similar. 'The victims had been asphyxiated, stab wounds had been inflicted, and the crime scenes had been cleaned,' he says. Bonnie might have been the only child victim, but there were enough similarities for Ron to strongly suspect the boarder of her murder.

If only the original investigators had seen it that way. Within minutes of finding her daughter dead, Marion realised there was only one person who could have killed her: the boarder, and she told the police so. He was the only person who knew how heavily she slept, and that Moomsie would not bark if he were in the house because she knew him. She also said he would have known she left the back door slightly ajar to let out a second dog, which was not housetrained. The boarder also knew the layout of the house and where she had placed little 'traps' – plants and the like – to alert her if there was an intruder.

So why did the police think Marion had done it? 'The original investigators thought she was an unfit mother because she would have a drink from time to time, or occasionally leave Bonnie with other people in the house,' Ron says. The reality was, Marion was a hardworking student and agency nurse who asked her boarders to watch Bonnie while she was at work, and Bonnie had never told her she was uncomfortable around Clarke. 'If she had have been afraid, she would have told me outright,' Marion insists.

Back then, there was no occasional childcare so even though Marion was doing her best, the police did not see it that way. 'Single mothers were not well looked upon,' she remarks. 'It was not as if I was on government handouts – I was working, and hard. I was working towards our future.'

Not surprisingly, when Tim Day first went to speak to Marion she was wary. Then he said he thought the early investigation had been botched. It was enough to make Marion break down in tears, grateful that, after all these years, there was finally some hope. She subsequently agreed to a polygraph test, which she passed with flying colours. 'By this time we were totally satisfied that she hadn't done it,' Ron says. He turned his attention more closely to Malcolm Clarke.

Ron and Day found out that Clarke was working as a nurse and also as a guard on the famous Dandenong Ranges steam train, Puffing Billy. Ron put in place a covert operation, arranging for an undercover operative calling himself 'Terry' to buddy up with Clarke. 'Terry offered Malcolm Clarke a lift home one day and after that they saw each other two or three times a week,' he says.

Meanwhile, Ron and Denis Clarke talked on the phone regularly. Ron was not at liberty to tell the dying father much about the investigation, but he did encourage him to keep the faith. 'As time went on I told him I was confident we could solve it but it created pressure which I did not need,' Ron admits. 'I think when you put yourself under that much pressure you have to be conscious you do not make a mistake or try too hard to get a confession. It always has to be about finding the truth of the matter.'

Despite the mounting pressure, Ron kept the investigation on track, and a few months into the covert operation, he arranged for Terry to take Clarke to meet another undercover operative calling himself Mark. That was when Clarke finally came undone, confessing in a covertly recorded conversation to having harmed Bonnie Clarke. 'I played with Bonnie,' Clarke told the undercover officer. 'I think she wanted to go scream or something and I covered her head. And I probably had a knife with me, I don't know. I was that fuckin' drunk.'

Clarke explained how he had entered through the unlocked back door before going into Bonnie's room where he had 'fingered' her. He said that when she had tried to scream he covered her head with a pillow. He stabbed Bonnie in the chest with a knife and panicked. He then pulled out the knife and left, having pulled up the little girl's pyjama bottoms and the bedsheet.

Ron and Tim arrested Clarke for Bonnie's murder just over an hour later. It was June 2002, some two-and-a-half years since Ron first agreed to look into the case for Bonnie's dad, and almost twenty years since Bonnie's mum was wrongly accused of murder.

*

During the video-recorded interview, Clarke recounted the whole, terrible story. 'To interview him with Tim Day was fascinating,' Ron says. 'Clarke was a quiet man, sometimes tearful. I'm not sure if it was because he'd been caught or the fact he felt sorry for himself. He said he'd confessed to the undercover officer because he liked him. That being said, he went on to plead not guilty.'

A Supreme Court jury found him guilty of Bonnie Clarke's murder and in December 2004, Clarke was sentenced to life in prison, with a twenty-five-year non-parole period. 'He then appealed to the Supreme Court in Melbourne, and eventually to the High Court of Australia,' Ron says. 'The issue was around the methodology used in employing an undercover operative, and the allegation he had made a false confession. In the end we won both arguments and his original conviction and sentence stood.'

It was an extraordinary result and, at the time, the oldest homicide Victoria Police had solved. It was also a relief, and while it wouldn't bring Bonnie back or take away the bitter memories of having been a murder suspect, Marion later remarked, 'My dark period is coming to an end. It's not as hard as it used to be.'

Getting justice for Bonnie, Ron acknowledges, was one of the highlights of his career. 'To vindicate an innocent woman was massively satisfying,' he says, his voice cracking with emotion. 'And to grant a dying man's wish . . . that's something I'll never forget.'

Denis Clarke – who ultimately saw a man found guilty of his daughter's murder – passed away a short time later.

23

PETER RULE'S TERRIBLE END

*'Leonard Borg committed this crime out of greed
so his drug business would not be put in jeopardy.
What he did to Peter Rule as a fellow human being
is difficult for me to comprehend.'*
– Ron Iddles

Peter Rule wasn't an angel, but no one could accuse him of being a bad dad. Separated from his wife, Rule wished he could have his son with him all the time, but he made do with access visits, picking up his boy Darcy from Southern Cross railway station every alternate weekend and during school holidays. Both father and son were mechanically minded, and would spend hours tinkering with Peter's car on access visits, happy amid the grease and spare parts.

In November 2009, Peter Rule went missing. It was out of character because he hadn't told Darcy he was going away. He'd also left behind his dog, which was peculiar as they went everywhere together. When local police determined Rule's disappearance was suspicious, they called on the Homicide Squad to find out what had happened to the single dad.

As soon as Ron spoke to Rule's family, there was no doubt in his mind that the fifty-six-year-old had been murdered. Before he disappeared, Rule lived alone in a public housing unit in the Melbourne suburb of Meadow Heights. He and his ex-wife, Judy Rule, shared custody of eleven-year-old Darcy. Every night without fail, Rule would ring Darcy to wish him goodnight. Bill Rule, one of his brothers, says he loved his son so much he used to think up fanciful ways of seeing him more often. Rule first shared his love of mechanics with Darcy when he was very young. 'Peter taught him to drive when he was probably about seven,' Bill recalls. 'Darcy is car mad and Peter was a car nut!'

Rule had something of a colourful past, however, but nowhere near as colourful as he liked to make out. 'We established that Peter was a guy that talked the talk; he always wanted to give the appearance of being tough, and inferred to people that he wanted to be a gangster, but he was pretty much the opposite,' Ron says. 'He did some debt collecting and repossessing of cars but relied predominantly on a disability pension.'

Rule – who was diagnosed with Attention Deficit Disorder just before he turned fifty – grew up in the rough Melbourne suburb of Glenroy in the 1950s and 1960s. When Rule was ten his mother died of an aneurysm, so his thirteen-year-old sister left school to look after her eight younger siblings while their father went to work. With no parental guidance, the young children did as they pleased, and some of the boys took to stealing other people's belongings – bicycles and the like. It was a habit they all outgrew, except for Rule who, as an adult, was convicted of minor dishonesty and drug offences. Yet his misdemeanours did not detract from the fact that he was a loving dad and brother, someone his family could always count on. 'He wasn't a bad person by any means,' Bill says.

Ron explains the circumstances surrounding his mysterious disappearance. 'One Sunday Peter told his son that late that night he was going to meet someone who was going to show him an old motorbike,' he says. 'I think maybe it was meant to be a BSA [Birmingham Small Arms Company] bike from the 1950s.' Peter would have been excited to see the vintage model because he loved motorbikes as much as cars.

Two days later, on Tuesday, 17 November 2009, one of his neighbours reported him missing after noticing the light on in his unit, and realising his much loved dog, Bella, was inside. Rule hadn't called Darcy either, which was so unusual that his brother Joe also alerted the police, who went to Rule's unit to look around. 'His car was there and the door was closed but unlocked,' Ron says. 'It was odd because inside was his mobile phone, his wallet and his dog.'

By Sunday, 29 November, with no sign of Rule, the Homicide Squad took over the case. It was up to Ron and his crew, including another talented investigator, Detective Senior Constable Paul Rowe, to find out what had happened to the missing dad. 'The local police had made some inquiries but they hadn't taken any statements,' Ron recalls. 'So we decided to conduct a doorknock.'

One of Rule's neighbours recalled seeing something unusual. 'A dark-coloured four-wheel-drive had stopped and pulled up out the front,' Ron says. 'The neighbour saw a man go to Peter's front door but didn't know who it was. A short time later the black four-wheel-drive left.'

Who was the man in the four-wheel-drive? Ron wondered. And did he have anything to do with Peter's disappearance?

Ron looked at the timeline on his whiteboard to consider Rule's movements before his disappearance. 'We knew on the Sunday night he'd dropped his son off at Southern Cross railway station, and spoken to his brother Joe at about 8.35,' he says. 'The other thing we knew was that he'd indicated he was going to meet someone.' *But who?*

Ron held a media conference and released Rule's photo in the hope that someone might come forward with information. 'No one had seen him, but we thought it might relate to the fact that he'd dobbed someone in for armed robbery,' he says. 'That person was in jail, but we eliminated him.'

Hoping Rule's worried siblings could shed some light on his disappearance, Ron drove to the country to see them. 'After speaking with them, I was confident Peter had met with foul play,' he says. 'He just wasn't the sort of person who wouldn't contact his son.'

Ron and his team also spoke to some of Rule's associates in the car-repossession business. 'We found out he was to meet someone called Potato Head,' Ron says. Ron wanted to know Potato Head's real name and eventually found out through a man at a car yard. 'Paul Rowe said, "I think Potato Head is a guy called Leonard Borg".'

Ron and Rowe discovered that Leonard Borg was twenty-five and lived in Melbourne's northern suburbs. 'We also found out that on 12 November – only a week after Peter had gone missing – Leonard Borg had gone to Malta,' Ron says. It was a planned trip, not a spur-of-the moment decision. 'We found that out from his mum,' Ron says, adding that the detectives asked if she could arrange for her son to call them upon his return. 'He did, and we took a statement. He admitted he knew Peter Rule.'

As it happened, the men were friends. Borg told the police that on the Sunday night in question he was working in Campbellfield at a factory owned by Corey Small. 'Leonard Borg was a boilermaker and had been doing some welding work there,' Ron explains. 'He said he could get some timesheets to verify he'd worked late that night.' By and large, that put Borg – who provided the timesheet as promised – out of the picture. 'And the investigation came to a bit of a standstill.'

But things changed suddenly on Tuesday, 6 April 2010, when nineteen-year-old welding apprentice, Michael Spiropoulos, walked into a police station in the early hours of the morning. 'He wanted to see the Homicide Squad,' Ron says. 'I arranged for Paul Rowe and another detective, Sally Leach, to go to the police station and see him.'

A short while later, Rowe called Ron back. 'He said that Michael's come in because he can't live with what he knows. He says Leonard Borg killed Peter, but he was involved in the disposal of the body and he wants to assist and help the police.' Ron advised Rowe to formally interview and caution Spiropoulos, but also to arrange for the young man to get some legal advice.

After receiving the necessary advice, Spiropoulos – who had met Borg through work – gave the detectives a detailed account. 'He said that on the Sunday night he received a phone call from Lenny, who asked him to buy him some bleach, then go over to a factory where they'd been doing some welding in Campbellfield. So Michael went to Safeway, bought ten bottles of bleach, some garbage bags and rags, then drove to the factory, where they had a conversation,' Ron says. 'Leonard told him Peter was dead and in fact he was still lying on the floor of the factory.'

Spiropoulos said Borg asked him to wait in the office. He then heard a forklift moving, followed by the sound of the boot of Borg's Volvo being closed, and assumed Borg had used the forklift to move the body before putting it in his car. The older man asked Spiropoulos to help him scrub the walls and floor of the factory with bleach. Spiropoulos did as he was asked.

A short time later, Spiropoulos noticed blood spatter around the entrance to the female toilet cubicle. 'Borg told Michael he'd shot Peter ten times with a .22 semi-automatic rifle,' Ron says. 'He told him he'd picked Peter up from home, they'd had dinner, and after driving around for a while, he'd taken Peter back to the factory. He said he'd shot Peter as he stood near the toilets. Lenny and Michael then found nine spent shells, which Lenny crushed with a hammer, wrapped in toilet paper and flushed down the toilet, but they couldn't find one.'

Once the factory looked spotless, the men put everything they'd used to clean it into Borg's Volvo. They then headed to a factory in Thomastown. Borg had leased the premises to cultivate cannabis, with Spiropoulos' help. 'He'd convinced Michael to borrow $35,000 to help fund it,' Ron says.

After that, Ron says, the pair drove to a service station where they bought firewood and filled a fifteen-litre jerry can with petrol. Borg returned to the Thomastown factory, where he had a bed, while Spiropoulos went home for the rest of the night.

'The following day, Michael came back to the factory, where Leonard was burning the body in a forty-four-gallon drum,' Ron says. 'There was black smoke everywhere and Michael said the smell was shocking.' The younger welder noticed that, around the bottom of the barrel, Borg had spread coco soil – used in the cultivation of the cannabis – as the barrel had begun to leak. Over the next few days the two men visited Bunnings to purchase various items including citronella oil to remove the smell, a hatchet and hydrochloric acid. 'They also bought a shovel, which was used by Leonard to keep poking the body down,' Ron says. 'He also dismembered the body with an electric chainsaw and the hatchet.'

Borg then emptied the barrel's contents onto the factory floor. 'He got a hammer and smashed the bones,' says Ron. 'Leonard had a view it would go to a powder.' Borg put what remained into a black plastic tub and poured hydrochloric acid over it. After placing the black tub into the boot of Spiropoulos's car, they loaded the coco soil into the garbage bags and put them on the back seat.

Spiropoulos told the police they drove to the Great Ocean Road, stopping about three kilometres from Anglesea. 'They went down a track near the beach and tipped out the garbage bags containing what was left of the body, after it had been burnt, cut, and put in acid,' Ron says. They then went to a beach about five kilometres east of Lorne, where Borg tipped the black tub into the ocean.

Not surprisingly, drops of acid from the tub had burnt holes in their clothes. 'So as they drove to Lorne they bought matching shorts and a top each,' Ron says. They later returned to the Thomastown factory, where they left the tub and the garbage bags in a corner. They also drove their cars through a car wash. 'And they re-painted the floor of the Thomastown factory.'

Borg headed off for his trip to Malta on 21 November, leaving Spiropoulos to tend to the cannabis crop. 'He also instructed Michael to get rid of his Volvo, which he did, and he removed the number plates,' Ron says. Upon Borg's return the following January – around the time police first interviewed him – the men took all the incriminating items and dumped them in a skip in Campbellfield.

*

On the day of his confession, Michael Spiropoulos accompanied Paul Rowe and a colleague to the factory site in Campbellfield where he'd said they'd dumped the suspicious items. The skip had gone, but among some rubbish on the nature strip were several pieces of broken plastic tub and a piece of plastic, flecked with blue paint. There was also a cigarette butt and a substance that looked like soil. Forensic tests later showed that the blue paint on the melted plastic was the same as the paint on the floor at the Thomastown factory.

The following day, Spiropoulos led the investigators to the hatchet, and two days after that, he accompanied them down the Great Ocean Road. Rowe told Spiropoulos to point out the locations he'd told them about. Spiropoulos led them to a tea-tree grove near Aireys Inlet where they found piles of coco soil containing burnt plastic, other burnt items and flecks of blue paint. 'In some of it was a piece of bone which turned out to be human,' Ron says. Again, the blue paint matched the paint on the floor at the Thomastown factory. Among the debris they also located a burnt mobile phone. 'It had a partial model number that was the same type of phone Peter last used,' Ron adds.

Other members of the team executed a warrant at the Campbellfield factory where Rule had been murdered. Rowe spoke to the owner, Corey Small, who had supplied Borg's timesheet in good faith and had no idea what had gone on in his premises. 'He'd thought Leonard had been welding, until we went and saw him,' Ron explains. 'He remembered coming in on the Monday morning and it had all been cleaned, especially around the toilet area. Leonard had said he'd spilled something and he'd accepted it.' The crime scene investigators ended up finding microscopic blood at the scene that turned out to be one and a half billion times more likely to belong to Peter Rule than anyone else.

Armed with more than enough evidence, Ron and his team had closed in. 'I arrested Leonard Borg as he was driving home around eleven one morning,' he says. 'I got a team of detectives to execute a warrant on his factory and his home. He came back with me to St Kilda Road.'

On his arrest, Borg came across 'as if he was shocked', Ron says. 'He wanted legal advice. After that he answered some very basic questions.' Ron put Spiropoulos' story to him, to which Borg had no comment. Ron attempted to engage Borg, but he was not talking.

When the paperwork was finished, Ron told Borg police were searching his factory and had found his dog. 'I told him the police shot him,' Ron says, the tougher side of the veteran detective, apparent. 'He goes, "What?!" I said, "Yeah, it's been shot".' The comments visibly upset Borg who, like Rule, loved his dog. 'I said, "I'm only joking",' Ron continues. 'But I said, "You're worried about a dog when I've accused you of shooting someone, cutting him up and burning him? For goodness sake!"'

During the search of Borg's Thomastown factory, police found, among other items, the hydroponic cannabis set-up, two fired .22 calibre cartridge cases, a shovel and a tin of blue floor paint.

At one stage, Spiropoulos walked the detectives through the scene and showed them where Borg had burnt Rule's body. When Rowe looked up, he saw black soot on the ceiling, which supported Spiropoulos' story. Spiropoulos also revealed that Borg's firearm was kept on the mezzanine level, and while it was not there, the investigators did find a box of .22 ammunition. It was missing ten rounds, the exact number reportedly used to shoot Rule. They also found damaged number plates that had come from Borg's discarded Volvo. 'Michael had chopped them up, but forensic scientists were later able to put them back together,' Ron says. 'Investigating this case was like putting a jigsaw together.'

At the house where Borg lived with his unsuspecting parents, police found several tins of blue paint, a photo that indicated he was familiar with the Great Ocean Road, and the LBAY brand shorts he had bought after the acid burnt his clothes. 'We'd been to the clothing shop in Lorne and the lady had gone back through the cash register,' Ron says. 'One day during the time period we were interested in, she had sold two pairs of shorts and two pairs of tops. It was the only place in Australia where you could buy the shorts which matched those in Leonard's bedroom drawer.'

During a subsequent visit to Borg's home address, police found, quite by accident, a firearm poking out of a piece of PVC pipe in Borg's ute. They also found a silencer, spent cartridge cases and empty cartridge boxes. 'In his factory we also found a piece of PVC pipe which was about three feet long,' Ron says. 'It [the cut end] matched perfectly the pipe in the back of the ute.'

Thanks to some nifty forensic investigation, and the help of Michael Spiropoulos, the pieces of the puzzle had well and truly fallen into place. 'Everything Michael had told us, we were able to corroborate,' Ron says. 'Come Leonard Borg's trial, Michael had pleaded guilty to the charge of accessory to murder. In other words, he'd assisted in the disposal of the ashes and so on. He was given a three-year suspended sentence on the basis that he gave truthful evidence for the Crown.'

Ron says that during Borg's trial in 2012, Spiropoulos gave evidence for a week and 'didn't miss a beat'. He also had the opportunity to explain why he had helped Borg. 'I didn't really feel I had much of a choice,' he said in court. 'He wasn't just going to let me go after I had seen what he had done. I felt I either had the choice of helping him do it or have the same sort of fate happen to me.'

At the end of the six-week trial, the jury found Leonard Borg guilty of murder. At the pre-sentence hearing Judy Rule read out a victim impact statement by Darcy, then aged four-teen. In part, it read: 'When I found out the news about my father and what had happened, all I could do was cry and cry because I missed him so much and I wish and wish that none of this had ever happened,' the statement began. 'For a while I didn't know what to do with myself because I wanted to be with him so very much.'

Borg was sentenced to twenty-three years in prison with a non-parole period of nineteen. But the investigators and the Office of Public Prosecutions didn't think that was enough. 'We appealed it and he got more,' Ron says, explaining that in July 2013, the sentence was increased to twenty-eight years and nine months with a non-parole period of twenty-four years and nine months. Ron felt the nature of the crime demanded the longer sentence. 'It's one of the most horrific murders I've investigated,' he comments.

Why did Borg do it?

'He thought Peter Rule had dobbed him in for a cannabis crop he used to have in another location,' Ron says. 'Peter knew about his set-up at Thomastown and figured Peter was too big a risk, so he lured him – probably by saying he wanted to show him a motorbike – and killed him. The ironic part of it was, Peter Rule had never dobbed him in at all. And if Borg hadn't involved anyone else, he might have gotten away with it.'

While nothing was going to bring Rule back, Ron was satisfied that he and his team could solve the case for the Rule family and, in a way, help them to grieve. 'In the end one of the greatest things was to give back to the family a piece of bone so they could at least have something to bury,' he says.

24

THE IDDLES EFFECT: CONNECT

*'If people reached out to me I always wanted
to respond and help where I could'.*
– Ron Iddles

You could call it the Iddles Effect: the unique way in which Ron has touched the lives of those he met, including fellow police, the media and, most significantly, victims' families.

Armed Robbery Squad detective Allan Birch's life changed the day he met Ron Iddles. Birch's superiors said he needed greater levels of supervision, but who, in the high pressure world of the Crime Department, was going to take him on? Ron. Of course.

Soon after joining Ron's crew, the outspoken newcomer found himself impressed by his new boss's investigative skills and compassion for the victims. He realised he was under the tutelage of the finest cop he had ever met – and was smart enough to know he could learn from the best. Ron recognised his new sergeant was 'a great strategic thinker and brilliant operationally'; all he needed was 'a bit of polish'. With Ron's guidance, Birch went from the bad boy of the Crime

Department to one of Homicide's most valuable investigators. Together, they worked on around 70 cases and became life-long friends.

*

Twenty-five-year-old Mersina Halvagis was stabbed to death by serial killer Peter Dupas as she tended her grandmother's grave one spring day in 1997. Her father, George Halvagis, says Ron didn't even work on Mersina's case, yet always lent him a sympathetic ear. 'He personally ensured that my daughter Mersina's case remained open and all evidence was re-investigated,' George says. 'This resulted in a conviction and a measure of closure for the family now that justice has prevailed.'

Halvagis says Ron dedicated his life to making society 'safer and better', and has helped many families of victims in his personal time. 'He's a humane and compassionate person who deserves public recognition. He's mixed with so many broken-hearted victims.'

'He's the greatest, Ron. He's a man of great character and victims just love him,' says Noel McNamara, who runs the Crime Victims Support Association with his wife, Bev McNamara. Noel and Bev's eldest daughter, Tracey, was murdered in 1992 and the couple have since devoted their lives to helping other families in similar circumstances.

'People never forget Ron once he's helped them,' Bev says. '[As the family member of a murder victim] you know he's very interested in you. He gives you everything. You've got his whole attention and he's so gentle to people and follows through. He answers every phone call. He tells you things as they are, and that's what I like about him. And you know you can trust him with your life.'

Jo-Ann Adams, whose seventeen-year-old son Gary was murdered in 2003, is grateful to Ron for cracking her son's case when it might otherwise have gone unsolved. In 2011, the desperate mum approached Ron at a fundraiser and persuaded him to look into the case. At the time Gary was listed as a missing person, but Ron discovered that the teenager had been killed, and later that year arrested Gary's stepfather, John Xypolitos, for the murder. In 2013 a jury found Xypolitos guilty of bashing Gary to death with a hammer, and he was sentenced to a non-parole period of twenty-four years. 'If it hadn't been for Ron, Gary's case might still be sitting in a box somewhere,' Jo-Ann says.

A result like that might not have been possible had it not been for Ron setting such high standards for himself and his crew. 'He did keep a very high bar, which was fantastic when you achieved it,' Birch says.

It earned Ron the nickname 'The Great Man'. He didn't care for the moniker because he maintained he was just doing his job, but as the guilty verdicts stacked up, he lived up to the title.

Former Homicide detective Tim Peck met Ron in 2005. One of the cases they worked on together was the cold case disappearance of twenty-two-year-old Elisabeth Membrey, a casual bartender who was hoping to embark on a career as a journalist. 'For me the most outstanding feature that Ron displayed was "accurate empathy",' he says. 'I came across this phrase while studying a psychotherapy course and each time the phrase was used in context it reminded me of Ron. It is about the ability to show humility, to accept another human being for what they are, and to provide a space for that person to feel safe regardless of the circumstances. There are many counsellors, therapists and other mental health professionals who spend their whole career trying to develop this skill – Ron has it in spades.'

As time went on, Ron became far more than a mentor and boss to Peck. 'There is a bond that is created when dealing with such sensitive and emotional issues that arise in homicide investigations that goes further, in my view, than "normal" police camaraderie. This was particularly the case when dealing with Ron. He became the sounding board for all sorts of work-related issues and was available to provide advice or support, regardless of his own busy commitments. He was available at times to his own detriment, tremendously giving, but always open, transparent and dependable.'

When Peck went through a dark period in his personal life and left the force in 2014, his former senior sergeant did not let him down. 'It was Ron I went to in crisis and he has since helped me through the rehabilitation process and continues to provide unconditional support and guidance,' Peck says. 'The accurate empathy was evident but this time I was the recipient, and I took great comfort from that. The outcome may have been tragically different but for his influence, support and presence.'

*

The media also noticed there was something exceptional about Ron, and it wasn't just because of the high number of cases he took to trial but about the way he behaved. The results naturally followed.

Leading Australian crime writers, John Silvester from the *Age* and Keith Moor from the *Herald Sun*, both agree that one of the things that made Ron so special was the way he treated everyone with respect. 'He goes beyond the call of duty,' Moor says, revealing that Ron has been known to stay in contact with victims' relatives for thirty or forty years.

Silvester remembers driving to a fundraiser with Ron, who spent most of the trip on the phone to an informer who had given evidence in a case some ten years earlier. 'He was having trouble with his neighbours over a fence,' Silvester says. Ron was trying to help him. 'It was an old case and this bloke was no longer of any use to him,' Silvester explains. Yet there he was, 'trying to negotiate some little thing'.

Silvester is also aware of an occasion in which Ron may have prevented bloodshed. After a man was killed during a feud between rival crime families, Ron approached the victim's mother. 'He said words to the effect of, "I'm not promising I'll solve it but I'm not interested in your [criminal] background. I will give it all I can",' Silvester reveals. 'And she spoke to the sons and said, "You let this man do his job". So he might have stopped a war.'

Moor says Ron recognised early on that the media is not the enemy and that it can be used as an investigative tool. 'He's old-school in that he believes in telling people as much as he can about the crime,' Moor explains. 'Ron is a great believer that it only takes one call to Crime Stoppers to solve a case.'

The way Ron sees it, a good police officer makes a connection with the person they're talking to, whether colleagues, victims' loved ones, suspects, witnesses, or members of the community who may be able to help crack a case.

How an investigator talks and the kinds of questions they ask can be critical. It is the very basis of how they gather information.

And, of course, crimes can only be solved, Ron insists, through information. While information may come from forensics, it also comes from people. Keep people onside, be straightforward and do not backflip on promises: that is the key to a police officer's success. It was certainly the key to Ron's. In his twenty-five years at Homicide, Ron estimates around seventy-five per cent of all the suspects he interviewed either made admissions or full confessions, an astonishing figure and a direct result of his progressive approach to formal interviews. While some have raised an eyebrow at what they consider a 'touchy-feely' style, the numbers do not lie.

For Ron, it was about giving much-needed answers to those who needed them most – the families of the victims.

*

Question, answer. Question, answer. When Ron first started in the job in 1974, that was how interviews were conducted. Officers would ask a question, wait for the interviewee's answer, type it on a clunky Facit typewriter, then move on to the next question. There was no connection between the police officers and suspects, and the rudimentary three-page records of interview, containing questions and answers, reflected that.

By the late 1970s, police were permitted to take slightly longer statements, and suspects were required to read them back before signing off on their statement. If a suspect was illiterate, another police officer would read back the interview before getting their assent.

Ron noticed that his Homicide boss, Detective Senior Sergeant Brian McCarthy, had a different approach. 'Brian had a good manner in the way he spoke to suspects,' Ron says. 'As I've said before, it was like someone coming to a priest for a conversation. He'd have a fairly relaxed manner. He showed me that if you were authentic and straightforward, you had a better connection with them.'

Once Ron was granted permission to conduct interviews at the Homicide Squad, he followed his boss's example. 'Prior to sitting down and doing a typed interview we'd often have a conversation where the suspect was cautioned and we'd take copious written notes of what they were saying,' Ron says. 'The person might actually admit to the crime before you got to the more formal stage.'

The pre-interview, if it could be called that, was controversial. 'There were allegations that the conversation before the formal interview didn't take place,' Ron says. 'It was often put to you that it was a fabrication of what was said.'

Around the mid-1980s, Victoria Police began tape-recording every interview. 'People were cautioned, the tape recorder was put on and everything that was said in the room was recorded,' Ron says. The new process led to longer interviews, yet Ron noticed that officers still overlooked key aspects of cases. 'By the late 1980s I'd realised there was no formal training in interviewing other than the question–answer, question–answer approach. You either picked up good traits from good operators or picked your own style and put it together.'

Ron believed the force could do better. 'By 1994, when I returned to the Homicide Squad after leaving the job, the Homicide Squad alone had moved to video-recording interviews with audio.'

It was around this time that Ron started to develop and reinforce his own style, predominantly based on what he'd seen McCarthy do. 'It was about treating people you're interviewing – especially suspects – fairly, and having some sort of connection with them.' In practice it meant that Ron often started an interview by offering a suspect a coffee, or asking if they wanted to smoke. 'Most would say no, but then when I said I would have a coffee and ask, "Are you sure you don't want one?" they would nearly always have one with me,' Ron says.

When Allan Birch joined Ron's crew in 2005, he'd never seen a detective take such an informal approach. Initially, the former Armed Robbery Squad detective found it 'distasteful' when he saw Ron put his arm around a suspect. But he quickly realised that humanity was the secret to the experienced homicide investigator's success. Plus, not all suspects are guilty. 'Ron would always say, "Do not bring your prejudice. Don't bring your hypothesis and try to make the evidence fit it",' Birch recalls. It didn't take long for Birch to realise that by following Ron's example, investigators could get more information out of suspects than by standing over them.

From 2007, conscious that Australia did not have an interview model, Ron began studying interview techniques, which took him overseas and started conversations with police in other countries.

Meeting police from around the world was enlightening. 'I found out that London had had an interviewing model for several years, Brazil had had one for around eight years, and New Zealand had adopted a model similar to London's,' Ron says.

It's about time Australia got up to speed, he thought. Upon their return to Australia, Ron and Detective Senior Sergeant Chris O'Connor arranged for an expert from London to share their method with a small group of Victorian police. 'One thing about Ron, he would never sit back on his laurels. He's always developing himself,' Birch says, adding that everything Ron learnt led to better outcomes.

Ron was highly impressed by the overseas models and believed techniques from both England and Canada should be implemented in Victoria. 'So Chris O'Connor and I got together again and we developed an interview training package,' Ron says, adding that he had already started using aspects of both models in his own interviews.

In customising the training package, Ron and O'Connor meshed the first three elements of the English PEACE model – Preparation and Planning, Engage and Explain, and Account – with the second part of the Canadian model, which was Interrogation. It wasn't about yelling and screaming at a suspect. 'The interrogation, or monologue, is about having a one-on-one conversation with the suspect,' Ron says.

'During this process, you might have a break, then come back into the room. The first part of what you might say is an accusation. For example, "There is no doubt in my mind that you're involved in this death".' The investigator might then go from standing to sitting and is most likely looking the suspect in the eye. 'I might then say something like, "I've spent some time with you. I don't think you're a bad person but you've made a bad choice. Your emotions have outrun your intelligence".' At that point, the investigator might find a way to connect with the suspect. 'So you might say something like, "I know you've been having financial trouble, and I know you've been fighting with your partner".'

During the accusatory phase, Ron says an innocent man will react strongly – Peter Smith was a good example. 'But the person who's involved won't protest,' Ron says, 'because they're only confirming what they know.'

Ron started to teach his crew the method he and O'Connor had adapted and fine-tuned. Then Ron did something that rattled a few old-school investigators: he removed the table from the interview room. 'What I'd learnt from the study I did was that a table is a barrier to communication,' he explains. 'And I also went to a method of conducting interviews on your own.' In the past, two detectives had always been present during interviews but it was no longer necessary as a video camera captured everything. Ron's new approach gave interviewers an opportunity to have a one-on-one conversation with their suspects.

The key, Ron told his troops, was authenticity. Suspects could smell insincerity a mile off. Ron didn't want his crew mimicking him either: they had to be themselves. 'You've got to be present in the room. Sometimes you've got to show a bit of yourself and be genuine, because if you don't, you'll never be successful.'

Ron had two other pertinent sayings: 'There are two things that cost you nothing – the ability to listen, and the ability to understand.' He encouraged those he taught not to interrupt the suspect, and to put themselves in their shoes.

Around 2010, Victoria Police started to formalise the training method, and Ron led a three-day course teaching practical interviewing skills to officers from the Crime Department. It was very popular and, over four years, he trained 386 detectives.

The new interviewing method was not without opposition. It came as a great surprise to some of the state's more conservative lawyers when they saw Ron wearing jeans and a t-shirt during a videotaped interview. 'Again, it was about having a connection, about coming to the suspects' level, but still being professional,' he says. 'I explained it had been done in London for sixteen years and we had a similar legal system. I was totally complying with the *Crimes Act*, which included telling the suspects their rights and cautioning them.'

In one instance, Ron purchased two armchairs and placed fishing magazines and a packet of cigarettes on a coffee table. It was unorthodox, but Ron knew his suspect liked fishing and smoked, and figured he might open up if he was in a familiar environment. Ron thinks he flicked through the magazines during a break; it seemed to relax him.

Ron was no Mr Plod when it came to cautioning suspects either. 'I've gotta tell you what your rights are,' he'd say. 'You might've watched a lot of television. You might've watched a lot of American shows. I've gotta tell you, you're a suspect in this person's death. You've got a driver's licence – that's a privilege, and it's something you could lose. But I want to tell you that your rights are something no one can take from you.' Ron would then tell the suspect they had a right to total silence. 'You don't have to tell me anything,' he'd continue, 'but what you do tell me could be used in evidence against you.'

As Birch had witnessed early in his career at Homicide, Ron would sometimes put an arm around the suspect. 'The [teaching] material says it's high risk but it's also high gain,' Ron says. 'If the suspect feels it's not genuine, that's it. They'll pick it up.' But, as Ron learnt from experience, if suspects recognise it as a sincere gesture, they sometimes spill the whole story. 'You've got to be empathetic but not sympathetic,' Ron used to tell his students.

Birch is full of praise for Ron's interview technique. 'It served me exceptionally well in my career at Homicide,' he says. 'We managed to get people who were last known to have seen a missing person alive admit to the killing, and take us to the body.'

Ron also taught Birch how to read when a suspect wanted to get their crimes off their chest. 'Many killers are not happy that they've killed someone. They're terrified of the public outcry,' he says. 'But you can see in their demeanour and body language they want to admit to it.'

The way Birch sees it, The Good Cop has no equal. 'He would have to be the gun of homicide investigation and the most forward-thinking about possible interview techniques. He wasn't scared to try something new if it was going to better the outcomes. It's extremely unique in coppers.' Ron's methods were a means through which he could help others through his work. 'In his career, those who really mattered in priority were the deceased and those who loved the deceased,' Birch says.

'He was so successful,' Birch continues. 'How can you not be won by that?'

25

NO LOOKING BACK

*'By February 2014, I had prepared myself
mentally to leave Homicide. I had to close
the door behind me and move on. It was now
about the next chapter in my life.'*
– Ron Iddles

Sometimes, says Ron, it's not about what is said but what is not said.

When he told senior police he would be happy to spend another three years at the Homicide Squad before retiring, they said very little. 'They told me I'd be a great secretary for the Police Association,' he recalls. He took their silence to mean that he would probably be rotated out of the Homicide Squad, just like his fellow team leaders had been.

Despite the feeling of standing on shifting sand, Ron remained focused on solving homicides. In 2013, he investigated seven violent ice-related murders in a row. Some of the cases involved torture, suffocation, dismemberment and fire. 'They were disputes over drug trafficking and payments,' Ron says, 'or the accused were affected by ice.' The extreme level of violence shocked him, which was saying something.

Ice had become an epidemic, so serious that the former Chief Commissioner, Ken Lay, was heading a national task-force to tackle the problem. 'I guess after twenty-five years at Homicide, I was now dealing with a different sort of murder investigation,' Ron explains. 'I was getting to the stage where, if I was moved, I would probably have accepted it and said I'd had a good run.' And he realised if his application for the job at the Police Association were successful, it would provide him with the chance to reinvent himself.

But still, he thought, it would be good to have the choice.

*

On Christmas Eve 2013, Ron was toiling away at Homicide. He was looking forward to the end of the day, when he planned to enjoy a glass of his favourite Barossa Valley shiraz with Colleen and put the last of the presents under the tree. He loved seeing the grandchildren's faces light up when they receive a gift they'd been hinting about all year.

That day, Ron's superintendent had invited him to a meeting at 1 pm. It wasn't for a kiss under the mistletoe. 'There was a discussion about my future,' he recalls. 'I was told I was going to be moved and it was based around my welfare.' The super-intendent asked him where, in the police force, he might like to work and explained that there were excellent opportunities open to him – just not at Homicide.

Ron told his boss, 'Come March next year I'll go, and if I don't get a position at the Police Association, I'll go and lecture at the academy.'

The superintendent thanked Ron for all he had done. 'And I still remember the statement, "As your supervisor, I cannot afford to give you back to your family a broken man".'

Ron accepted the decision, but could not understand the rationale. 'I'd done the job for nearly twenty-five years and I believed I was the best person to judge my emotional state,' he says. 'I thought I had done fairly well over a long period of time and if I was going to fall down, I would have done so by then.'

What made the decision even harder for Ron to understand was that he had just solved ice murder after ice murder, and they weren't easy jobs. 'To me it didn't make a lot of sense,' he says. 'Surely it was good for the Homicide Squad and the Crime Department to show we had the ability to solve these really complex investigations?'

Ron steeled himself to tell his colleagues. 'The hardest part was to say to my crew members who were there that day, "The journey's over. Come March next year, I won't be here. I've been told I can have any position I want but it won't be at Homicide. It's happened and I've accepted it. It'll come to an end".' He sent his crew home early to enjoy Christmas, but he knew there would be a dark cloud over their festivities.

Allan Birch was particularly stunned by the inference that Ron had nothing more to give. His crew felt differently. Birch recalls how, in the lead-up to the decision to let Ron go, the crew had been cautious of their every move. 'Everything we did, we thought, *How would this impact on Ron?* We'd rather leave than have him leave. That's how much we valued him.'

But the deed was done.

On the drive home, Ron called Colleen. 'I said, "I've basically been told my time's up",' he recalls. She was almost speechless. 'Happy Christmas,' she managed to say.

Colleen had seen the writing on the wall since Ron showed the photo of Jill Meagher a month earlier. 'It was the saddest thing, because he lived and breathed doing homicide investigations,' she says. 'That's what he'd always wanted to do since he was a child. All he wanted to do was be a good cop and do a good job.'

And even though, Colleen says, Ron will never forget the timing of the meeting, he forgave those responsible for the decision. 'He was shattered,' she says, 'but he doesn't hold a grudge.'

*

Christmas Day that year was a sombre affair in the Iddles household. The following day, Ron was back investigating a man's suspicious disappearance in Bendigo – another ice murder. 'He'd also been cut up,' Ron recalls.

In the new year, the *Age* newspaper called him. 'The journalist said, "I hear you've been asked to leave and your career's finished at Homicide",' Ron remembers. He suggested they call Police Media instead.

'I then had a meeting with the head of Homicide, Detective Inspector John Potter, and my superintendent to discuss their response to the newspaper,' Ron says. 'The formal response would be that we had met on Christmas Eve and this was not unusual as senior managers often met with their staff,' he explains. The following day the *Age* expressed that fact, and ran the story under the headline, 'Homicide Detective Ron Iddles Asked to Move On'.

It did not come as a surprise to the *Age*'s John Silvester. It was not his article but, as the chief crime reporter, he knew that, with the other senior sergeants already moved out of the squad, it was only a matter of time. 'Ron was the last. He lasted longer than any of them. It was inevitable he was going to go,' he says.

Silvester believes Ron's superiors had been genuinely worried about his emotional health. 'There were serious concerns at a higher rank that after investigating case after case after case, that could squash him,' Silvester says. 'We'll never know if that was true or not. His emotionalism might have been misinterpreted as a sign he was not coping.' Silvester suspects that Ron's emotional nature actually suggested he *was* coping, and that, coupled with driving buses, actually relieved the stresses of the job.

When Chief Commissioner Ken Lay saw the newspaper article he immediately called Ron. 'He said, "You can stay as long as you like at the Homicide Squad",' Ron recalls. 'He said, "I don't want there to be any ill feelings".'

Admittedly, there were other considerations, with Ron in the running for Greg Davies' position at the Police Association. 'So there were now others who I would disappoint if I withdrew,' Ron says. 'But if I did not get Greg's job, then I had assurance from Ken Lay that I could stay at Homicide.'

In February 2014, Ron made his decision. He was offered the job at the Police Association and, seeing it as a new way to make a difference, decided to take it. He would start the following month.

On his last morning as a homicide investigator, Ron dropped in at the home of convicted killer Bruce Nicholls. Perhaps it was a subconscious way of saying goodbye to murder. Nicholls was among the long list of people who felt deeply saddened that the squad had lost its finest investigator. 'He deserves great recognition for putting so many years into the police force,' Nicholls says.

But it was people like Mark James, who first met Ron when he'd worked on his mother Maria's murder in 1980, who were hit hardest by the news. 'I think what happened to him was very unfair,' Mark says. 'It was vexatious.'

'I could have got bitter and twisted, but would it help the team?' Ron asks. 'No. Would it help me? No. When I knew I was going to the Police Association, I got my head around the fact that my days at the Homicide Squad were over.'

Arriving at the familiar St Kilda Road office, Ron packed up his belongings and shredded sensitive documents he no longer needed. He and Colleen then treated his crew to lunch at the nearby George Hotel in South Melbourne. He told his colleagues there were to be no speeches or presentations, but Ron being Ron, he made an eloquent speech, thanking his crew for their hard work, loyalty and dedication to the job.

The only time Ron's crew ever defied him was a couple of weeks later. Despite his orders, there was no way they were letting him leave without something to remember them by. 'Allan Birch had made up a collage of snapshots of me at crime scenes,' Ron says. They also gave Ron and Colleen a generous gift voucher to Melbourne restaurant Vue de Monde. 'And they gave me a bottle of Penfold's Grange,'

Ron adds. It was from 1980, his first year at the Homicide Squad.

'I always said, when I walked out the door, I won't look back and I won't come back,' Ron says. 'And to this day I haven't been back.'

He would miss those guys, but it was over.

26

STEERING THE SHIP

'The history of the Police Association shows it is a tough job and many have failed or been removed from office. History will be the judge of my time.'
– Ron Iddles

They say that when one door closes, another one opens. In Ron's case, behind an oak-panelled door in East Melbourne, a new future awaited.

Ron had never run an organisation. Yet here he was, in the corner office of the Police Association of Victoria, a CEO with thirty-seven staff and answerable to 14,000 members. It was a lofty position and he soon found himself in regular meetings with the premier, the leader of the opposition, and the chief commissioner.

After a two-week handover with the outgoing secretary, Greg Davies, in March 2014, it was up to Ron to shape the association as he saw fit. He remembers his first day at the helm.

'I felt sick,' he says. 'I was totally out of my comfort zone. I remember going home to Colleen and saying, "I feel so far out of it".'

But things quickly changed. 'I decided I couldn't just sit back and not get a handle on everything that was happening,' Ron says. 'So I spoke to each staff member on a one-to-one basis to find out what they did and the association could do better.' They were enlightening meetings that also helped the new boss remember his employees' names.

Ron discovered his colleagues were as eager to help him as he was to learn about them. 'Without the support of the staff, but in particular the assistant secretary, Bruce McKenzie, it would have been difficult to make the transition,' Ron says. 'They were fantastic.'

Ron then turned his focus to the members, who were other police just like him. 'While we're not a union as such, we're often referred to as one and realistically we operate as such even though we're a business,' he explains. 'So I developed a road map for where the association was going over the next three years.' The three-year strategic plan was published online for all members to see.

Most importantly, Ron chose to emphasise that the association existed for officers' welfare. 'I made a decision when I took over that if a member was involved in a critical incident such as a fatal police shooting or a pursuit which ended up being a fatality, I would personally go out and attend those incidents, but not in an investigative capacity,' he says. 'The decision was solely about showing the members of the Police Association that we were there to support them, to make sure they got the right legal advice if required, but mainly to be there for their welfare.'

Ron made it clear that he was personally available to members twenty-four hours a day. It was a move embraced by the membership. 'Currently there are twenty-two members a month who are going off on sick leave related to depression, issues with alcohol or post-traumatic stress disorder,' he says. 'So there's a real need to focus on that and get members to say, "I'm struggling, I need help", and for us to provide a good, personalised service.' As part of that service, Ron decided to introduce a sophisticated phone app in conjunction with Victoria Police and the state government. It enables officers to self-assess how they are coping with the demands of the job and determine whether they need any help.

In order to provide the association's members with the level of service to which he'd committed, Ron had to resign from his job as a part-time bus driver for Firefly. His boss, Joe Bono, was disappointed. 'I was in shock,' Joe says. 'I said, "You're kidding?" But he said it was for the members. He'd have to put all his focus on the job, which I understood.'

As ever, Ron did the job his way, including working the switchboard on Fridays, which was also an effective way to find out more about the members' needs. 'I don't consider myself the boss there,' he says. 'I just see myself as a worker who comes in and steers the ship. But I'd like to think that when I leave the organisation, it will have a bigger focus on member welfare.'

Ron sees the opportunity to lead the Police Association as a privilege. Colleen points out that, as its secretary, her husband had become one of the two most powerful police in Victoria and yet, as usual, he has remained unassuming. If you ask Ron, he'll say, 'I'm only just a policeman.'

Few people consider Ron 'just a policeman', and on Australia Day 2015, he was awarded a prestigious Order of

Australia Medal by Victorian Governor Alex Chernov, for his contribution to charity and his years of work for victims and their families.

The former police guard at Government House had come a long way.

*

Although he was focused on police officers' welfare, Ron couldn't just forget the hundreds of cases he had investigated over the years. Never more so than when those cases threw up new developments. Even during his first year at the Police Association, one of his cold cases went to trial. It was the Michelle Buckingham murder.

It was a distressing case. Sixteen-year-old Michelle Buckingham, who lived alone in a caravan park, had gone missing in October 1983. A fortnight later a farmer stumbled upon her body amid long grass at Kialla East on the outskirts of Shepparton. She had been stabbed up to nineteen times.

A local, Gregory Gleadhill, was charged with her murder but it was dropped. Ron could clearly see that police had charged the wrong man. Buckingham's mother, Elvira, did not think Gleadhill had killed her daughter either, but doubted she would ever find out who had.

But in 2012, Tammy Mills from the *Shepparton News* got the ball rolling again. Eager to find a way to help the victim's mum Elvira, the cub reporter called and urged Ron to reopen the case. She knew that for a year, he'd been heading a new cold case unit. 'I said we wouldn't have the resources to take it on right then,' he remembers. But Mills wasn't giving up that easily and called him again a month later. He drove to Shepparton to see her, and the plucky twenty-five-year-old convinced him to take on the case.

Ron thought the media coverage could help. 'When Tammy wrote her first story about the case, saying it had been reopened and that I was investigating, thirty-five pieces of information came in,' he recalls. But with no available staff, Ron had to investigate each report on his own.

After Tammy's story was published, Ron was working from the Shepparton Police Station when a local police officer told him a man had called Crime Stoppers with information. 'The caller said I should speak to a man called Norm Gribble because he knew who had killed Michelle Buckingham,' Ron says.

Ron contacted Gribble who suggested they meet at the Shepparton East Football Ground. *Another clandestine meeting with a stranger*, Ron thought. 'Silly as it sounds, I went with no gun or equipment. I never took one unless I was going to make an arrest.' He always hoped words would work better than a gun.

As Ron waited for the enigmatic Gribble, tumbleweed might as well have rolled across the football ground. 'There was no one else around,' he remembers. 'Then a ute arrived. There were two people in it and one got out.' But Gribble – who Ron estimated was about sixty-five – was not at all threatening. 'He said, "I can't live with what I'm going to tell you",' Ron recalls. 'He said he had lived with this secret for some thirty years.'

'Gribble said his brother-in-law, Stephen Bradley, had come to him one Saturday morning,' Ron begins. 'He was very upset and had blood on his hands.' Bradley was too upset to say what was wrong, so Gribble suggested the pair go for a drive. They bought some beer, then sat in a picnic area, where Gribble said his brother-in-law Bradley told him what he'd done.

'I stabbed Michelle Buckingham last night,' Bradley reportedly told Gribble. 'He said he'd picked her up and driven her to the Pine Lodge Hotel in Shepparton East,' Ron says.

According to Ron, Bradley's story continued like this: 'It was dark. I put the hard word on her and she didn't come across,' he said. 'I stabbed her.'

Bradley told Gribble he drove to Violet Town Road and dumped Buckingham's body. 'Later, he sat beside a river thinking about what he should do.' Bradley wondered if he should drive into the river and kill himself. But he unburdened himself on his brother-in-law instead.

'It put Norm in an unenviable position,' Ron says. 'Norm said, "You have to go to the police."' At first Bradley did not want to but on the drive back to Gribble's house he ultimately agreed to take care of it.

'And that was probably the last time Norm saw him,' Ron says, adding that almost straightaway, Bradley got rid of his 1973 green HQ Holden and bought a different car. 'He also moved out of the area and never really returned.'

Ron says that when Buckingham's body was found about two weeks later, Gribble realised what Bradley had told him was true. 'He said he could never do anything with that information because he was married to Bradley's sister, so he felt he couldn't tell,' Ron explains. Gribble feared it would destroy his family.

Ron asked Gribble if he had told anyone else. 'Yes, about four years ago,' he replied. He had told Stephen's brother, Lawrie Bradley, and it was Lawrie who'd made the call to Crime Stoppers.

After all these years, the police were making progress. The only problem was that – even though Gribble couldn't live with the secret any longer – he didn't want to make a statement. Ron hoped to persuade him.

The day after speaking to his new informer, Ron went to meet Elvira. 'I was a bit apprehensive because I was going to tell her I was going to solve it,' he recalls. She told him that was what police had told her in the past. She wasn't expecting a miracle after all these years.

'Why should I trust you?' she asked him.

'I said, "You're going to have to".'

Ron then revealed the new information and will never forget Elvira's emotional reaction. 'She said, "While I accepted my daughter had died, for sixteen years I still waited for her to come in the door. Then after twenty years I went to the doctor because I was still struggling. The doctor said, 'Get over it, move on, look after your family', and that's what I've done. But now, you've come and knocked on my door, and it's as raw as if it was yesterday".' Seeing the misery etched on the German-born woman's face, Ron silently vowed to do everything in his power to help her.

Next, Ron spoke to Bradley's brother, Lawrie. Ron explained to Lawrie that he had a moral obligation to tell him what he knew. 'The following day, as a result of the phone call, I met Lawrie Bradley, who told me what Norm had told me, and he spoke of a comment Stephen had made at their mother's funeral. It had something to do with Michelle.'

Back in Melbourne, Ron and his team started investigating Bradley. 'We had many conversations about how to progress a case that was almost thirty years old,' he says. 'What tactics are we going to use?'

Ultimately, Gribble agreed to make a statement. 'That became the crucial piece of the puzzle because we were going to dredge up evidence about what the accused had said to him,' Ron explains, adding that part of his initial investigation was covert, and the second part was overt. He and his team thoroughly interrogated the original file. Interestingly, Bradley's name was in there but the original investigators had set their sights on Greg Gleadhill. The wrong man.

More than a year of intense investigation passed during which Ron and his team felt they had gathered enough evidence.

Ron was geared up to arrest Bradley just as the Jill Meagher controversy was about to break. 'I arrested Stephen at a bus-stop in November 2013,' he remembers. Bradley was on his way back to the boarding house where he lived after working as a cleaner at a veterinary surgery. 'When I arrested him, I said I was reinvestigating the death of Michelle Buckingham and thought he could help. He didn't question it. He was quiet. I would say he looked like a shy person.'

At the offices of the Brisbane Homicide Squad, Ron asked Bradley if he knew anything about Michelle Buckingham's death. 'He said, "No, I've never heard her name".'

Ron asked Bradley if he had been in Shepparton at the time of the murder, to which Bradley said he thought he had been. Ron pointed out that would make him the only guy in Shepparton who had never heard of her. The detective asked if Bradley had been to the caravan park where Buckingham had lived, or the Pine Lodge Hotel in Shepparton East.

'Then I asked, "Have you ever told anyone you killed Michelle Buckingham?"' Bradley said no, he had not.

Ron noticed Bradley's uneasy body language. 'He had his hands on his knees and couldn't control his feet,' he remembers. 'Then I said, "Your brother-in-law, Norm, has come forward and says on a Saturday you told him you'd stabbed Michelle Buckingham".'

Bradley said he could not remember.

'Is it possible,' Ron continued, 'you did it and can't remember? He said words to the effect of, "I think you would remember if you'd stabbed someone. Surely I'd remember if I did".'

As the interview continued, Bradley claimed he did not remember telling his brother-in-law he had stabbed Buckingham. But after about an hour, his tone changed. 'At the end it was like, 'I might have done it but if I had I would remember,' Ron says. 'I guess he agreed to a proposition that he might have done it but for whatever reason he'd blocked it from his memory.'

Ron released Bradley, but told him the investigation was not over. Two months later, in January 2014, Ron returned, armed with a video of Gribble talking about what Bradley had told him on the night in question. He waited at Bradley's boarding house, knowing he was a creature of habit who would return home from work around 6 pm. 'Sure enough, he came around the corner,' Ron says, and spotted the police who wanted to take him in again.

Back at Brisbane's police headquarters, Ron cautioned Bradley and explained that he had the video containing what Gribble had told him. 'You don't have to watch it,' he said, but Bradley agreed to look. 'He sat there for ten minutes glued to the screen. He did not move.'

Once it was over, Ron asked Bradley if he had anything to say. 'He said something like, "I might've done it".' He said he had been having dreams for twenty years in which a young girl with long black hair sat on his chest and was having trouble breathing. 'In the dream, he took the knife and plunged it into the girl. He recalled the knife going in like butter, and cutting his hand.'

He also said he dreamt of being at the back of the Pine Lodge Hotel. 'Then he said he dreamt of driving very fast in the car,' adds Ron. 'I said, "Well, put the dream to one side, what do you actually remember?" He said, "That's the difficult part. I have trouble distinguishing between dreams and reality".'

As it happened, Bradley had received psychological treatment for disturbing dreams for about thirteen years, so Ron tracked down his counsellor. 'While he'd spoken to her about having bad dreams, he'd never told her about what was in them,' Ron says. 'I had been hoping in the counsellor's file he'd have made admissions to killing Michelle.'

But it didn't matter. Once Ron and his crew put together their brief, the Director of Public Prosecutions believed there was enough evidence on which to charge Bradley. 'So Allan Birch, Simon Hunt and I went back to his boarding house around 6 am,' Ron says. The detectives arrested him and said they were taking him back to Melbourne. Bradley asked if he could pack up his room, which was barren except for a few clothes and a twenty-inch flat-screen TV. He also asked if he could go upstairs and farewell his mate. Ron said he could.

'To some extent I felt a bit sad,' Ron admits. 'He was in his early fifties and walked out of that boarding house with all his worldly belongings in one small bag.'

'When the arrest came I was really quite emotional,' Tammy Mills says. 'I remember Ron ringing me about it. I think he was crying over the phone and I was crying too.'

Back at Brisbane's police headquarters, Ron interviewed Bradley once more. Bradley was still having troubling distinguishing reality from his nightmares. Ron arranged for two counsellors to see him and he was taken to the city watchhouse, where he was charged and remanded, before being flown back to Melbourne.

At the committal hearing in Shepparton, Bradley was ordered to stand trial for murder. Before the trial, he contacted Ron's Homicide Squad colleague, Detective Senior Constable Simon Hunt, and asked to be re-interviewed. 'He then said he remembered the night and said, to the best of his recollection, Michelle was probably killed at the hotel that Saturday afternoon and placed in the back of his car,' Ron says. He said he probably slid his hand down the knife, which is how he cut himself.' He claimed, however, that he had just been pretending to stab her. At the trial, he would plead not guilty.

But Elvira would not live to see justice done, dying of heart failure five days before the trial began. 'Emotionally, I didn't cope,' Ron admits. 'I'd spoken to her just a week before her death. I was asked to go to her funeral, but I just couldn't. They say you shouldn't get emotional when you're investigating jobs but I knew I was going to solve it. And I'll never forget how she told me she trusted me.'

The heartbroken mum had been right to trust him: in October 2015, a jury found Stephen Bradley guilty of her daughter's murder. It was by this time the oldest solved homicide in Victoria and the last case of Ron's career. 'I was sad that Elvira didn't get to see the result,' he says. 'But her daughter and son did, and they were most grateful they got an answer. They say that their mum will know from above what the result was.'

'He makes me believe in the police force and the job they do,' Tammy Mills says of Ron. 'He cares so much about his work. To have someone like that representing victims, people like Michelle who don't have a voice – you couldn't have anyone better than him. He gives a bit of himself. It's not a contrived, planned thing. That's him.'

Bradley was sentenced to twenty-seven years behind bars with a non-parole period of twenty-one years. During sentencing, Justice Robert Osborn praised Ron's finely honed interview technique. 'What probably gave me the most satisfaction was that the judge said the interview was "masterful",' Ron says. 'So, after twenty-five years at Homicide, I had mastered interview technique.'

He says the sad thing now is that exact technique is no longer taught at Homicide. 'You don't build something up then watch the wall get torn down,' he says wistfully. 'But I wasn't part of the future of that office.'

*

Over a career spanning more than four decades, the man

who'd once dreamt of becoming like his TV idols on *Homicide* left a lasting legacy for police. 'I'd like to think that the legacy I left Homicide was around the way in which I dealt with the families of victims and my commitment to a strong work ethic. I'd also like the techniques and interview skills we developed to continue on and become standard practice,' he says. 'I'd also like to be remembered for treating criminals with respect – for trying to understand things from their point of view.'

Ron does not speak poorly of those who let him walk out the door of Homicide, nor will he admit he wishes he were still there. But those close to him suspect he will never get it out of his system. *He might have physically walked away,* they say, *but there will always be a part of Ron that is still there.*

Ron Iddles gave twenty-five years of his life, at significant personal sacrifice, to the pursuit of justice. His integrity was incorruptible. He put victims and their families before himself at every turn, and solved more cases than any other homicide investigator in the country. He never said no to anyone who reached out to him for help, especially fellow police. He is a titanic figure in the history of Australian policing.

Now, at the Police Association, Ron wants to help other officers enjoy robust careers by encouraging them to balance their lives. 'This is something I am now passionate about,' he says, 'helping members understand how they change once they become a police officer. We see everything from a very negative lens: everything is bad, so the whole world is bad, when in actual fact 99 per cent of people are good. It is understanding that concept, and developing skills to survive as a police officer. Exercise, diet and having interests outside the police force are all important. If you do not do those things, then relationships will not survive.'

Ron hopes that when his five-year term with the Police Association comes to an end, he will have left it as a modern business that comprehensively serves its members. 'And I'd like the focus to remain on their welfare and support,' he emphasises.

Tim Peck – who was once on the receiving end of Ron's care – knows his old boss will make a lasting impression. 'Ron's greatest legacy may well be the path of change he has initiated at the Police Association to bring greater under-standing and insight to the mental health issues faced by serving members,' he says. 'I recently obtained employment with Beyond Blue, and Ron remains a close friend and ally in creating networks to address the member welfare issues identified within Victoria Police.'

Ron often refers to his extraordinary career as his 'journey', and says it is one that he could not have made without his wife, Colleen. He says this is as much Colleen's story as it is his, and that it's ultimately a love story. 'For more than forty years, regardless of what I did or what decision I made, she always supported me, even if she did not agree,' Ron says. 'Without her, I would have been nothing.'

'I never knew I was going to have this kind of life with him,' Colleen says. 'I am living such a good life and it's because of a decision I made when I was sixteen. It was the best decision I could have made.'

The next big decision, however, will be what to do once Ron retires. 'I have a simple view that I came quietly and I want to go quietly,' he says. 'As a Homicide investigator, I could never predict what my next case would be, but in my mind, I was always an average guy doing a difficult job. Despite my public profile, I am a reserved person and, to some extent, I like the private life. When my job here is done, I look forward to being a private citizen again.'

What Ron knows for sure is that he'll be taking more time out to relax with Colleen and the family. 'We'll go on a lot more caravan trips,' Ron says. 'There will definitely be driving involved.'

Any *bus* driving trips? 'Well,' Ron laughs. 'Maybe just *one* . . .'

ACKNOWLEDGEMENTS

I have had numerous approaches for my story because of my public profile. My move from the Homicide Squad to the Police Association generated an article written by Justine Ford in the *Age*, from which came an approach from Pan Macmillan Australia.

To Justine Ford, thank you for your patience, commitment and brilliant work in writing my story. I am aware you moved to the great state of Victoria to do this, and that was a personal sacrifice that cannot be repaid.

Thanks to Pan Macmillan for believing it is a story worth telling.

To my wife of forty-one years, Colleen, what can I say? Without you and your total support, I could never have achieved anything. I know there have been difficult times over the journey, but you have always been there regardless, and I cannot express my gratitude enough.

To my children, Joanne, Matthew and Shae, I know at times I have failed you and on many special days in your life I was not there. That is not something I can change now.

The comment still rings in my ears, 'You built the sandpit but you did not play in it.' This is something I will forever regret. Yes, I may not say it a lot, but I love each of you dearly and will always be there for you.

Thanks to Victoria Police for giving me opportunities to work for the community but, above all, to investigate some of the most serious crimes in this state for thirty-seven years. It has been a fantastic journey that has taken me around Australia and many parts of the world. I have worked with many police officers and some have become lifelong friends. It is difficult to name them all, and if I tried I would no doubt leave some out and that is not my intention.

I should mention two of those officers – Paul Delianis, who was in charge of Homicide when I first arrived there in 1980, and Brian McCarthy, my senior sergeant. Both officers helped to shape my career, and provided me with role models.

The families of victims were a central part of my twenty-five years at the Homicide Squad, and you will not be forgotten. I may not have provided all the answers but I hope my team were able to ease some of your pain.

The legal fraternity, Office of Public Prosecutions and defence counsel, judges of the Supreme Court: thank you for your guidance, wisdom and knowledge. I learnt more during the trials than any classroom could teach me. Court was the arena where every decision I made came under scrutiny. It taught me 'the decision you make today you will have to justify'.

To all facets of media: without your stories, many of the crimes would not have been solved. I thank you for the support you always offered. Someone once told me that police cannot do without the media, and the media need the police. It is a partnership that has stood the test of time, but maybe of recent times this has not been fully understood by our decision makers.

To friends and acquaintances, now that you have read my book you may understand why I did not attend your dinner, barbecue or function, or why Colleen came alone. I hope I was there in spirit.

Ron Iddles

At an Iddles family barbecue, I said to Ron, 'You have to be a pretty special person to have a biography written about you.' Typically humble, he didn't know what to say, so he acknowledged with a smile that he knew it was something to be proud of.

The information Ron has so generously imparted in our weekly meetings has been eye-opening, sad, funny, heart-warming, astonishing and, most of all, inspiring. So it is you, Ron, I must thank, first and foremost, for being an extraordinary subject, an incredible detective and community leader, and an exceptional human being. You are one in a million and it is a great honour to tell your story in this book.

To the beautiful and gracious Colleen Iddles, who has largely shunned the spotlight until now – thank you for the fascinating stories you have shared with me. (Not to mention the books of Ron's press clippings you have so lovingly compiled!)

To Ron's children, Joanne Zammit, Matthew Iddles and Shae Iddles – my enormous gratitude to you for telling me about the dad you so obviously love and admire. I hope this book will be something you can hand down to future generations.

Thank you to Ron's dad, Bill Iddles, who, at eighty-eight years old, spoke to me from a hospital bed and told Ron that he'd 'hang on' so I could interview him. It was a privilege to talk to the father of The Great Man. And to Ron's brother Barry Iddles and sister, Nancye Lees, thanks for all the funny anecdotes and endearing family photos.

To John Silvester, thank you for generously sharing your expert knowledge of Ron in the foreword. It is an enormous honour to have one of the greats of True Australian Crime contribute in such a meaningful and insightful way.

Anne Stanford from the Supreme Court of Victoria – you are a champion. Thanks for all your time scouring records and going 'across the road' to dig up old files.

Special thanks to Julia Taylor and The Five Mile Press, as well as Mary-Anne Toy and *The Age* for permission to reprint quotes from my previously published stories.

Much gratitude is owed to all the other contributors to the book, whose personal stories and tributes have helped to tell the Ron Iddles story. Thanks to: Jo-Ann Adams, Allan Birch, Joe Bono, Jenny Burke, Louise Burke, Ted Coleman, Paul Delianis, Harry Derix, Paul Evans, Bob Falconer, Leigh Gassner, George Halvagis, Paul Hatton, Glenn Heaton, Judy Ip, Mark James, Brian McCarthy, Lindsay McMinn, Bev McNamara, Noel McNamara, Carl Mengler, Tammy Mills, John Moloney, Keith Moor, Mick Long, Bruce Nicholls, Ken O'Connor, Geoff O'Loughlin, Tim Peck, Sal Perna, Margaret Read, Sharon Relf, Ray Relf, Bill Rule, John Silvester, Amanda Sinclair, Ivan Smith, Keith Sutherland and Marion Wishart.

To my publisher, Angus Fontaine from Pan Macmillan, I am ever grateful for the opportunity to tell this special story and for your continued help and guidance. It has been a privilege to write for you.

Thank you also to my brilliant editors – Senior Editor Mathilda Imlah, Foong Ling Kong, Rebecca Hamilton and Mark Evans. What a gun team!

As always, I wish to acknowledge my wonderful agent, John Timlin, who has championed my work from the start. I hope you like this one, John!

Enormous thanks also to those whose enduring love and support encourages me to keep writing – my family and friends who push me ever onwards. I could not appreciate it more.

And thanks to you, dear readers. Because of you, I get to tell amazing and enduring stories like this.

Justine Ford

If you have any information about any of the cases featured in this book, contact Crime Stoppers on 1800 333 000.

Need help?
In the case of an emergency, contact 000. If you or someone you know are affected by crime, contact police immediately.

For help with mental illness, contact your trusted healthcare professional. Other organisations, such as Beyond Blue, can also help: www.beyondblue.org.au

If someone you know goes missing, report it to local police straight away.